Web Analytics Demystified

A Marketer's Guide to Understanding How Your Web Site Affects Your Business

Eric T. Peterson

Parts of this book are supplemented at the author's Web site:

www.webanalyticsdemystified.com

Web Analytics Demystified: A Marketer's Guide to Understanding How Your Web Site Affects Your Business

Editing by Maura K. Hallam | Hallam Creative Services
Cover design and original illustrations by Chris Garlotta
Published by Celilo Group Media and CafePress

International Standard Book Number: 0-9743584-2-8

This book is dedicated to Chloe Michelle Peterson

Acknowledgements

This book would not have been possible without help from the following people:

Jim Sterne for paving the way and providing endless encouragement
Bryan Eisenberg for advice regarding how to get this book published
Terry Lund and Dylan Lewis for their review of early versions of this book
Rand Schulman for his comments and encouragement
Maura Hallam, Chris Garlotta and Nik Blosser for technical assistance
Amity and Chloe Peterson for understanding that Chloe's daddy had to write

Additionally, the author would like to thank John Breese, Dustin Robertson and the entire BackcountryStore.com crew for allowing me to use their Web site and data in examples throughout this book.

About the Author

Eric T. Peterson has worked in the field of Web analytics since 1998 as a Web developer, Web marketer and Web analytics specialist. As the director of professional services for WebSideStory, creators of HitBox, Mr. Peterson has had the opportunity to provide analytics consulting for some of the largest and most recognized brands in the world. More recently, Mr. Peterson has joined Jupiter Research as a Site Operations and Technology analyst, advising Jupiter customers on many of the technologies and ideas presented in this book. Mr. Peterson lives in San Diego, California, with his wife, daughter Chloe and a menagerie of animals.

Foreword

Eric Peterson asked me to write the forward to *Web Analytics Demystified* because, well, I'm one of three people in the world who was written a full-length book on the subject (Hurol Inan from Australia is the third writer). The question I wanted to answer when I wrote *Web Metrics* in 2002 was "What is Web Analytics All About?" I wanted the average business person to stop being fearful of what they didn't understand and start availing themselves of the rich information at their fingertips.

Web Analytics may seem like the counting of click-through, page views and (if you're lucky) revenue. But beyond that, it is a collection of data elements that reveal the mind-set of your marketplace. Web analytics gives you a front-row look into the hearts and minds of your customers and prospects, helping you to answer questions like "How do they feel?", "What do they gravitate toward?" and "What holds their attention this week?"

The ability to strap the analytics EKG onto the world at large and see how it reacts to your advertising, your product descriptions, and your persuasion process is simply too valuable to stay a secret. To spread the word that this kind of information was available I wrote the first book on the subject of Web Analytics, *Web Metrics: Proven Methods for Measuring Web Site Success.*

I consider myself a professional explainer; I am a marketing guy with a degree in Shakespeare who started out selling Apple IIe's and VisiCalc in the early 80s and never looked back. When I meet executives who just don't get it, I do my best to put it all into terms they can understand and I get very excited when the light bulb goes on and they see the potential.

Because I am a published author on the subject and a consultant, these executives invariably turn to me for help. They have excellent questions like "What should we measure?", "How do we educate the rest of the company?" and "How do we convince the top brass that the information we're getting off our website is far more probative than anything we've had in the past?"

Invariably, corporations reach that point where they want to choose the most appropriate technology, implement the systems and start reaping the rewards; three very different steps. They are ready to move on to the next question: "How Do I Get it Done?" This is where I fall back on the two most important phrases in consulting: "It depends" and, "Trust me".

How you get it done depends on what you have in place at the moment, how enthused your technical staff is by the prospect of yet another initiative, and how well the resulting reports will be received and put to use by the business people who have the most to gain. It all depends. And trust me; I've been through this with enough companies to know that this phrase always resonates as true.

Most clients have already passed my book around and are prepared for more specific education – the down and dirty details of why some data elements will reveal great insight and how others won't. Where the data stream leaks and why the ecommerce engine disagrees with the campaign management systems. Phone calls, PowerPoint presentations, workshops, personal attention and repeated explanations until the information finally sank in and became gospel – a process that often took much longer than any of us wanted to spend. That is, until now…

Now, I will be able to hand my clients a copy of *Web Analytics Demystified* and say, "Read Chapters 4 and 11 through 16 and call me in the morning. Then we can get started." Now I have a definitive reference for the "how" of Web Analytics, an authoritative work that is the perfect compliment to the "what" and the "why" that I have already explained in *Web Metrics*.

Regarding the author, I've never met anybody as bursting with enthusiasm about Web Analytics as Eric Peterson. He is high energy, highly focused and a true believer. The only way I know to get his mind off the subject is to mention his daughter. He really wants the world to understand the nitty-gritty of how it works. He really wants people to be able to roll up their sleeves and dig in and do the actual work involved in continuous improvement, making their Web sites more valuable to their customers and their companies. While I'm looking out over the horizon and pointing the way, he's tuning the engine and checking the fluids.

I believe that the Internet has given us a new window on the world, a window where we can keep an eye on our customers and prospects. Eric Peterson makes sure you understand the process of turning grains of sand into panes of glass and keeping that glass as clean as possible in order to keep the picture of your customers and prospects as accurate and valuable as possible. In *Web Analytics Demystified* Eric has effectively "demystified" the process of making this data work for you, doing his part to share the secret with the rest of the world.

Jim Sterne
Author: *Web Metrics: Proven Methods for Measuring Web Site Success*
www.targeting.com
www.emetrics.org

CHAPTER **1**
WHY WEB ANALYTICS
DEMYSTIFIED?

**"I know that half of my advertising budget is completely wasted,
I'm just not sure which half."
Lord Leverhulme, founder of Unilever**

Web Analytics Demystified - A Marketer's Guide to Understanding How Your Web Site Affects Your Business is intended to be exactly that, a useful guide to help you get more out of your current online investments. While there are several good books about *why* you would want to set up a Web analytics program, and hundreds of different vendors to sell you the tools you will need, there has been a lack of information about how to actually extract useful information from these applications once they're installed.

Enter *Web Analytics Demystified*—a book that will demystify the marketing mumbo-jumbo that vendors provide and look behind the curtain, to help you discover that Web analytics doesn't have to be difficult or confusing at all

After reading this book you will take three things away with you:

Awareness of what Web analytics is, from a practical perspective, and what a Web analytics program can and cannot tell you.

1. An understanding of which tools and statistics are actually useful to a Web analytics program.
2. Knowledge of which available statistics are most useful to your particular online business, and how, ideally, those statistics should be used.

The goal of this book is to elucidate which statistics, ratios, and comparisons are most likely to help you improve the overall quality of your Web site for your visitors and customers. Independent of your online business model, *Web Analytics Demystified* presents each set of measurements as they relate to the standard customer life cycle—reach, acquisition, conversion and retention.

Intended Audience for This Book

If you are reading this book you probably fall into at least one of the following groups:

1. Web marketers, those challenged with bringing visitors to the Web site and enticing them to complete some valuable activity.
2. Web operations managers, those challenged with providing a high-quality Web presence to improve the likelihood of success for the Web marketers.

3. Web executives, or just executives in general, those ultimately responsible for their company's business success.

These are three very broad groups, and that you may belong to one or more of them. The key to taking something away from *Web Analytics Demystified* is that you, the reader, have some vested interest in the success of the Web site. If part of your job function is to monitor and improve your company's online return on investment, this book is for you.

Parts of *Web Analytics Demystified* are technical, but you don't need a background in PERL, C and UNIX to get value from this book. Sections of this book delve into the business value of your Web site, but you won't need an MBA to understand why you'd want to want to take a particular measurement. Hopefully you are lucky enough to work with two smart people, one technical and the other business-focused, with whom you can work with collaboratively on your Web analytics program.

If you are still wondering if this book is for you, turn to any page in Chapters 11 through 14 and confirm that at least some of the statistics look familiar to you. If you have never thought about the difference between a "new visitor" and "returning visitor," wondered about the difference between a "hit," a "page view" and a "unique visitor," or struggled to figure out what "top paths" can tell you, then perhaps this book is not for you.

If you have been asking yourself those kinds of questions repeatedly, however, keep reading.

What This Book Is Not

Web Analytics Demystified is not a book describing *why* you would want to establish a Web analytics program for your online business. It is assumed that if you are considering purchasing this book that you have already invested time, effort and at least some money trying to understand where your Web site visitors come from and what they do when they get there.

We'll waste no time describing the "characteristics" of a good Web site analyst as the only requirement for this position is desire: The desire to improve the quality of one's Web site.

Web Analytics Demystified does not present a comprehensive history of traffic analysis applications starting with Wusage™ and WebTrends Log Analyzer™. This book does little to compare the currently available applications as applications come and go, but it will occasionally mention a vendor's specific solution if that solution provides some type of information that is unique in the marketplace.

Web Analytics Demystified also does not attempt to describe how you can build a recency, frequency and monetary value (RFM) model of your visitors or customers or outline more than just the barest of steps you would want to take to integrate multiple sources of data; this book is a practical guide. This it not to say that RFM models and data integration are unnecessary or impossible to implement. The decision to skirt these subjects or avoid them altogether was based on the relative difficulty of implementation compared to the number of potential readers likely to benefit from their description. For more information on the RFM model, the author points you to

Chapter 11 of Jim Sterne's book *Web Metrics: Proven Methods for Measuring Web Site Success.* For a cursory introduction to data integration, please see Chapter 16 of this book.

This book is also a vendor-neutral guide. The author has made a conscious decision to discuss only those metrics that should be available in *any* well-designed Web analytics application. The concept of "well-designed" is an important one, especially considering that there were an estimated 80 companies selling some type of Web analytics solution at the time this book was completed. Obviously all 80 of these companies are not providing all of the metrics needed to build the key performance indication reports listed in Chapter 15. If the reader is cautious when choosing an analytics solution, preferentially choosing a vendor with A) a proven track record of success in helping customers and B) an application that is not brand new or completely revolutionary, it is safe to assume that the metrics you need to make use of this book will be available to you.

Use of Examples and Web Analytics Tips throughout This Book

The examples used throughout this book have been graciously provided by the kind people at BackcountryStore.com, the Internet's fastest growing retailer of outdoor gear. The author was introduced to BackcountryStore.com through his position at WebSideStory, creators of HitBox™, and has worked closely with management at BackcountryStore.com to help them optimize their Web site and analytics program using many of the concepts presented in this book. The author is deeply indebted to everyone at BackcountryStore.com for their permission to use their site and data in examples throughout *Web Analytics Demystified.* More information about BackcountryStore.com can be found at www.backcountrystore.com.

Figure 1: BackcountryStore.com home page, a shining example of how to drive visitors to purchase online.

Unless otherwise noted, images used in examples have been taken from the HitBox Enterprise and/or HitBox Commerce interface, the analytics package that BackcountryStore.com has standardized on since 1999. More information about the HitBox family of services can be found at www.hitbox.com or www.websidestory.com.

Additionally, throughout this book the author has included several "Web Analytics Tips." Presented in the first person, these tips are intended to supplement the examples in order to help you better understand exactly how this information is practically applied.

CHAPTER 2
OVERVIEW OF "WEB ANALYTICS"

"If you build a Web site, you must have a solid reason for doing so. Once the Web site is operational, it is crucial to understand how well it works—failure to do so is a waste of time and money."
Hurol Inan in *Measuring the Success of your Web site*

Web analytics is a term that is easy to banter around when discussing your Web site but more difficult to truly understand. It is a complex interaction between human beings, machines and code that often generates large amounts of data that then need be mined, manipulated and presented in meaningful ways. Don't be misled, a Web analytics program can be very difficult to implement successfully—but reading this book will provide insight that will make your life a little easier.

What is "Web Analytics"

Depending on whom you ask, Web analytics can have a wide variety of definitions but is ultimately focused on a single goal: Understanding the online experience such that it can be improved. A few select examples of how Web analytics is described:

- According to Guy Creese of the Aberdeen Group, a noted authority on the subject, Web analytics is "the monitoring and reporting of Web site usage so enterprises can better understand the complex interactions between Web visitor actions and Web site offers, as well as leverage that insight for increased customer loyalty and sales."

- Sarner and Janowski of the Gartner Group state that "Web analytics uses a variety of data and sources to evaluate Web site performance and visitor experience, potentially including usage levels and patterns at both an individual and an aggregate level. Data and sources may include click-stream data from the Web server log, Web transaction data, submitted data from input fields on the Web site and data in the Internet customer repository. The goals are to improve site performance, both from a technical and content perspective, enhance visitor experience (and thus loyalty), contribute to overall understanding of customers and channels, and identify opportunities and risks."

- Webopedia from internet.com states that "(Web analytics is) a generic term meaning the study of the impact of a Web site on its users. E-commerce companies often use Web analytics software to measure such concrete details as how many people visited their site, how many of those visitors were unique visitors, how they came to the site (i.e., if they followed a link to get to the site or came there directly), what keywords they searched with on the site's search engine, how long they stayed on a given page or on the entire site, what links they clicked on and when they left the site. Web analytic software can also be used to monitor whether or not a site's pages are working properly. With this information, Web site administrators can determine which areas of the site are popular and which areas of the site do not get traffic and can then use this data to streamline a site to create a better user experience."

For the sake of this book, we will define the study of Web analytics as such:

> *Web analytics is the assessment of a variety of data, including Web traffic, Web-based transactions, Web server performance, usability studies, user submitted information and related sources to help create a generalized understanding of the visitor experience online.*

The underlying assumption is that the information gained from this assessment will be used to improve the overall quality of said visitor experience, although we now know that many times there is a disconnect between having the data and knowing exactly what to do with it. The reader should immediately recognize that this definition is sufficiently broad to include a multitude of data sources not listed above. The following sections further define each of the data sources listed above.

Techniques and Technologies Used in Web Analytics

Web Traffic Data

Without a doubt the most popular source of Web analytics data is Web traffic data. Traditionally mined out of Web server log files and more recently derived from Web clients via JavaScript "page tags," traffic data is often looked upon as a goldmine of information. Generically speaking, this data source is informed by an application (such as page tags) making a record of the request for information being received (such as clicking on a link to see a Web page), and it is this record of information that is analyzed.

As Web traffic data is one of the focuses of this book, later chapters and sections will cover this data source in much greater detail.

Web Transactional Data

Any business conducting commerce online likely has access to information derived from these transactions, similar to the Web traffic data described above. Data points such as number of customers, number of orders and average size of transactions should be available to the Web analytics process. Like Web traffic data, this data source will be covered at length in following chapters.

Web Server Performance Data

The Internet is a complicated piece of technology. Designed to allow applications from anywhere on the planet to quickly connect to resources and make them available via a variety of protocols, the Internet has quickly evolved from a military/academic experiment to become an integral part of our daily lives. This explosive growth has not come without a price. While the number of global Internet users is increasing every day, technology often lags behind this usage, especially in rural areas and developing nations. The effect this technology lag has on the visitor experience can be examined within the context of Web performance data.

Web pages and applications are made up of constituent parts—text, script, images, multimedia files, banner ads, and so on—which are reassembled within a visitor's browser based on a system of rules called the Hypertext Markup Language (HTML). For a very complete explanation of HTML, please see the description provided by its inventor, Tim Berners-Lee in his book, *Weaving the Web*. Regarding performance, the general idea is the larger a Web page is in terms of overall kilobyte "weight," that is, the size of the page's component parts, the longer it will take to download and render on a visitor's computer.

From these concepts comes the very valuable "10-second rule," often cited by usability experts, including Jakob Nielsen. Nielsen, in his book on Usability Engineering states that:

- One tenth of a second (0.1) is the limit for a user to feel that a system is responding immediately when engaged in a task.
- One second (1) is the limit for a user's flow to remain uninterrupted, allowing them to notice a delay but not losing the feeling of direct connection with the task.
- Ten seconds (10) is the upper limit for keeping users focused on a single task. When faced with delays of ten seconds or longer, users have a tendency to engage in side tasks or become frustrated with the lack of system response.

A good way to think about this is by imagining a conversation that you may have with anyone. Rather than simply engaging in regular conversation, often beating the 0.1-second response by talking over each other, imagine that you had a 10-second pause between each statement. By the end of every pause you would likely need to take an additional second just to reorient yourself to the last statement made, especially as the conversation went on over time.

Compare this to the visitor experience on the Internet, where people commonly engage in side tasks while waiting for pages to load. In 10 seconds, while waiting for the next page to load, any user could potentially:

- Switch to their email browser and read email
- Switch to another Web browser and surf another site
- Start a conversation with a nearby person
- Answer or initiate a phone call
- Take a short walk
- Close their browser or simply navigate to another site

The reason that all this is so important is that on an average speed connection (56Kb modem), a Web page of only 65 Kb can take eight to ten seconds to download. While many of us have broadband connections to the Internet and performance is typically not a concern, it is important to consider that most of the global Internet audience still connects using a modem.

To put the "10 second rule" into context, here is a small sample of home page weights for popular Internet destinations:

Web Site	Page Weight	Load Time (28K / 56K / ISDN)
Amazon	113 Kb	34 sec / 17 sec / 7 sec
Wal-Mart	164 Kb	49 sec / 25 sec / 10 sec
Microsoft Network	61 Kb	18 sec / 9 sec / 4 sec
Yahoo!	55 Kb	16 sec / 8 sec / 3 sec
ESPN	206 Kb	61 sec / 31 sec / 12 sec

Table 1: Example page load times, measured in October 2002.

As you can see, only Yahoo! even really comes close to hitting the 10-second target for visitors using 28K modems and only Yahoo! and the Microsoft Network hit the target for 56K modems. Keep in mind, the "10-second rule" describes the *high-end* target, the absolute maximum for keeping a visitor engaged with what they're doing.

Of course there are excuses for making mistakes like this. "Our users like all this information, they don't mind the wait" or "We have an obligation to corporate to use these images, it is part of how we build our brand." The author's personal favorite is, "My CEO likes how the page looks and he doesn't want to attract visitors that use modems anyway…" These are all fine excuses, but keep in mind that is all that they are—excuses that contribute to a poor overall visitor experience.

To make a long story longer, one of the key factors to consider when analyzing the visitor experience on your Web site is, "How long do our pages take to download?" Since the answer is different for different types of connection, you need to take this one step further and ask, "How do our visitors connect to our Web site?" and use that answer to answer the first question. While not advocating unattractive Web pages, smart Web managers must consider download times as part of their overall Web analytics program.

One vendor that has demonstrated time and time again their knowledge of Internet performance and the download times as a component of Web analytics assessments is Keynote Systems. At the time of publication there were several interesting white papers on this subject available for free, including, "The Economic Impacts of Unacceptable Web-Site Download Speeds," "Fundamentals of Internet Measurement: A Tutorial" and "Web Page Design and Download Time."

Web Analytics Tip: Examining Page Weights

Whenever I'm analyzing a client's Web site, the first thing I do is check the page weights of their home page and three or four key pages on the site. This allows me to establish a baseline for likelihood of success. If page weights are high and I run into other problems, I tend to worry more—design issues plus potentially high download times equals real trouble. Conversely, if page weights are low, I tend to worry less about other problems.

The logic here is simple; if you make a process needlessly difficult *and* make the user wait long periods of time to try and get through said process, said user is much more likely to abandon the process. Use an inexpensive service like such as Keynote System's NetMechanic (www.netmechanic.com) to monitor page performance as you develop new pages.

Usability Studies

Usability studies are less of a Web analytics data point and more of a science of their own, having been more or less an established practice for decades in software engineering. Briefly, usability studies involve working with real human beings, typically likely visitors or actual customers, to better understand how people expect to use one's Web site or Web-based application.

Usability studies are a necessary component of a Web analytics program but this book does not delve deeply into this topic for two reasons. First, while usability studies can be frustrating, difficult and expensive to perform, there is no substitution to seeing how people really interact with the content and navigation systems that you have built. One cannot describe the feeling you get when you have spent weeks building a sophisticated navigation system that takes advantage of the full spectrum of available technology, only to have eight out of ten study participants fail to understand how said system works. Conversely, one can also not describe the feeling one gets to see real users interacting with a system you have designed and finding the information they seek in a timely manner.

Second, there are a handful of well-written books on the topic of Web usability, allowing the author to defer to the expertise and wisdom of others on this subject. For more information on Web site usability the author recommends two extremely well-written books; Jakob Neilsen's *Designing Web Usability* and Steve Krug's *Don't Make Me Think!* The former is the recognized bible on the subject, written by the elder statesman himself, Jakob Neilsen. The latter is arguably one of the best books written about Web sites ever, both humorous and useful.

User Submitted Information and Related Sources

User submitted information and related sources includes information collected via polls and surveys, direct user entry forms and non-Web based systems such as CRM databases and ERP systems. As with all Web analytics data sources there are a number of different vendors able to help collect this kind of information and dozens of applications to help you collect survey data from your visitors.

The value of user survey and polling to the Web analytics process is the ability to collect more than just raw data; you are actually able to collect user opinions and feedback. This is the difference between knowing that 8,000 people visited your home page on Monday and knowing that four out of five visitors thought your home page was slow to load. The downside of this data type is that often there are no clear patterns in the data, surveys can be very difficult to write well and often visitors complain about unwanted pop-up windows or being asked to complete forms that they did not specifically request.

If you are going to survey your visitors or user base the recommendation is to do so as unobtrusively as possible. If you are careful, this data source can add a rich component to your overall Web analytics program; if you are not careful you can seriously damage the already tenuous relationship you have with your visitor. Ways to succeed at this include:

- Partner with a vendor that has experience producing well-written surveys so that you can avoid asking too many questions, asking questions that will likely lead to "noisy" answers or producing a survey that will do more damage than good.
- Survey only participants who opt-in. Entice these visitors using some kind of "bribe" —offer discounts, access or freebies to people who will take the time to complete your survey. Most people will take the time to offer their opinions and feedback to any company that offers something they can use personally (the most useful and enticing bribe is often simply a gift certificate to any popular online retailer for any amount over $10 USD).
- Use a low-impact method for conducting the survey, such as OpinonLab's Online Opinion System (www.opinionlab.com). This Chicago-based company offers a data collection system based on a subtle little icon that floats in the lower-right portion of the Web pages you choose to instrument with their code. At the time of this writing, OpinionLab customers included Gateway Computers, Sprint, Overture, Dell Computers, Novel and Intel.

Perhaps the most useful user-collected data is the forms-based type, direct user answers to specific questions. Depending on the traffic analysis solution you have, this type of data can enable complex segmentation strategies such as demographic segmentation and rules-based segmentation. Imagine being able to sort all registered visitors to your site into "men" and "women" based on their answer to the question "what is your gender?" asked during the registration process—and then being able to see if visitor activities differ by gender. Carry this one step further and be able to see if one age group (based on the answer to the question "when were you born?") is abandoning a key process more frequently than other age groups. Imagine the powerful analytic opportunities that this type of data creates.

It is beyond the scope of this book to describe the complex interaction between customer records and anonymous customer visits using data from traditionally non-Web based systems such as CRM and ERP systems. The information provided in Chapter 16 on data integration approaches this topic briefly, but you may also contact your specific CRM or ERP vendor and asking them how they recommend you integrate the data they supply with information collected from your Web site.

Web Analytics Tip: Integrate Forms-based Data

Whenever I'm helping a client implement a traffic analysis solution I am always thinking about how to integrate forms-based data, usually with visitor segmentation in mind. My thinking is that any strategy I can find that brings disparate sources of data together *easily* is valuable.

Successful form-based segmentation strategies that I've implemented in the past include variations on demographics (age, gender, family income level, presence of children in the household, indicated preferences, indicated likelihood to purchase, and son on).

Most advertising sales groups would rather tell potential advertisers that "they had 8,000 visitors in the male, 18-to-25-year old demographic segment visit content group "A" last week and these visitors generated a combined total of 15,000 page views" rather than "we had 27,000 visitors to content group "A" last week who generated a total of 43,000 page views, and many of those visitors are in the 18-to-25-year old male demographic you are targeting…"

Where This is Going

As mentioned briefly above, the focus of the balance of *Web Analytics Demystified* will be traffic and transactional data, with performance data included as appropriate. Why?:

- Traffic analysis applications, such as WebTrends™ family of products, Fireclick's Netflame™ and even Wusage™, are far and away the Web analytics applications that most online business are already familiar with and likely own.
- While most online business already own some type of traffic analysis application, few of these businesses are likely using these applications to the full extent possible, and many are not using these applications at all (even though they have already made significant investment in said software).
- Of all the data types listed above, traffic and transactional are typically the most voluminous and by extension potentially most useful for understanding the wide variety of visitor interactions possible on a given Web site.
- It is the author's belief that the greatest possible gains for the least possible cost online revolve around developing a firm understanding of what traffic and transactional data can tell us. While it can be prohibitively expensive to continuously conduct usability studies, and you risk damaging the relationship you have with your online visitors to survey them again and again, traffic and transactional data is collected quietly behind the scenes. This quiet and constant data collection enables a fundamental Web analytics strategy, the continuous improvement process.

The Continuous Improvement Process

The continuous improvement process, sometimes referred to as the continuous improvement methodology or simply *kaizen*, is the most fundamental component of a Web analytics program for your online business. It is an idea that has been used informally for some time, but has more recently been better elucidated. The basic tenet of continuous improvement, and by extension, Web analytics, is that *measurement without thoughtful action is wasteful*. Yes, it is important to have information about how many people visit your Web site and what pages they look at when they visit but if that is all you get from your analytics package you will soon be asking yourself why you made such a significant investment. Jim Sterne, one of the godfathers of Web analytics, clarifies the need to measure and act quite well in his book, *Advanced Email Marketing*:

> "The secret to truly successful marketing is *actionable measurement*. Measuring your results alone isn't enough; the key is feeding them back into your sales and marketing processes to make continuous improvements. Many marketing projects fail in this regard."

Supporting Sterne's comment about marketing projects failing to act upon what they measure, is a recent ClickZ article by Jason Burby of the Web business consultancy ZAAZ, Inc,. citing the following three reasons that analytics fail companies :

1. The goals for the analytics program are ill- or undefined.
2. Information generated from analytics projects are ineffectively shared within the organization.
3. Companies don't take action based on the data they collect.

(See the original article on Clickz at
http://www.clickz.com/res/analyze_data/article.php/3307121)

Fortunately, continuous improvement is an established framework to help companies avoid all three of these problems. Fundamental to the continuous improvement process is the notion that no changes are made on the Web site without a reason for making the change and expectations about what effect the changes should produce. By tying continuous improvement to the key performance indicators discussed in Chapters 11 through 15 of this book, the effects of changes can be observed by individuals throughout the organization. If you can convince your company to truly use this process you will never have to make another useless measurement on your Web site again.

The Process, Defined

The following five steps define the continuous improvement process:

Define

First establish the key activities and actions on which you want to focus your efforts. It is impossible to state that you want to simply "increase traffic to your Web site" and successfully work towards that goal. It is much more useful to define a goal of "increasing visitor traffic by 10 percent and visitor conversions by 50 percent from June to July by refining the marketing message delivered in our email campaigns." The former is vague and you will never be 100 percent sure what changes affected an increase or decrease in traffic. The latter is very specific, defining which parts of your site will change (email campaigns) and the expected changes (10 percent increase in traffic, 50 percent increase in conversions from June to July).

Measure

Taking baseline measurements is the only way to understand whether any of the changes you implement are successful. Using the above goal definition as an example one would start by recording the percentage-wise response and conversion of visitors arriving from email campaigning activity in June. Ideally you will take these measurements and roll them into a key performance indication program similar to those described in Chapter 15 of this book. Rolling these measurements into a regular report that is shared within the organization is critical to ensuring that everyone understands the changes you are about to make and that they are able to see the effect of these changes.

Prioritize and Change

As there are often several different solutions to a given problem, as well as several different component problems, it is smart business to assign priority to each component and potential solution so that resources can best be allocated. Continuing with the aforementioned example, it is reasonable to assume that two possible explanations for response being low are poor targeting and poor messaging. While it is sometimes difficult to find lists of appropriate email addresses for blind campaigns (in other words, spam) it is reasonable to create three different messages and test the individual efficacy of each message.

It is this step that is nearly always the most time-consuming; the point where you have to actually sit down and create new wire-frames, design new pages, consult existing personas, work with outside agencies, and so on. In order to make this step as painless as possible you should consider breaking changes up into reasonable "chunks" of work. If people start making statements like, "We should redo the entire Web site" or "We should hire an entirely new advertising agency" in order to reach the defined goals, perhaps everyone should take a deep breath. The chances that you will be able to measure the effects of large changes like these are not good. More often than not when a complete redesign occurs all you do is create a whole new suite of problems that need to be addressed.

Instead it is much better to try and break the perceived problem down into as many small actions as possible and tackle them in order of likelihood of returning the desired effect. Doing so is not nearly as difficult as it sounds as long as you keep the following in mind:

You will only be able to truly understand the effect of a change if you make one change at a time. Often it is the smallest thing that has the most significant effect.

Web analytics is not rocket science. On the contrary, Web analytics done well is more like private investigation – by looking closely for clues and forming micro-hypotheses that can be easily tested, often times the larger problem is solved with a minimum of effort.

Verify

Before you deploy your changes to the entire online universe and risk making costly mistakes it is wise to test your changes against a smaller audience and verify that results are visible. In this example it would be wise to send each of the three different emails to a subset of your blind audience to test that response rates have not gone down compared to the baseline data measured in June. If you are making changes to your Web site proper, it is strongly recommended that you run A/B tests such as those described in Chapter 6 and make sure that A) you can see the effects of the changes and B) that the effects are significant enough to be propagated throughout.

Analyze

This is the final step, taking measurements to determine how successful the changes you made actually were. It is this step that allows you to refine future business strategy, essentially learning from your successes and failures. Provided that you have successfully verified that a positive effect can be observed based on the changes and have rolled the changes out to your entire site or audience, you then want to continue to measure their effect over time. The analyze step would essentially be the "after" reporting in your key performance indicator (KPI) report and the percent change would then be compared to the desired goal described in the first step in this process to measure success or failure.

Strategies for Success

As you can imagine this is a cyclic process – as soon as you get the results of your analysis it is time to define the next set of changes based on evolving business goals. A few strategies for success when employing the continuous improvement process include:

Think Micro, Not Macro

Put another way, don't bite off more than you can chew. A well-established Web analytics program will be continuous in its own right and there will be plenty of time to put all of your business goals through this cycle. The biggest mistake businesses make is trying to change too much at once and then not being sure what actually caused any observed results. Give yourself a fighting chance! There is more than enough variability inherent in the Internet itself without adding more complexity to the mix.

Test for a Reasonable Amount of Time

You don't want to spend too much time on any one step, especially the "analyze" step. There is a tendency to keep watching, measuring and waiting in the hopes that whatever you are watching will magically "get better" on its own. The problem with this is that the effect of most changes is seen quickly, especially on high traffic sites, and so waiting and watching essentially becomes opportunity lost. Keep the pressure on to figure out what combination of flow and presentation works best for your customers, especially if you are trying to affect abandonment and conversion rates by changing flow and design through a specific process. This is not to say change your site every day to try and find the magic formula. Be judicious about making changes; your business model and existing infrastructure will likely constrain your ability to make and deploy changes. Still, you want to fight the temptation to only make changes once a quarter, hoping that your defined goals will be met sometime in the next year. The key performance indicators discussed in Chapter 15 will likely be extremely helpful in determining when a reasonable amount of time has passed and that the results you are seeing are the results you are going to continue to see.

Keep Careful Track of What Works and What Doesn't

The single most wasteful act in continuous improvement and Web analytics is making the same mistake over and over again. Assign someone the role of gatekeeper and ensure that he or she has intimate knowledge about changes that have been made in the past and the effect of those changes. If the author had a nickel for every time he heard someone say "hey, isn't this the same change we made to this part of the site last year?" he wouldn't need to write this book *or* work.

It is difficult to emphasize enough the importance of making use of the continuous improvement process in your Web analytics program. Many of you will likely recognize the close relationship between continuous improvement and the Six Sigma process; more of you should realize that continuous improvement and kaizen are only more interesting terms to describe the scientific method – forming and testing hypotheses by collecting data and objectively analyzing said data. Most, if not all, of the greatest gains of humanity have been realized by some application of the scientific method; is there any reason to expect that your Web site cannot benefit from the application of a strategy this tested and valuable?

Very few online businesses are fortunate enough to simply stumble upon the correct combination of language, presentation and flow to maximize profits or optimize the visitor experience. Truly successful businesses apply a methodology like continuous improvement or Six Sigma to systematically test ideas, looking for those that are good and ferreting out those that are "less good." If you take nothing else from this book at least consider applying the continuous improvement process to whatever Web analytics you already do.

Web Analytics Tip: Applying the Continuous Improvement Process

With every new business I work with doing any kind of Web analytic work, be it training, implementation or analysis, I always spend time helping them to institute the continuous improvement methodology. The most important thing for everyone to know, or at least anyone who is serious about their online business, is that the Internet is not a static entity. Customer preferences change, the competitive landscape changes, technology changes, everything changes. If you accept the fact that everything changes and that the Internet is a dynamic entity you can immediately see the value in being aggressive about implementing and testing changes on your Web site.

Case in point: One customer I work with had been requiring registration to move through their purchase process. They were doing so because other companies did it and they were reported to be very successful (I often refer to this as the "Amazon syndrome"). What this customer didn't stop to consider was the negative effect this would have on visitors who were unsure they would ever make a repeat purchase;

people want to make sure that you're a good vendor from end-to-end before they're willing to commit to having a relationship with you.

To make a long story short, we implemented the continuous improvement process to test the theory that removing the registration step would have a positive impact on the site's overall conversion rate. Turns out we were right—when they removed the registration step, making it optional and opt-in, the site-wide conversion rate went up more than 20 percent. Encouraged by this simple, but very significant, win the customer kept applying continuous improvement and was able to make additional gains without outside support or encouragement.

In addition to the continuous improvement process, I also encourage my customers to track key performance indicators (KPIs) such as those described in Chapter 15 of this book. The combination of KPI reporting and the continuous improvement process provide a structured and powerful strategy for improving nearly any critical metric of online business success.

CHAPTER 3
DIFFERENT WEB
TRAFFIC DATA SOURCES

**"With so much data available, what's the most important thing to measure?
The most important metrics is that which helps improve your site."
Jim Sterne in *Web Metrics***

One of the most unique things about *Web Analytics Demystified* is that this is the first book known to its author that provides a moderately technical comparative analysis of Web-server log files and the more recently emerged client-side page tags. These page tags, sometimes referred to as "web bugs," have been touted in 2003 as "the future of Web analytics data collection" and analysts like Matthew Berk have declared that "the Web analytics war is over and page tags have won the battle." While statements such as these may be premature it is important to understand the strengths and weaknesses of the common data sources for Web analytics measurement.

The Two Most Common Sources plus One Uncommon One

The history of Web traffic analysis typically begins with the sentence "in the beginning there were Web server log files, and Web server log files were good…" While it sounds like the beginning of a bad joke, this is pretty much the truth—Web traffic analysis began with the server log file. Because of this, Web traffic analysis is often referred to as "log-file analysis," which is often no longer the case. WebTrends Corporation of Portland, Oregon (now NetIQ), did a great deal to promote log file analysis, originally selling their Log Analyzer™ product to the many emerging Webmasters of the world during the Internet boom of the 1990s. Since we've already stated that *Web Analytics Demystified* is not a history book, let's just leave it at that.

At some point the engineers at WebSideStory of San Diego, California, observed that JavaScript could be leveraged on individual Web pages to transmit interesting information about the page a visitor was viewing and the browser application they were using to view the page. In essence, the JavaScript would build a series of variables populated with a snapshot of visitor and page information and then pass that information to a data center via a small "gif" image. The combination of JavaScript and the image request was initially referred to as a "page tag" and page tagging started the era of client-side traffic data collection.

At this point in time, log files and page tags are the two most common Web traffic data sources globally. Log files still enjoy the widest usage, thanks in large part to the hard work of WebTrends sales force and distribution channels through the mid-90s. However, page tagging is rapidly becoming more popular, thanks in part to the application service provider (ASP) model that allows for faster implementations and lower in-house costs of ownership, and the number of business sites employing client-side data collection grows daily. Both of these data sources will be explored in great depth in this chapter.

There is a third source of data available to Web analytics reporting, that of network data collection, which was Pioneered by Accrue Software, Inc., in 1996 and later copied by Andromedia in their ARIA product and Marketwave in their Hit List family of products. A network data collector, in the words of Bob Page, founder and CTO of Accrue Software, is "the moral equivalent of a protocol analyzer, except it's tuned for HTTP, and built for folks who are content developers and marketing executives, instead of protocol engineers." Put in perhaps more friendly terms, Accrue's network data collector sat on the same network as the Web servers and passively watched data flow between the Web server and the Web clients (that is, visitors' Web browsers) making requests.

Some of the purported advantages of network data collection included the ability to measure how often visitors were hitting the "stop" and "reload" buttons in their browser, the ability to measure a visitors effective Internet connection speed including how long it took for an entire page to load (HTML plus all component objects) and the ability to determine how much of a Web page was actually transmitted to determine whether pages were loaded completely into the visitor's Web browser. Vendors not supporting the network data collection often complained that the model was not scalable and that it would have serious performance issues. While scale is a potential problem for any analytics product, Bob Page related to this author in a personal email that the Accrue G2 product was measuring 1.5 billion "hits" a day using network collection.

While each of these does seem to be advantageous, the network data collection model never really took off in a big way. In the first wave of consolidation, around the approximate time that NetIQ purchased WebTrends, Inc., Accrue purchased Marketwave and Macromedia purchased Andromedia (Macromedia has since ceased supporting the ARIA product). More recently, as Accrue's stock price fell and stayed below the $1.00 per share minimum for membership on the NASDAQ exchange, Accrue declared bankruptcy and was purchased by a new company, Datanautics, which has been reported to be made up completely of the previous owners of Accrue. While this author has little direct experience with network data collection, it is safe to say that he is not alone in the world and that *very few* people have direct experience with network data collection as a Web analytics data source.

Focus on Web Server Log Files as a Data Source

According to the most recent survey by the Aberdeen Group, companies selling log file analysis solutions share about 41 percent of the available revenue in the Web analytics market. Companies in this market segment include the WebTrends division of NetIQ, SPSS (having purchased NetGenesis in 2001), Accrue, IBM's SurfAid, Revenue Sciences and a handful of others. The 41% market share is down significantly from the 1990s when log-based solutions were "the only game in town." When the Internet craze of the mid-90s hit and business after business clamored over themselves to get online, it became obvious that some solution was needed to help understand what visitors were doing on these Web sites. At the time, the only easily available data source was the Web-server log file.

A Web server exists to do essentially one thing—serve resources to requesting clients. Resources are objects like HTML pages, images, multimedia files, script files and the like. Requesting clients are most often Web browsers being used by people but can also be automated agents like search engine spiders, performance monitoring applications and other related applications. A Web server is "successful" as long as it is able to respond to all requests for information in a timely fashion without losing track of requests. Problems occur with Web servers when try to respond to too many requests at one time; the most common result in this case is a failure to respond. To keep track of the "how, when and why" these problems occur, Web servers offer logging capabilities.

The Web-server log file is roughly what it sounds like, a text file that is written as activity is generated by a Web server. According to the folks at Apache, whose servers currently enjoy more than 60 percent of the market share, "in order to effectively manage a Web server, it is necessary to get feedback about the activity and performance of the server as well as any problems that may be occurring." Microsoft, whose Internet Information Server (IIS) holds roughly 30 percent of the market share have this to say: "Microsoft (Internet Information Server) uses log files to track information about events that occur when users access IIS Web sites and applications. Information such as the number of visitors to your site or application, the number of bytes sent and received, and the referring page is invaluable for Web managers, who can examine the data to discern trends and patterns."

The log files are able to collect a variety of data about requests for information coming to your Web server. The most common pieces of information collected are the Internet Protocol (IP) address of the client requesting the resource, the authenticated user name of the requestor (if known), the date and time of the request, the method of the request and the resource being requested, the status code sent back to the client and the size in bytes of the object sent. A typical log file entry in common log format (CLF) looks like:

```
127.0.0.1 - frank [10/Oct/2000:13:55:36 -0700] "GET /apache_pb.gif
HTTP/1.0" 200 2326
```

Most, if not all, currently available Web servers offer additional (or extended) logging capabilities. A complete list of data available to common and extended logging includes:

Request Property	Explanation
Resource requested	The actual file being requested via HTTP (HTML, GIF, JPG, PDF, and so on)
Date	Date of the request based on the server time
Time	Time of the request based on the server time
Client IP Address	IP address of the browser making the resource request
Referrer	The URL containing the link to the resource being requested. This is usually only available if a link is actually clicked, although not always
User Agent	The browser or application making the resource request
Service Name	Name of the service, such as, Web server application
Server Name	Name of the Web server serving the resource
Server IP	IP address of the Web server serving the resource
Method	GET or POST. Both are methods for sending information to scripts running on the Web server and for making requests

URI Query	The query string appended to the end of the URL. Not always present but typically used to pass information to dynamically generated Web pages
HTTP Status	Numerical values describing the Web server response. Common codes include "200" (ok) and "404" (file not found). A complete list can be found at http://www.w3.org/Protocols/rfc2616/rfc2616-sec6.html
Win32 Status	Similar to HTTP Status but referring to Microsoft's proprietary list of codes
Bytes Sent	Total bytes transferred by the Web server
Bytes Received	Total bytes received by the client browser or application
Time Taken	Total time taken from request to delivery
Protocol Version	HTTP protocol version used in request and transfer
Cookie	Text to be written to browser cookie, typically used to store identifying or session "state" information

Table 2: Information commonly collected by Web server log file extended file format.

This example contains information in the combined log file (CLF) format with the addition of referrer and user-agent

```
lothlorien.ncsa.uiuc.edu - - [19/Sep/1995:15:19:07 -0500] "GET
/images/icon.gif HTTP/1.0" 200 1656 "http://hoohoo.ncsa.uiuc.edu/"
"NCSA_Mosaic/2.7b1 (X11;IRIX 5.3 IP22)  libwww/2.12 modified"
```

An example from a Microsoft IIS Log file format collecting user's IP address, user name, date, tie, service name, server name, server IP address, time taken, bytes received, bytes sent, status code, Win32 status, request type and the resource being requested:

```
172.16.255.255,anonymous,03/20/98,23:58:11,MSFTPSVC,SALES1,192.168.114
.201,60,275,0,0,0,PASS,intro.htm
```

As you can see, different Web servers offer slightly different data points and collect the information in different formats. Keeping track of this information for *every* request coming to a Web server can quickly add up in terms of disk space. Because of this, Web servers offer the ability to both selectively collect data and to rotate logs on a regularly occurring basis. Selectively collecting data is a good thing, and log rotation is simply a fact of life.

Consider Table 2, describing the data available to extended logging. While it is nice to have some of this information, one must consider the question, "What is the business value of knowing the Win32 Status of a request?" More often than not the answer to this question is, "What is a Win32 Status?"—which is another way of saying that there is no business value. It is important to remember that logging does not come for free and the more you collect, the more you have to process. With this in mind, here is an assessment of the business necessity for each of the data points described in Table 2.

Request Property	Value	Explanation
Resource Requested	Yes	This is the actual document that the visitor is requesting
Date	Yes	The date of the request is necessary to put the request into a temporal context

Time	Yes	The time of the request is necessary to put the request into a temporal context
Client IP Address	Maybe	Often used to determine uniqueness of visitor; cookies are better but require additional set-up
Referrer	Yes	Knowing what Web sites are linking to you and sending you traffic is a key component in understanding reach and acquisition
User Agent	Maybe	If reporting end-users are developers responsible for ensuring that Web site is tailored for most common browser then "yes," otherwise likely "no"
Service Name	No	Non-actionable, uninformative information
Server Name	No	Non-actionable, uninformative information
Server IP	No	Non-actionable, uninformative information
Method	No	Non-actionable, uninformative information
URI Query	Maybe	If your Web site makes use of dynamically generated pages and passes information to these pages in the URL then "yes," otherwise, "no"
HTTP Status	Yes	For tracking errors and broken links.
Win32 Status	No	Non-actionable, uninformative information
Bytes Sent	Maybe	If your analysis application is able to compare the difference between bytes sent and bytes received then "yes"; otherwise "no"
Bytes Received	Maybe	If your analysis application is able to compare the difference between bytes sent and bytes received then "yes," otherwise, "no"
Time Taken	Maybe	If your analysis application is able to report on the average time taken for clients to download resources, or even better the distribution of these times, then "yes," otherwise, "no"
Protocol Version	No	Non-actionable, uninformative information
Cookie	Maybe	A much better strategy to determine the uniqueness of a visitor is to use cookies (rather than IP address) but cookies require additional set-up. If your server supports cookies as a unique user identifier (UUID) then "yes," otherwise, "no"

Table 3: Business necessity and value of data available via Web server log files.

In general, whenever you are going to collect data it is advised to collect only the data you are sure you will need to answer the specific questions being asked. Many data analysts subscribe to the notion that every possible data point should be collected so that different hypotheses can be tested after the fact. This is fine if you are conducting an experiment that will be difficult or costly to reproduce (such as sending people into space) but never the case when collecting Web data. Changing log file formats is very simple and can typically be done in a matter of minutes. Reconfiguring log file analyzers can be slightly more challenging but is not rocket science. Since the Internet is always on, if you add some data points to your collection it should only be a matter of hours or perhaps days until you have enough relevant data to study.

Remember that a fundamental aspect of the continuous improvement process, and therefore Web analytics, is to define and measure. By carefully defining the question you hope to answer you will very likely also define the data that you need to collect. If you only collect the data you need to answer any given question you will save yourself the trouble of having to wade through meaningless data, thereby decreasing the time required to analyze and increasing your likelihood for success.

Advantages of Web Server Log Files as a Data Source

When traffic analysis applications were first being deployed by online businesses, the advantage of using Web server log file data was that it was the only data source available other than network data collection. With the emergence of client-side data collection online businesses now have a choice as to which data type they will use. Some advantages of using Web server log files as a data source include:

Ownership of Data

Since your Web server is creating the log file as requests are being served, the data is collected and contained on your own machines. Regardless of the location of these servers, unless your online business is served from a shared hosting environment (see disadvantages, below) your log files can be stored on the same network serving your Web pages, and so on. While it is your responsibility to rotate, backup and maintain these files, you theoretically always have access to the logged data and even if you switch reporting applications you will likely be able to analyze historical data from said log files.

Flexibility of Data Collection: Types of Data

As previously mentioned, your Web servers can be instructed which data to collect and which to ignore. If you have determined that all you need to answer your fundamental Web analytics questions are the referring source, requested object and date/time of the request then you can simply instruct your Web server to log only that information. Most Web servers even give you the ability to log only certain types of requests, such as those for HTML documents but not for images or scripting files. An advantage this flexibility provides is the ability to keep track of non-HTML pages downloaded (such as PDF, multimedia or executable files) as well to track different types of server errors (500s, 404s, and son on) and some server-based redirects.

Ease-of-Implementation

Unlike page tagging there is no need to instrument every page on your Web site to take advantage of a log file solution. Since request logging is part of the Web server process, not the pages or objects being served, no additional setup or implementation is required to create Web server log data.

Ability to Log Directly to a Database

Some Web servers (such as Microsoft's Internet Information Server) allow you to log requests directly to a database application. The advantage of doing this that if you have smart SQL developers you may be able to answer many of your Web analytics questions without needing an expensive analysis application. Since logging directly to a database can be resource-intensive it is not recommended to use this method in high-volume request situations. In these situations it is likely better to batch import Web server log data into the database on regular intervals.

Ability to Determine if Downloads Complete

One advantage Web server log files have is that they are able to report on the total of "bytes sent" when a request is made. Log-file-based applications are able to take advantage of this information and report on the percent of requests that successfully downloaded. From this information it is possible to determine roughly how often visitors A) click the browser's "stop" button or back up before the page download is completed and B) successfully download non-HTML objects such as executable files and Adobe PDF documents. Many companies in the business of providing applications or content have a very real need to know not only how many people begin to download a document but also how many of those downloads complete.

Ability to Measure Traffic from Robots and Spiders

Because non-human traffic is not usually excluded by default, most software solutions using Web server log files as a data source also provide reporting on which robots and spiders are visiting and with what frequency. While it is extremely important to exclude this traffic from regular reporting about the use of the Web site, it can be very useful in helping to determine the effect of search engine optimization (SEO) projects. The goal of SEO projects is to attract more search engine-indexing agents and have them traverse the site deeply and broadly. Having this information can help the online business quantify the effect of SEO, especially when the work has been outsourced, and make decisions about future SEO efforts.

Disadvantages of Web Server Log Files as a Data Source

An historical disadvantage of Web-server log files, and one that does continue to plague the highest-volume Web sites, is disk space. If you are collecting all available data, and your number of daily page requests is up in the millions, the necessary disk space to keep daily logs can be quite large. In this instance the online business would likely need to have a structured program for moving logs on a regular basis—which can then impact the ease-of-reporting. Fortunately, most online businesses aren't faced with this volume of traffic and since the cost of disk space and disk I/O has come down significantly in the past few years, storage is less of a disadvantage.

Still, Web-server log files as a Web analytics data source do have some significant disadvantages worth noting:

Proxy Caching

Before the "broadband revolution" began the most pressing issue faced on the Internet was long, frustrating download times. In the home environment dialing up to the Internet using a modem, users would constantly, and justifiably, complain about how long it took to get information. An early solution to this was caching—keeping often requested information in a location that was closer to the end-user to speed the delivery time. Proxy caching is a technique employed by Internet Service Providers (ISPs) to keep frequently requested content on their own machines which are very close to the user, as opposed to the content's original site which can be "far away" (on the Internet, far away is both relative and real). Proxy caching in essence takes a snapshot of a Web page when it is requested the first time and keeps that image for a set period of time. If another user requests this page before it "times out" then the page is served from the proxy server to speed delivery. Proxy servers are a great idea really, but the negative impact on Web server log files is that the request for content never actually comes through to the Web server. Proxy servers are less of an issue for dynamically generated Web pages, which typically are delivered with a "no cache" directive.

Browser Caching

Related to proxy caching is browser caching, or the ability for your Web browser to store frequently or recently viewed information on your computer's hard drive for speedy retrieval. The most frequent use of the browser cache is demonstrated by using the "back" and "forward" buttons in one's Web browser. When an end-user visits a Web page, they get that page and the objects it is composed of via the Internet (whether the page and objects are delivered from the businesses Web server or a proxy cache is impossible to know). As the user clicks through a Web site, each of these pages and their components are usually stored locally on the user's hard drive. When a user then clicks the browser's "back" button, the page is quickly loaded from the hard drive, saving the necessity for another request through the Internet. The end result to the Web server log file is lost information. If, when the user backs through a site in the attempt to find information, the requests for these pages are never even sent to the originating Web server, no record can be created and information is lost. Unfortunately, the use of the "back" and "forward" buttons is common among Internet users and the knowledge of how visitors truly navigate is commonly invisible to the Web server log file.

IP Address as a Unique Identifier

As mentioned above, one element that is always available to the Web server log file is the IP address of the client making the request for information. One would reasonably expect that this IP address would then be a good identifier to help determine the uniqueness of a visitor on a Web site, right? Wrong. The same proxy servers mentioned above that speed information along to end-users are also often used to pass requests for information along to Web servers. The end result is that many different users in different geographic regions may be identified by the same IP address. The most frequently asked question that arises from this issue is, "Why are 40 percent of my visitors from Virginia?" The answer is, "Because the AOL proxy servers are located in Virginia and they have some 35 million users on the Internet." According to the AOL Webmasters, "AOL Members' requests for Internet objects are usually handled by the AOL Proxy system. When a member requests multiple documents for multiple URLs, each request may come from a different proxy server. Since one proxy server can have multiple members going to one site, Webmasters should not make assumptions about the relationship between members and proxy servers when designing their Web site." If you look closely at the AOL proxy and client IP addresses, you will discover that most of their 35 million users are connecting to Web sites via roughly 50 IP addresses. Multiply this problem by the number of multi-user portals working to build market share currently and you will start to realize that IP addresses can be a dangerously misleading indicator of the uniqueness of a Web site visitor.

These three issues are the most serious disadvantages of using a Web-server log file as a data source for your Web analytics program. Some estimate that the information loss as a result of proxy and browser caching approaches 40 percent or more (meaning you would undercount traffic to your Web site by 40 percent). The information loss as a result of using IP addresses to determine the uniqueness of a visitor is a function of the volume of traffic your site receives from proxy servers, which can be measured, but is frequently quite high depending on your business model.

The first and third issue can be overcome with careful and thoughtful implementation when setting up your Web server and Web analytics reporting application. The second issue, to the best of the author's knowledge, is impossible to overcome without page-by-page instrumentation, discussed below under page tagging as a Web analytics data source.

Some additional but slightly less serious disadvantages of Web server log files include:

Robots and Spiders and Crawlers, Oh My!

Traffic from search engines is something that most Web managers strongly crave. Having your Web site appear at the top of the first page of search results for a particular search term is something that a company can spend thousands of dollars to achieve. The basic strategy for achieving this success is to create "search friendly" pages and submit them to the search engines for indexing. It is this indexing process that can cause problems for Web server log file analyzers. The indexing applications, often called "crawlers" or "spiders" or "robots" but generically referred to as "non-human user agents," make requests to your Web server for content to index. The issue is that, while these requests show up in Web-server log files as nearly identical to the same requests that normal "human" visitors send, they are not traffic that most businesses want to measure, at least not as part of a Web analytics program. These user agents can be excluded from the Web server log file analysis (see "best practices …" below) but if they are not, depending on the type of Web site, robots and spiders can significantly inflate traffic and page request numbers.

Report Generation Time

Because Web-server log files can grow quickly, especially when not instructed to limit the data that they collect, it can also take significant time to parse these files and generate necessary reports to inform the Web analytics process. Some vendors have discovered ways around long reporting times, but for many the wait to generate reports for months or years worth of log files can be days or weeks. Another common issue is the time it can take to physically move the log files from the machine they're being created on to the machine they're being analyzed on.

Multiple Log Files from Multiple Servers

As traffic to Web sites grows it is common to serve requests from more than one physical computer. Web traffic load balancing devices are able to distribute requests in a variety of ways, the most common being the "round robin," but can also include logical distribution based on the type of request or the actual processor load on the Web servers at the time of the request. The end result in a multi-server environment (often called a "cluster" or "server farm") is that Web-server log files for the exact same time can be housed on physically different machines. Consider cases where Web sites are mirrored geographically—that is, multiple Web servers serving the same information from separate geographic locations—and the problem increases. In order to get a clear picture of the traffic to a Web site at any given time you need to combine all of these resulting log files into a single file. Additionally, depending on the strategy that a load balancer uses to distribute traffic, a single visitor's click-stream can be spread across multiple Web servers. If the online business hopes to examine click-stream data they will definitely need to stitch the multiple log files together and ensure that the clocks on each machine are exactly in-sync; if they are not, the traffic analysis application will not be able to reassemble the exact order of requests for information from the end-user. Depending on the exact goals of the Web Analysis being performed it may be acceptable to only analyze data from one or few machines, but more often than not this strategy can lead to misleading conclusions and is not recommended. Fortunately most log file analysis applications have tools to manage multiple log file situations but the solution almost always comes at a cost—longer report generation time.

Access to Web Server Log Files

Some smaller online businesses, especially those just getting onto the Internet, contract with ISPs who host many different Web sites on a single machine through a single Web server. In low-traffic volume situations this is often a cost effective solution, one that makes good overall sense. The downside can be that many of these ISPs will not log traffic data to separate files for each business, either because they are unable or unwilling to do so. Occasionally these ISPs will force the online business to use a Web analytics package that they provide, one that may not be adequate to answer the kinds of questions said business has. The key question to ask your ISP if you are considering shared hosting is, "How do I access my Web-server log files?" You want to make sure that they can provide log files for your Web site (and your site only) via FTP and that you are free to analyze them with software of your choosing.

Up Front Costs

The final disadvantage often associated with using a Web-server log-file analyzer is the fact that you typically have to purchase all of the software, hardware and expertise in advance. This differs from the ASP model most frequently associated with client-side data collection, where you "pay as you go." This may or may not be a disadvantage to your online business but it is one that is frequently cited.

While it may look like the disadvantages of using Web-server log files as a Web analytics data source heavily outweigh the advantages, keep the following in mind. Many of the disadvantages can be overcome through careful and thoughtful implementation and your online business likely already has much of what you need to take advantage of this data source. It is likely that you have a spare computer or two around to install whichever software package you choose and to store archived log files. It is also likely that you have someone on your IT staff that can help you install the necessary software and make changes to your Web server so that you are able to collect the data you need. Finally, it is extremely likely that you already have Web server log files somewhere on your network that you can use to set historical baselines and get more familiar with the analysis package you choose without having to modify your Web pages in any way.

Best Practices When Implementing a Web Server Log File Solution

Considering the risks and rewards associated with using a Web-server log-file-based Web analytics solution, the author recommends the following "best practices" for implementing such a solution. Most of these recommendations revolve around data collection and filtering and are relatively easy to implement.

Configure Carefully

Extended log files are able to capture a variety of different data, including server name, service name and server IP address, which are likely of no use to your Web analytics program. Collecting everything for everything's sake will do little more than slow down your analysis. A better strategy is to carefully consider the available data and decide which information to collect and which to ignore. Modifying your server configuration file to exclude data is trivial and will cut down on processing time and drive storage space. Consult Table 3 for help in deciding which fields to include or ignore based on business value.

Exclude "Non-Human" Traffic from Your Analysis

Web-server log files cannot, by default, differentiate between human visitors and software agents. While the goal of any Web analytics program is to measure the activity of human visitors, failure to filter out automated traffic will artificially inflate traffic and page view numbers. Most applications have an option to exclude based on the "user agent" string that should be exercised to ensure accurate data collection.

Plan for Multiple Log Files from Multiple Servers

If you incorporate a server cluster or multi-server environment it is likely that recorded traffic is spread out among different log files. Unless you are able to recombine this traffic you will end up with gaps in path or click-stream analysis and inaccuracy in page, visit and visitor counts. Most log analyzer applications have options for "stitching together" multiple files and these features should be taken advantage of to ensure data accuracy.

Plan for Rotation, Storage and Backing Up

Most Web server log files are created on a daily basis and given a unique file name. As time passes these files will likely consume too much drive space and need to be moved elsewhere for long-term storage. A common problem that results is that if you then would like to look back at dates contained in archived log files you will have to either move those files back into a format that your log analyzer can access or develop a strategy for analyzing archived log files.

Employ Cache and Proxy Busting Techniques

It is a good idea to attempt to implement some type of dynamic platform on your Web site, if for no other reason than to increase the likelihood that your site's Web pages will not be cached in proxy and browser caches. The HTTP/1.1 protocol supports cache control and a complete description of this protocol and its use can be found at the World Wide Web Consortium site (www.w3.org/Protocols/rfc2616/rfc2616-sec13.html). The easiest way to implement this is to use the HTTP META tag and setting:

```
<META HTTP-EQUIV="Expires" CONTENT="0">
<META HTTP-EQUIV="Pragma" CONTENT="no-cache">
<META HTTP-EQUIV="Cache-Control" CONTENT="no-cache">
```

While this method is not entirely perfect, and it will cause your visitors some additional headaches (every time they want to see a page it will have to be downloaded again) it will result in a more accurate measurement of the information requested by your visitors. This recommendation should only be followed if a significant percentage of your Internet audience is visiting using a broadband connection, thus decreasing the likelihood of complaints about poor page load time.

Work With Your Application Vendor

Compared to client-side page tagging solutions, getting a "best practices" implementation for a Web-server log-file-based solution really involves careful setup and data validation. Each of the current vendors selling Web-server log-file analysis solutions will have specific tips and tricks to ensure the highest quality data collection and analysis. Don't be afraid to ask, or even force, your solution provider to explain this to you. If they are committed to your success with their application they'll be more than happy to help you out.

Exclude Internal Traffic from the Analysis

By default most log file analyzers *do not* exclude internally generated traffic to the Web servers, that traffic generated by your developers and other employees making use of the business Web site. This traffic should be excluded or segregated out of the final analysis because it is not necessarily representative of your visitor's interests. Depending on your particular business model, internal traffic can be a significant component of the traffic to a given page or content area.

Most Web analytics applications will allow you to exclude traffic from reporting and analysis based on at least the IP address of the visitor. While IP address is a poor indicator of uniqueness, it is often useful for excluding groups of visitors as most corporate firewalls will identify internal users as having coming through one or several unique addresses.

Examples of When to Use a Web-Server Log-File Application

Provided you take the time to ensure that you are doing everything you can to increase the accuracy of data, there are a handful of scenarios when you would likely choose a Web-server log-based solution. These include:

When You Need to Incorporate Historical Data

It is extremely likely that your IT staff has been collecting Web server log files and storing them somewhere on your network. This does not mean that these files are "clean" or that the data is in the best format for your analysis, but the files do almost certainly exist. Still, if you want to start a Web analytics program off and have baseline data, or look back at the effects of changes you have already made on your site, historical log files are about your only option.

When You are Unable to Instrument Your Web Pages

This will be discussed in the next chapter at great length but a requirement of client-side data collection is adding additional code to each of the Web pages you want to track (hence the term "page tag"). In some situations it is impossible to do this, in others, impractical. If your IT staff can provide a suitable explanation as to "why" you cannot implement page tagging, Web server log files are the way to go. One caveat to this is be sure to ask your IT staff exactly *why* a page tagging scenario would not work—the worst thing for a Web analytics program is having to work through another department that is unable or unwilling to help.

When Ownership of Data is Extremely Important

One clear advantage of Web server log files is that all of the necessary data to conduct an analysis is yours and is contained in-house. Contrast this with page tagging where more often than not the data is collected into a remote data warehouse owned by the vendor (the exception to this is described in the next chapter under the heading "tags into logs"). If it is important to your organization to absolutely own the data underlying your Web analytics projects then Web server log file are most likely the right data source for you.

When Privacy of Data is Extremely Important

While it is very, very unlikely, there is always the possibility that a malicious soul could intercept the transmission of data from a page-tagging solution and somehow determine the identity of the person making the request and the object being requested. Most client-side data collection technologies either encourage their users to not send any personally identifiable information, or if they do—as may be the case in a commerce environment—they encourage their users to only pass obfuscated user IDs. Web-server log files circumvent this issue by simply not transmitting data (in most cases, but see "exceptions, caveats, and so on," below). Typically the furthest distance that log files are transmitted for analysis is from one network resource to another without making use of the Internet itself.

Exceptions, Caveats, and so on

The information described regarding the use of Web-server log files as a data source for Web analytics programs for the most part assumes the traditional software model, that is, you own your log files and you purchase or license an application to analyze those files on your own hardware, network, and so on. There is another model for analyzing Web-server log files, that of the application service. While application service providers (ASPs) are most often associated with client-side data collection, there are now a number of vendors who are willing and able to "grab" your Web server logs, among other data sources, and process them in their own environments.

Two of these vendors worth mentioning briefly are Revenue Sciences and IBM's SurfAid. Both companies have built a reputation on being able to combine multiple data sources and connect them to data stored in Web-server log files to answer complex business questions. A clear advantage of this type of solution is that the need for hardware, technical support and software licenses is outsourced, lowering the total cost of ownership significantly. A disadvantage of this type of solution is that the analysis and reports are typically limited to what the vendor can provide and the cost of integrating multiple data sources is potentially high. More information about these vendors and data integration is presented in Chapter 16.

Focus on Page Tags as a Data Source

As mentioned previously, many companies providing Web analytics are now doing so using a JavaScript "page tag" to collect data instead of using the Web-server log file. Because the visitor's Web browser enables the data collection, this type of collection is often referred to as "front-end" or "client-side." The Aberdeen Group reports that in 2002 the market share of companies employing some type of "front-end" data collection technique grew from just more than 12 percent in 2000 to more than 15 percent in 2002. Often vendors providing page tags are referred to as providing "outsourced Web analytics," which may or may not be the case (see "tags into logs" below). Aberdeen reports that more than 43 percent of the vendors in the Web analytics market are offering solutions that incorporate both types of data sources, page tags and Web-server log files. Companies that provide client-side data collection solutions include WebSideStory, the WebTrends division of NetIQ, Coremetrics, Omniture and a host of other, smaller companies.

This market segment is growing quickly for two fundamental reasons. First, in the case of completely outsourced vendors, the barrier to entry for an application service provider (ASP) is much lower than that for a traditional software company. The ASP doesn't have to build a software product and manage packaging and shipping— everything is delivered electronically. Second, companies are beginning to see the value of outsourced data collection as a way to lower up-front costs while still providing Web analytics data. Rather than having to purchase software licenses, hardware, network space and human resources to manage and maintain the application, the outsourced solution allows companies to "pay as you go."

It is worth noting at this point the differences in the use of "outsourced" and "client-side" when discussing this particular data type. Often vendors and authors, this author included, will use these terms interchangeably to describe data collected via a JavaScript page tag. While the use of the page tag is truly "client-side data collection," the use of a page tag does not necessarily imply that the analytics program has been outsourced; there are more and more vendors providing client-side data collection that can be run from within the businesses own IT infrastructure (see "tags into logs" later in this chapter). A truly "outsourced analytics program" is one in which the data is hosted and analyzed in another location, usually the vendor's data center. Some vendors (Revenue Sciences, IBM SurfAid, some others) have become adept at grabbing Web server log files via FTP and analyzing them in-house, the definition of "outsourced analytics." Confusing, yes. Truly important? No. All you really need to know in the context of JavaScript page tags is the difference between Web server log files and client-side page tags as a data source, regardless of the business model of the application provider.

For the most part, companies providing client-side solutions work like this:

1. You sign up for a service, agreeing to pay some type of up-front installation or set-up fees and a monthly cost based on the total volume of traffic and transactions to your Web site.
2. The vendor provides you with a set of JavaScript "tags" designed to detect information about the visitor. These tags need to be added to any of your Web site pages you wish to track.
3. You add the code to your site somehow, setting variables in the code depending on the exact vendor solution.
4. When your visitors come to your site, they download your Web pages, which now include the "page tag."
5. When your pages are downloaded in the visitor's browser, the page tags are executed and information is sent to the vendor's data center, most often using an image request for a very small image or another small file, by appending a long query string to the image request. This is the component often referred to as a "Web bug."
6. The data center receives the image request and parses the query string into the vendor's particular data model.
7. The image is sent back to the client and the transaction is complete.
8. You log into a secure online interface and view the data in pre-defined reports, or, depending on the vendor, get customized reports delivered directly to you via email.

While this is a significant oversimplification, fundamentally that is how the process works. The differences between vendors providing this type of solution are usually as follows:

JavaScript Variables

Some vendors are proud of the fact that they rely very little on post-processing of data and so their solutions are very fast and scalable. Other vendors are proud of the fact that their tags are very small and require little or no modification to function properly. The number and complexity of in-page JavaScript variables is something that each vendor in the outsourced analytics space has resolved in a slightly different way and there is really no "best way" for this to be done. If the author has any guidance on this subject it would be that the JavaScript and variables be A) flexible, so they can be set independently, broken up on the page or removed entirely if they're not being used and B) designed with page size considerations in mind.

Amount of Data

Again, some vendors provide very flexible solutions that are able to gather many different types of data, including multiple content groups and custom data types. Other vendors provide more rigid data models where only certain data types can be collected. Still other vendors accept the entire query string as a parameter, which can then be parsed and explored after the fact.

Vendor Data Architecture

Here, some vendors have made a living by providing highly scalable but relatively flat architectures to store incoming data, often in aggregate format. Other vendors collect all data into a relational database on a session-by-session basis. Still others store data in a combination of the two, depending on the incoming data type.

Reporting

For the most part, outsourced Web analytics vendors provide a static set of reports, grouped logically via a secure Web-based application. Each vendor puts their own spin on the data and organizes the information in their own particular way. Additionally, most vendors provide some type of "custom reporting" to allow data to be combined in different ways as to be more meaningful for your own business.

Price

Within the outsourced market it is likely that, depending on the volume of traffic and transactions you hope to measure and data you hope to get back, you will be able to find solutions ranging in price from "free" to "very, very expensive." While overall prices seem to be coming down, the cost per million page views model of pricing for client-side data collection is still all over the board.

Likely Longevity of the Vendor

This difference between vendors is likely a function of the downturn in the technology market at the time this book was being written; while there was a general trend towards consolidation in the analytics market in 2000 and 2001 that activity has more recently slowed. Every vendor will insist that they are doing "better than ever" and that their own long-term outlook is extremely bright but reality dictates that not every business can be successful and some vendors currently providing Web analytics solutions may not be around in two or three years.

With all these factors in mind, the general strategy when getting involved with an outsourced Web analytics vendor is to find one that has reports you can read and understand, a tag you can implement and a reputation you trust. It is very easy to see if your competitors or companies that you respect are using this type of data collection, you just go to a page on their Web site and do a browser "View > Source." If the company is using client-side data collection you will see their vendor's JavaScript somewhere on the page. Some common strings you can search for to verify this include:

Vendor	Search for	Example URL
WebSideStory	"websidestory"	www.backcountrystore.com
WebTrends	"netiq" or "webtrends"	www.webtrendslive.com
Coremetrics	"coremetrics"	www.victoriasecret.com
Omniture	"site catalyst" or "omniture"	www.ebay.com
IBM SurfAid	"stats.surfaid"	surfaid.dfw.ibm.com
VisitorVille	"plgtrfic.js.php"	www.visitorville.com
Fireclick	"hints.netflame.cc"	www.fireclick.com

Table 4: Commons strings used in Web page code to identify vendors supplying page-tagging solutions.

Advantages of Page Tags as a Data Source

As mentioned in the previous section, Web server log files have long been the *de facto* data source for Web analytics programs and traffic analysis applications. This is changing, however, as the popularity of page tagging and client-side data collection continues to grow. Some of the advantages of client-side data collection include:

Accuracy

Because data is collected directly from the end user, not from the Web server, client-side data collection is typically much more accurate than Web server log files. Most page tags rely on cookies to determine the uniqueness of a visitor and have cache-busting code that ensures that data is collected regardless of where the page was served. Client-side data collection is also typically able to measure the use of the browsers "back" and "forward" buttons because the code is executed every time.

Accuracy, Revisited

As mentioned in the previous section, non-human user agents such as search engine indexing spiders and crawlers can negatively impact the accuracy of Web-server log-file analysis applications. Fortunately, because *most* of these user agent applications do not actually render the Web page once it has been downloaded, client-side data collection applications are generally thought to be more accurate than Web server log files. Put another way, even though your Web server sees the request from the search engine robot, the robot never builds the page, does not execute the JavaScript page tag and therefore the information about the request is never passed along to the data collection application.

Speed of Data Reporting

While Web-server log files are arguably a less-obtrusive data collection technique, many client-side technologies are able to report data in real time or nearly so. Since there is no need for a log file that needs to be parsed at a later date, client-side data collectors typically parse the information into their respective data structures as the data comes in. This real-time parsing usually translates into information available via the reporting mechanism a few seconds to a few minutes after the page view is seen. While real-time data reporting can be very valuable in a handful of instances, see the section on "About 'real time'" below to determine how much of an advantage this may be to your actual business.

Flexibility of Data Collection: Variables

Since this technique depends entirely on a vendor-defined model for data collection and storage, client-side data collection typically allows for a greater range of variables that can be collected from any given page. Most client-side technologies require variables defining "page name" and "content group" but also allow for "campaign ID," "visitor segment," "product," "category," "brand," "price," and so on, depending on the application and the type of page containing the tag. While these variables are fixed from vendor-to-vendor, the flexibility provided by the methodology allows online businesses to define the type of data they want to collect and then pick a vendor that can accommodate their needs, rather than simply making due with log files or building complex workarounds.

Lower Upfront Costs

Since nearly all client-side solutions are delivered via the application service provider model (however see "Tags into logs" below), the upfront costs associated with implementing this type of solution are lower. As mentioned earlier most vendors make their customers pay some type of setup fee based on the specific solution, number of accounts or type of data collected and then charge monthly for actual traffic measured. There is no need to purchase hardware or hire IT staff to maintain the hardware and software—all of these costs are built into the price for an ASP solution.

Disadvantages of Page Tags as a Data Source

While on the surface client-side data collection appears to be a more accurate, more informative source for Web analytics projects, there are a handful of disadvantages, some of which can be significant. The notable disadvantages include:

Dependence on JavaScript and Cookies

All currently available page tags of any value rely heavily on cookies and JavaScript. Typically, JavaScript is the mechanism to determine necessary information about the visitor (what pages they are looking at, what browser they are visiting on, and so on) and the cookie is the session-to-session storage mechanism. Additionally, cookies are used to determine the uniqueness of the visitor. If a visitor has either of these technologies disabled, the quality of information collected is diminished. Most page tags make use of some type of <NOSCRIPT> code that passes part of the available information to the data center, but this is most often limited. Similarly, most page tags can detect the acceptance of cookies and will report back on their acceptance or denial but in their absence will report little or nothing about the visitor's session and previous activity on the Web site.

Dependence on Cookies as a Unique Identifier

While this is only loosely a disadvantage considering there really is not a better alternative, it is worth noting the problems associated with cookies as a unique visitor identifier. Page-tag vendors nearly always pitch their solutions as collecting information about "human visitors" when they're really collecting information about Web browsers. Client-side data collection assumes the following about visitors to make a one-to-one relationship between visitors and Web browsers:

- Every person uses only a single Web browser to surf the Internet.
- Every Web browser is used by only a single person to surf the Internet.
- People rarely disable cookies when surfing the Internet.
- People rarely, if ever, clear their browser's cookie cache.
- People rarely, if ever, switch between browser types (for example, Internet Explorer to Netscape)
- People infrequently upgrade their computers entirely.

As you can see, several of the assumptions listed here have the potential to be incorrect from time to time. The most obvious exceptions are for items one and two—many people surf the Internet using one computer during the daytime and another evenings and weekends, and in certain situations a large number of individuals may use the same computer/browser/login combination to surf the Internet (schools, public kiosks, and so on)

Regarding item three, while there is a seemingly cyclic pattern in the news media proclaiming the "dangers of Web cookies and their ability to invade your privacy," services that measure the acceptance or denial of cookies put the global acceptance rate at more than 99 percent. Data suggests that problems resulting from items four through six are less significant but are always a possibility. The author refers the reader to the section on "cookies and their use in Web analytics" later in this chapter for additional information regarding cookies.

Adding Page Tags to Every Page

Fundamental to page tagging is the need to add a JavaScript tag to every Web page you want to track. This is not necessarily a huge disadvantage depending on the vendor you choose and the type of Web environment you have but is potentially a time-consuming problem. The best case is where you have already built a "header/footer" structure for your entire site, one containing a common header and footer file into which the page tag can simply be inserted. The worst case is where you have an entirely static Web site with no opportunity for server-side includes, necessitating the manual inclusion of the page tag on *every* page you want to track.

Complexity of Tag Implementation

Depending on the vendor you choose you may be faced with a more complex implementation than you'd hoped for. Some vendors provide very simple tags that are the same regardless of the type of page you want to track. Other vendors provide very complex tags that need to be modified heavily and are different depending on the type of page you want to track. It is not uncommon for page-tag implementation projects to take a matter of hours, but also not unheard of for said projects to take weeks or months to successfully complete.

Performance Issues

No matter how small the JavaScript code is that needs to go on each tracked page it is never "zero weight." It is a simple fact that anything you add to your Web pages will increase the total download time to your visitors. Regardless of how emphatically a vendor claims that "our tags result in no additional delay in loading and rendering your Web pages" they are not being completely honest. While the execution time for a page tag may be very short, typically measured in milliseconds, the additional time to download the page over a modem connection may be noticeable. It should, however, be noted that in most instances this additional wait to your visitors is offset by the valuable information gained by including the page tag in the first place, especially if you have no Web analytics program already in place

Measurement of Robots and Spiders

While we've listed exclusion of non-human user agents as an advantage of client-side data collection, there are of course exceptions to this rule. The most often observed exceptions are performance monitoring user agents, such as those from Keynote Systems, Gomez and Mercury Interactive. Because these types of user agents are specifically designed to measure the download and render time of Web pages they do execute scripts on pages including the JavaScript that controls a page tag. Additionally, because these services are designed to repeatedly test response times for key pages on a Web site, if their requests are not excluded these requests can artificially inflate traffic and page activity metrics. If you plan on using services like Keynote alongside a client-side Web analytics solution, make sure that the solution you choose allows you to exclude the traffic coming from this type of user agent.

Length of Time Data Can Be Stored

Unlike Web server log files, which you are free to keep and store for as long as you like, some page-tag vendors do not keep your data forever. Because there is a cost associated with disk space, and an even higher cost associated with database storage, some vendors limit the length of time that data is made available after its initial collection. Note that not all vendors do this, but this is something you want to check into very closely when choosing a vendor if you think that having access to historical data is important.

Types of Data that Can Be Collected

Unlike Web server log files, page tags are limited in their ability to report on non-HTML views, such as those to downloadable file types, error pages and redirects. Some client-side collection solutions are able to track views of different file types (such as PDF, zipped files, executables, or multimedia files) but do so by tracking clicks as opposed to successful downloads. Many client-side solutions are able to record information about error pages as long as these pages allow the necessary JavaScript to be included. Some client-side solutions can also be tricked to count certain types of redirects. Needless to say, none of these data types are easily or automatically collected with any significant accuracy and this should be considered when choosing a solution.

Inflexibility in Reporting Formats

One disadvantage of outsourced Web analytics solutions that the software vendors often cite is the fact that, for the most part, "what you see is what you get" for analysis and reporting from outsourced solutions. Since ASPs run the same application for most, if not all of their customers, the reporting interface is typically standardized for all customers. This can be seen as a disadvantage if you really know what you are doing and you only want a particular subset of reports, want reports in a different format (Excel, Adobe PDF, and so on) or would like different language used in your reports. Since the software vendors have been saying that this is a significant limitation for the last few years, outsourced vendors have more recently begun to incorporate a variety of solutions to this problem in their applications. Some examples include customized language in reports, alternate themes or views in reporting and completely customized reports delivered either on an ad hoc or scheduled basis, typically in Excel. It should be noted that any vendor providing a "tags into logs" solution will likely provide the same flexibility in reporting afforded to software-based solutions while still making use of data collected directly from the browser client.

The Sticky Question of Who Owns the Data

One of the biggest disadvantages associated with outsourced solutions of any type is the question of "who owns the data if we decide to cancel the contract?" While vendors will assure you that you own the data, most will charge you some additional fee to allow you to export the historical data so that you can create a data backup "just in case" you ever leave the particular vendor. According to Guy Creese of the Aberdeen Group, there appears to be a trend of companies trying two or three different vendors before finally settling in with the one that is the best fit for their needs. If this is true, there will always be a question of "how do we keep track of historical data when we move from vendor to vendor?" While some outsourced solutions can facilitate the import of Web-server log-file data, this author is not aware of any service that allows the import of data from another outsourced solution. Unfortunately, most companies accommodate this problem by manually building Excel spreadsheets of basic historical data "just in case"—a tedious and time-consuming task.

Privacy Issues

Internet privacy is an extremely popular subject, especially as Internet viruses and identity theft cases continue to be reported with alarming frequency. Issues surrounding what types of data are collected, how they are passed around and where they are stored are common. Because of this nearly every Web analytics vendor providing an outsourced solution offers some kind of privacy policy, recommend that their customers adopt some part of their privacy policy, and even, in some cases, go so far as employing a Chief Privacy Officer (CPO). The core argument regarding privacy and Web analytics is that you are obligated to tell your visitors that you are using some kind of client-side data collection solution, describe what is and what is not collected and provide your visitors the ability to "opt-out" of this data collection if they so choose. But as long as the online business works with their outsourced solution to implement an appropriate privacy policy covering the client-side data collection there is little to worry about, at least at the time that this book was being written.

Again, while it seems like the list of disadvantages of outsourced Web analytics solutions are many and may outweigh the relative advantages, one must keep in mind that none of the aforementioned disadvantages are insurmountable. Careful selection of an outsourced vendor and a thoughtful implementation that is reflective of your specific business needs is usually all it takes to negate most, if not all, of the issues listed above. It is recommended that any company carefully consider the following best practices, especially those surrounding the selection of an outsourced vendor, before committing any money to a Web analytics project if it has been determined that a client-side data collection is the methodology of choice.

Best Practices When Implementing a Page Tagging Data Collection Solution

While the author believes that page-tagging data collection is a very useful, powerful and accurate source of data for any Web analytics program, there are a handful of "best practices" that should be followed when setting up this type of solution. Most of these suggestions deal with implementation and vendor selection.

Provide "Human Readable" Names

As you can imagine, and in the author's experience, the more easy-to-read the names of pages and content groups, the more likely people are to make use of the available data. The difference between …

"pl_gp_12311_groc"

… and …

"Store Category View: Product List 12311"

… should be obvious in terms of the ability to quickly understand what information was conveyed to the visitor. Using the first example ("pl_gp_ …") there are without a doubt a group of users in your organization that will understand exactly what page or content group is being described. More often than not this is a small group of IT or technical people who built the pages or the system. In the second example ("Store Category: …") you can reasonably assume that *any* member of your organization who is familiar with your Web site and business model should be able to quickly determine which page is being described. Fight the temptation to take the easy way out and use "simple to generate" names; spending the extra time at implementation to provide "simple to understand" names instead will pay off in the long run.

Establish a Quality Assurance Program

Making sure that you have a well-defined process for testing the deployment of page tag scripts on new pages or sections of your Web site is critical. Fundamental to the way that most page tagging technologies work is the rule "if you don't tell us about it we have no way to know." Put another way, if you mess up the implementation and fail to collect data, likely that data is forever lost. To this end the author recommends working very closely with your application provider or other knowledgeable resource to implement and test any new code being deployed prior to pushing the code to your live servers.

Challenge Your Solution Provider

Many times in this author's experience customers have simply said "just send us the code and the manual and we'll get it all up and running" only to come back at later and say "we never felt like we got the full value of the application because we don't think we implemented it correctly." Any vendor you choose, no matter how small, should be more than happy to help you understand how to best implement their application so that your business makes use of all their bells and whistles. If the vendor you choose is not able to help you, find another vendor. Also, don't assume that you will be able to figure it out yourselves just to save a little bit of time or money. If you are reading this book it is very likely that Web analytics application integration is not your core competency. Take advantage of outside resources who implement that particular technology for a living and you will significantly increase your chances of getting more out of the solution in the long run.

Conduct Performance Testing

In all cases, using a page tagging solution will increase the physical time it takes to download your pages somewhat, but following this "best practice" will let you quantify this increase. Things to watch are total increase in kilobytes (most vendors will round down when describing the total weight of their scripts) and total increase in response time, especially for the image or object that is being requested from the vendor's data collection center. An important caveat to this is that download time should not be the absolute indicator of the effect on the visitor experience. Several vendors provide combinations of scripts, some that load every time to beat the cache and others that are highly cacheable to improve overall performance. While you should monitor the effect of download time it is also important to double-check this against some type of usability testing, asking the subjects if they perceive a difference between pages containing the script and those without.

Exclude Internal Traffic from the Analysis

By default most analytics applications *do not* exclude internally generated traffic to the Web servers, that traffic generated by your developers and other employees making use of the business Web site for whatever reason. This traffic should be excluded or segregated out of the final analysis because it is not necessarily representative of your visitor's interests. Depending on your particular business model, internal traffic can be a significant component of the traffic to a given page or content area.

Most Web analytics applications will allow you to exclude traffic from reporting and analysis based on at least the IP address of the visitor. While IP address is a poor indicator of uniqueness, it is often useful for excluding groups of visitors as most corporate firewalls will identify internal users as having coming through one or few unique addresses.

Do Your Homework Regarding Vendor Selection

Because most page tagging solutions are offered as an outsourced service, the single most important aspect of your success with an application will be the company that supports it. It is critical to ensure that you trust the vendor team that will be responsible for your success. The author highly recommends that at minimum you do the following:

1. While still in the sales cycle, ask to meet or talk to the team that will support you after you sign the contract, as this is almost always a different group than you talk to in the sales process.

2. Ask for customer references and actually call those references. Ask these people things like, "How long have you been with this vendor?" "What was the implementation like?" "How do you feel about the support they provide?" "Describe a situation where you didn't feel like the vendor responded as quickly as you would have liked." "Who is your primary point of contact at the company?" If the reference really likes their primary point of contact, ask the vendor if that person can work with you ask well. And keep in mind that *the vendor hand-selects these references to say the best things possible about them.*

3. Hunt down other customers that the vendor does not provide as references and call these people. Considering that the vendor will only provide references who give glowing recommendations and that you can pretty easily figure out whom else is using their technology (consult the "Our Customers" page on the vendor's Web site) it will benefit you to spend a little time trying to run down a non-reference customer. If you are able to find a reference that is in your line of business you will likely get more relevant and honest answers to your questions. When you identify the company, simply write to "webmaster@" the company and clearly explain what you are trying to accomplish and could they please pass your contact information along to the

appropriate resource. Include all of your contact information so the recipient knows you are serious and not just spamming them.

4. Ask the vendor what kinds of support and training they provide, how often it is available and how much it will cost. Any good vendor will be happy to sell you training and support after you have already signed a contract. Strong vendors will also provide free training and support, at least on a limited basis, to improve customer retention and satisfaction. If training and support is only available at an additional charge, ask what they recommend or provide to most other customers and then make them include this at no additional charge in the contract as part of the negotiation.

As you can see, because page tags were designed to collect true Web analytics data there are fewer recommendations here about how to ensure the data is good and more suggestions to help you leverage the solution you choose to your ongoing success.

Examples of When to Use a Page-Tagging Data Collection Solution

The following are examples of when you'd likely choose an outsourced Web analytics solution:

When Information Technology Staff Are Too Busy

The most common reason that companies switch from an in-house to an outsourced solution is a lack of resources to manage, maintain and update an internal solution. Whether the necessary staff is overworked, underpaid or simply disinterested in helping, attempting to make the most of an in-house solution without internal support is nearly always an exercise in futility. In contrast, outsourced solutions typically require very little internal support on an ongoing basis, usually only at the onset of a project where pages are being tagged or when data collection is being modified to suit specific measurement goals. Nearly all outsourced solutions eliminate the need for IT to be involved in the reporting process, thus speeding the information delivery to the end-user's hands.

When Traffic Volume is Very High

In high-traffic volume situations there is a tradeoff between having to pay more for an outsourced solution that can aggregate data from multiple machines and report data back quickly; or paying less but waiting long periods of time to get reports. Depending on the size and number of log files being generated by high volume sites, Web-server log-file analysis solutions can take hours, days or weeks to report back on information that can be generated in "real time" by outsourced solutions (but again, see the section on "real-time" reporting, below).

When Needs are Diverse

Because page-tagging solutions are more flexible in terms of the information they can collect, client-side data collection is typically preferred in situations where companies would like to tie traffic data to online purchasing data, perform complex visitor segmentation, or rapidly change naming conventions to accommodate different measurement needs. The ability to pass in customer-defined variables typically imparts additional measurement and reporting power that can be leveraged to answer more interesting questions than, simply, "How much traffic did the Web site get last week?"

When Accuracy is Very Important

Page-tagging applications are very accurate by default in terms of measuring unique individuals, busting proxy caches and excluding non-human traffic from measurement and reporting. All of these things can be accomplished using a Web server log based solution if great care is exercised when implementing and the solution is carefully maintained. Lacking this attention to detail, client-side data collection is the preferred method for accurate data collection.

Tags into Logs

A more recent entry into the battle between Web server log files and client-side page tags is the "tags into logs" solution. The rationale behind "tags into logs" is that while page tagging is recognized as a powerful and accurate method for collecting data, some businesses prefer the reporting flexibility of an in-house, software solution. "Tags into logs" gives the business both—the Web site is tagged as if the reporting were entirely outsourced except the data collection is collected internally through a mechanism that simply writes the request to a file. This file can then be parsed and analyzed using the same type of software solution one would use to analyze a traditional Web server log file.

The clear advantages of "tags into logs" are accuracy, ownership of data and flexibility of reporting. This "build a better log file" concept effectively neutralizes many of the disadvantages of a Web-server log-based solution. No more concerns about determining the uniqueness of a visitor, proxy or browser caches, no more concern over robots and spiders. Also, this type of solution consolidates activity across multiple Web servers, eliminating the need to stitch logs from multiple servers together prior to analysis and reporting.

The disadvantages of this type of solution are similar to those of any in-house solution. Unless you outsource the analysis application you will still need to have your IT staff install, monitor and maintain a software application, you still need to store and rotate log files, and you will still usually need to wait hours, days or weeks for reports to be generated. Also, unless the particular solution you choose stores the information collected in a standard log file format (such as NCSA combined) you are still stuck with the problem of "who owns the data"—even if you own and store the data on your servers, if it is in an incompatible format it is functionally lost if you change solutions (consider Beta videotapes and 8-track audiotapes).

About "Real-Time" Data Collection and Reporting

A marketing point that some outsourced solution providers go to great length to emphasize is the value of "real-time" data reporting—the ability to see visiting traffic almost immediately after it occurs. While this sounds great, there are only a few instances where an online business would actually need true "real-time" reporting.

When the Online Business is a Content Provider

If the online business is publishing content to create advertising views, engender loyalty and create site stickiness, there is something to be said for knowing the effects of content immediately after this content has been posted. The best example of this is the news portal content editor who wants to maximize the effect of a new news story. He or she would post a new story, watch the traffic flowing to that story, and continue to feature that story prominently until the percentage of traffic viewing that story slips below a pre-defined threshold based on the ratio of traffic to the story compared to overall traffic volumes.

Where the Business is an Online Retailer

Being able to see the real-time or near real-time response to product placement on key pages throughout a Web site, including product conversion rates and revenue generated, can help smart merchandisers maximize the value of product placement. An example of this would be the online florist testing three different flower arrangements just before Mother's day, closely watching the conversion rates for each in real time, rotating out the arrangement with the lowest conversion rate every thirty minutes until the most popular product spread is achieved, based on conversion rates that start high and stay high.

When You are Serious About Improvement

Because there are no minimums or maximums to the amount of time changes should be measured when using a strong Web analytics methodology, smart business managers can use real-time reporting to test the effects of changes to multi-step processes rapidly. Rather than run the risk of testing changes made to a process for a few days only to discover that the result is higher abandonment or lower conversion, real-time reporting can help identify this trend quickly so that these changes can be backed out, thus minimizing any detrimental effect.

Other than these three examples, real-time reporting is usually a nice feature that few people actually take advantage of, much like a software manual or online help system. Again, before you choose a vendor simply because they provide "real-time" reporting make sure that this is something you actually need, something you can take advantage of.

Cookies and Their Use in Web Analytics Applications

At this point in *Web Analytics Demystified* you have read about cookies and their use in analytics applications many times. Cookies have evolved into an important and controversial technology on the Internet—some demonize their use as an invasion of privacy, others praise their ability to simplify and personalize the browsing experience. We've already discussed some of the assumptions and limitations inherent to cookies as a tracking mechanism. Regardless of their limitations and how people feel about their use, cookies are critical to Web analytics applications and their ability to accurately track the uniqueness of a visitor.

Because visitors in most cases are not willing to log in to a Web site simply to allow the site to track them accurately, and since it has been shown repeatedly that IP addresses are inadequate to determine the uniqueness of a visitor, cookies are here to stay. While visitors are free to set, change and delete their cookies, especially using new privacy tools available in Web browsers such as Internet Explorer 6.0 and the growth of P3P privacy standards, data suggests that few people actually take advantage of this. If this is true, cookies will continue to be an effective tool to track visitor activity on a Web site.

One of the major concerns for privacy experts is the difference between first- and third-party cookies. First-party cookies are those cookies served directly from one's Web site, served directly from the Web site's own domain. Third-party cookies are those cookies served from another domain (such as DoubleClick or WebSideStory). Emerging privacy standards are different for each type of cookie and are generally stricter for third-party cookies. The issue that most privacy advocates cite is the third-party cookie's ability to observe visitor behavior across multiple domains—if I am tracked with the DoubleClick cookie I can be "seen" on any site tracked using DoubleClick's tracking technology. While this may be technically true, in the author's experience vendors providing outsourced solutions that depend on third-party cookies are *extremely* conscientious about not creating visibility across sites. Some go so far as to identify their cookies as being part of a combined domain using the sub-domain attribute—they set a cookie to "ehg-bcstore.hitbox.com" instead of just "www.hitbox.com." While there is really no difference technically speaking, and both URLs are from a third-party domain ("hitbox.com"), this combined assignment would, in theory, make it more difficult for someone other than HitBox to access the information contained in these cookies.

First-party cookies skirt this issue by being written directly from the business' own domain. Only applications and script running within that domain have access to the cookie, a privacy standard built into all Web browsers. While the use of first-party cookies protects the visitor slightly more, some perceive the fact that their use necessitates running software in-house as a disadvantage. Clearly there would be an advantage given to an outsourced analytics provider who was able to write first-party cookies, thus increasing privacy (or at least the perception of privacy to the visitor or customer).

Fundamentally, as long as the cookies you use to track visitors to your Web site do not contain any personally identifiable information and your vendor is not using third-party cookies to track visitors across multiple customer Web sites, cookies should be considered a safe and effective tool to enable your analytics program. Usually the kinds of Internet users that complain about the use of cookies by a Web site are either unsophisticated or overly sophisticated. The unsophisticated visitor has heard that "cookies are bad" and that they are an invasion of privacy and has taken this at face value. When their personal firewall pops up a warning about your cookies they become alarmed and more often than not fire off an email telling you to "keep your hands off my computer." The overly-sophisticated visitor is usually an IT professional or security expert, someone who should know better but has little else to do than stir up trouble for legitimate businesses. This type is more likely to actually create problems for you in that they may post the fact that you are using cookies on newsgroups or even report your use to the media in an effort to gain personal attention.

If you are using cookies, and it is strongly recommended that you do so, you do leave your business exposed to the aforementioned users. To protect against this exposure it is also strongly recommended that you work directly with your analytics provider to craft a privacy policy that describes *exactly* how you use cookies and what you use them for. While nobody actually reads privacy policies, it is important to have a document that you can point to if someone gives you trouble and say, "Well, we're sorry you feel that way but our privacy policy clearly states how and why we use cookies." In the author's experience, providing the policy is correct and up-to-date, this generally helps to minimize the fallout and encourages the problem user to move onto more important things like how to get a date to the prom, how to clean the lint from their belly-buttons, and so on

Consult your analytics vendor for more information about how cookies are used within their application and their suggestions for modifications to your privacy policy in this regard.

CHAPTER 4
WEB ANALYTICS
TERMINOLOGY

**"We measure this information based on hits in our traffic analysis program
which is different from the visits that we get from our advertising engine which
cannot be compared to the visitors described by our panel measurement service
and are also not quite the same as the page views that are cited in the recent
articles about the state of our particular market niche... Anyway, here are the
numbers."**
Anonymous Marketing Person

A good subtitle for this chapter would be, "Why the same words mean different things
to different people and what you can reasonably do about it!" Because Web analytics is
still very much an emerging discipline, different vendors have been free to define
words as they saw fit with little or no consideration for common usage or
standardization. This lack of attention to detail has resulted in common questions like:

- What the heck is a "hit" and what do "hits" tell me about traffic to my site?
- What is the relationship between a visitor, a visit and a view? What is the
  different between a "page view," a "total view" and a "view?"
- What is a "unique" and why wouldn't every visitor be a "unique visitor?"
- Why do some vendors measure some statistics by "views" and others by
  "visits" and others by "visitors?" Which vendor is right?!

This type of frustration goes on and on and on, especially when the group charged
with developing Web analytics programs within an organization is then tasked with
presenting their findings to non-Web analytics people. This would not be so bad if it
were as simple as educating the "outsiders" about a new language, one that was well
understood, such as mathematics or Spanish, you simply translate the term once or
twice and they're likely to figure it out. The problem with Web analytics is that you
end up giving people "the WebTrends/NetIQ definition of 'page view,' which is
different than the HitBox definition of 'page view,' neither of which are talking about a
'hit' but 'hit' is what we call a 'page view' here internally..." You may have already
experienced this type of frustration.

This chapter will provide standard definitions for the most commonly used Web
analytics terms, outlining what the words *should* mean, regardless of how vendors have
used them.

A Small Group of Mostly Useless Terms

The first group includes mostly useless terms that have managed to make it into the common parlance of Web analytics. Terms like "hit" and "click-through" only serve to confuse people, making them think they're measuring something that they are not.

Hit

"Hit" is a particularly bad word; people talk at length about the "number of hits" that their Web site received in such-and-such a timeframe. The common usage of "hit" appears to approximate "page view"—the number of times a Web page is actually seen by a visitor. Compare this usage with the definition provided by WebTrends/NetIQ on their Web site:

```
"(A hit is) an action on a Web site such as when a user views a page
or downloads a file."
```

At first glance the reader is tempted to agree that a "hit" and a "page view" are analogous. The definition states that a hit is an action, such as a "user view(ing) a page," does it not? This is not the problem; the problem is the second part of the definition, "or downloads a file."

Consider the makeup of a Web page; Web pages are simply an HTML description of the relationship between text and objects. The result of the assembly of objects around text is a rendered "page." Each of the "objects" that make up this "page" need to be downloaded along with the HTML description of the page and herein lies the problem. Most of the "hit" numbers that are reported by Web server log file analyzers include HTML pages *and* downloadable file types such as ."GIF," ."JPG" and ."CSS." This means that for any given "page" that is downloaded there can be dozens or hundreds of "hits" required to completely render the page. Talk about artificially inflating the numbers!

Another way to think about hits is using the pyramid model of Web analytics data presented later in this chapter. The pyramid describes the utility of data types in informing Web analytics projects, from least to greatest value in terms of unique visitors to a Web site. "Hits," if this data is even available, are the bottom of the pyramid.

Click-Through

"Click-through," or "click-through rate," is used to describe the number of people who click on a particular thing —a banner ad, a link, a keyword. Again, WebTrends/NetIQ defines "click-through rate" as:

```
"(The) percentage of users who click on a viewed advertisement. A
good indication of an ad's effectiveness."
```

While it is good to measure rates and percentages, as opposed to absolute numbers, using the percentage of clicks on a particular link as a measure of effectiveness can be misleading. Consider the number of banner ads that are now cleverly disguised as content on Web sites. Consider the number of times you have clicked on a link that looked useful, only to discover that link was taking you to a site designed to sell you something you don't need. Consider the number of times you have clicked on a search result, only to immediately back up when the response was slow.

A common experience on the Internet is the "click, oops, back up" method of browsing. The user clicks, accidentally or not, on a link but immediately thinks, "I didn't mean to do that" and uses the browser's back button. In most instances the "click" part of "click, oops, back up" is counted as a part of the "click-through rate." If people change their minds 5 percent of the time, your click-through rate would be inflated by 5 percent; if people change their mind 20 percent of the time, common when site response is slow, your click-through rate would be inflated by 20 percent.

A better measure than "click-through" is response rate, the measure of the number of visitors that actually arrived at the site after clicking on the link. The response rates for a particular ad or link can help you better understand one of the most useful measurements in Web analytics, the activity conversion rate.

In short, don't use "hits" or "click-through" when talking about Web analytics if you can help it. If someone else says, "We had 200,000 hits to our Web Site last month," ask them if they really mean hits or perhaps they're talking about page views, or visits or unique visitors. If they tell you, "Our click-through-rate from Overture is 95 percent," ask them what percentage of those clicks actually gets to their Web site and how many of those respondents actually do something important. If they aren't sure, please give them a copy of this book.

A Slightly Larger Group of Useful But Confusing Terms

The next group includes useful and necessary terms to Web analytics that are often confusing because different vendors define them in different ways. This group includes core Web analytics terms like "page view," "visit," "visitor," "unique" and "referrer."

Page View

Page views (or "views") are the next highest level of information in the pyramid model of Web analytics data. Page views are actual visitor views or requests for information, regardless of the number of images or objects necessary to construct said page. The following issues contribute to confusion regarding the definition of a page view:

- **The question of "what is a page."** Most systems are able to measure HTML pages with ease, either from a request logged in a Web server log file or via a page tag. Problems may arise when considering dynamically generated pages. It is very common for business Web sites to make use of a dynamic system to generate a large number of "pages" from a small number of templates and a database. In this instance, the definition of page can become blurred. If a single Active Server Pages template can define 100 different product views, do we measure 100 views of the template as a page viewed 100 times, or each different product view as a page viewed one time? Both strategies for measurement would contribute the correct number to a sum total of all page views for the site, but only the latter would provide the level of detail that most online business managers need.

- **Types of documents included in the definition of a "page."** Again, in general HTML pages are measured without problem. Problems can arise when different systems are used for content presentation, such as Cold Fusion, Active Server Pages or PERL/CGI. What if some of your ASP pages are designed to present content but others are for data processing? Do you count all ASP pages as "page views?" What if your catalog is presented using PERL/CGI but your Web analytics application does not recognize ".cgi" as a valid page name extension? In this regard, clear definition of which document types should be considered "page views" is necessary.

- **Repeat views ("resets" or "reloads").** It is unfortunate but some Web analytics application providers choose to deal with reloaded page views as different from the original page view. One vendor counts any page that is reloaded or refreshed within fifteen seconds of the original page loading as a "reload" and segregates the counting of the reload from the "page view." While it is perhaps interesting to know this, in most cases this information provides little additional value and only serves to obfuscate the definition of a page view.

- **Frames.** Easily one of the most confounding issues in Web analytics and the definition of a "page" is the ability for Web designers to use frames and framesets. Briefly, a frameset is a description of how other pages should be laid out in a browser to represent a "page" to the end user. While frames provide some very minor advantages to Web developers (static navigation elements, the ability to provide a common header and footer that aren't constantly reloaded), end users are often confused by framed pages.

The problem with frames in the context of Web analytics is the question of "what constitutes a page?" Is it just the content frame, or is it all frames considered together? If you are using a Web server log analyzer, frames can present serious problems when counting page views —should you count the frameset description and the non-content frames? If not, what is your strategy for excluding framesets and non-content frames from the analysis? Client-side data collection services have an easier time with frames since it is generally easier to define what is counted and what is excluded, but even then you cannot be 100 percent certain what the user was truly seeing when conducting an analysis.

With all of this in mind, the definition of a page view should be as follows:

> *"A page view is counted with the successful loading of any* **document containing content** *that was requested by a Web site visitor, regardless of the mechanism of delivery or number and frequency with which said content is requested."*

Note that this definition is very inclusive —content does not necessarily only denote text or HTML. If you have a Web page that loads a Flash file but you would like an accurate count of how many times that Flash file was loaded you can use page views (Flash can create different problems, however, dealt with below under "What about Flash?").

Using this definition it should be clear that if your Web site is built using frames you should only be counting the actual content the visitor is requesting, not the header, footer or navigation frame content. It should also be clear that no definition of page view should depend on whether the page was loaded once or many times in rapid succession.

Visit

Visits are the next highest level of data value in the pyramid model of Web analytics data. A visit, sometimes referred to as a "session" or "user session," is what a "visitor" is engaged in while generating "page views" on one's Web site. The most confusing aspects of visit are synonymy and duration.

Synonyms for visit are "session" and "user session"—all three terms mean the same thing. The authors prefer the term visit simply because it is convenient when describing the pyramid model, that is, *unique visitors visit* Web sites generating *page views*.

The duration of a visit is defined as any period of activity, as measured by page views or requests for pages, separated by 30 minutes of inactivity. This is why some vendors refer to visits as having a "30-minute timeout." Thirty minutes of inactivity was originally an arbitrary number but has become the *de facto* standard. The following examples attempt to illustrate how the 30-minute timeout should be applied when calculating visits:

- A visitor clicks to a Web site at 1:00 PM and surfs at random for 20 consecutive minutes before closing their browser and going offline. **One visit.**

- A visitor clicks to a Web site at 1:00 PM and starts putting items in a shopping cart. At 1:15 PM the telephone rings and for 31 minutes the visitor does not click any links on the Web site. At 1:46 PM the visitor ends their phone call and completes their purchase transaction by 1:57 PM. **Two visits**—the first from 1:00 PM to 1:15 PM, the second from 1:46 PM until the transaction is completed at 1:57 PM.

- A visitor clicks to a Web site at 1:00 PM and randomly surfs for 45 minutes. At 1:45 PM the visitor notices a link to another site which, when they click, opens a new Web browser (leaving the existing site open). The visitor surfs the new site for 31 minutes, at which time they close the newly opened browser and continue to surf the original site. **Two visits**—even though the browser containing the original site was left open, if there is no activity on that site the visit will have timed out at 2:16 PM (1:45 PM plus 31 minutes on the new site).

- A visitor clicks to a Web site at 1:00 PM and randomly surfs for three hours without any break in activity. At 3:00 PM the visitor makes a sandwich but is back surfing at 3:29 PM, at which time they surf for 30 more minutes before closing the browser and logging off. **One visit**—the longest period of inactivity was 29 minutes, one minute shy of the 30-minute timeout.

The definition of a visit should be as follows:

> *"A visit is counted when a unique visitor creates activity on Web page—which are being measured via a page view statistic—regardless of the duration of this activity as long as the period of inactivity between page views does not extend beyond thirty minutes."*

Note that the key to the definition of a visit is that the pages the visitor is browsing are those being measured as part of the page view statistic. This is covered by the third example above, where the visitor was browsing page on a different Web site, but this could easily extend to pages on your own site not being tracked by your Web analytics package.

Visitor or Unique Visitor

Visitors, commonly called "unique visitors," are the next highest level of data value in the pyramid model of Web analytics data. A unique visitor is the person visiting the Web site, generating page views. Human beings are visitors, search engine indexing agents and performance monitoring applications are not.

The fundamental problem with unique visitors is the method used to determine uniqueness. As previously discussed, strategies for determining uniqueness of a visitor include IP addresses and cookies. The section in Chapter 3 on Web-server log files discusses the disadvantages of using IP addresses to determine uniqueness at length. The section in Chapter 3 on client-side data collection discusses the disadvantages of using cookies to determine uniqueness. While cookies are not perfect for determining the uniqueness of a visitor, they are the preferred method for identifying anonymous visitors.

The definition of a unique visitor should be as follows:

> *"A unique visitor is counted when a human being uses a Web browser to visit a Web site, regardless of the number of pages visited or the duration of the visit. A visitor can be unique for different periods of time, and the individuality of a visitor is defined, preferably, by the presence of a cookie stored in the visitor's Web browser."*

Note the differentiation of uniqueness for different periods of time. Web analytics applications often provide distinct measurement for daily, weekly and monthly unique visitors. This concept necessitates an addendum to the definition of a unique visitor.

"A daily unique visitor should be counted the first, and only the first, time a unique visitor visits a Web site on any given day. A weekly unique visitor should be counted the first, and only the first, time a unique visitor visits a Web site in a given week. A monthly unique visitor should be counted the first, and only the first, time a unique visitor visits a Web site in a given month."

This definition can be simplified somewhat when considering any arbitrary timeframe:

"A unique visitor for any arbitrary timeframe should be counted one time and one time only on their first visit between the start date and the end date."

This way, if a person visits a Web site for the first time in a month, they should be counted as a daily unique visitor on the day of the visit, a weekly unique visitor in the calendar week of the visit, and a monthly unique visitor in that calendar month. If they return the next day, the visitor would only be counted as a daily unique visitor for that day, unless the day in question is in a different calendar week or month than the previous day.

Referrer

The term "referrer" is used to describe the source of traffic to a Web site. Most often referrers are reported as "referring URL" or "referring domain." The former is the complete URL describing the Web page containing the link to one's Web site. The latter is only the domain portion of this URL (the "amazon.com" portion of http://www.amazon.com?bookID=12345). The referrer is information contained in the HTTP header when the visitor is passed to the Web site being tracked, information that is available to both Web-server log files and client-side page tags.

Common problems with referrers include what to report when there is no referrer and how referrers are grouped. Often, when there is no referrer, Web analytics applications will report that the link came from a browser "favorite" or "bookmark" or that the visitor typed the URL for the Web site directly into the browser. Occasionally, the absence of a referring URL means that the click was passed through some technology that stripped the referring URL; most non-HTML based email applications and some banner-serving network software are known to do this.

Any groupings of visits that do not contain referring information make assumptions. One assumption, if this traffic is referred to as "Bookmarks or Directly Referred URLs," is that people often bookmark Web pages on the site being tracked, or perhaps that marketing activity is effective—people know the URL and type it in directly to the browser. The problem with these assumptions is that they are assumptions—one has no way of accurately knowing which answer is true. Because of this, it would be better to describe visits that do not contain referring source information as having "no or unknown referrer."

Name
Bookmarks or directly referred URLs
www.google.com/search?q=kaizen&hl=en&lr=&ie=UTF-8&oe=UTF-8&start=20&sa=N
» search.msn.com/results.aspx?ps=ba%3d(9.7)0(.)0.....1.0.%26oo%3d(0.15)4(0.1...
www.clickz.com/sales/traffic/article.php/2239681
» www.google.com/search?sourceid=navclient&ie=UTF-8&oe=UTF-8&q=web analytics...
www.google.com/search?q=kaizen&hl=en&lr=&ie=UTF-8&start=20&sa=N
search.yahoo.com/search?p=kaizen&ei=UTF-8&cop=mss&fr=fp-tab-web-t&b=21
www.wilsonweb.com/cat/cat.cfm?page=1&subcat=ms_Metrics
dmoz.org/Computers/Software/Internet/Site_Management/Log_Analysis/
www.emetrics.org/resources.html
» search.msn.com/pass/results.asp?RS=CHECKED&FORM=MSNHM1&v=1&q=&q=kaizen&cp=...
www.google.co.uk/search?q=kaizen&hl=en&lr=&ie=UTF-8&oe=UTF-8&start=20&sa=N

Figure 2: Example referring URLs driving traffic to the author's Web site, www.webanalyticsdemystified.com.

In terms of grouping URLs, Web analytics applications have a tendency to consider traffic from the top search engines as "traffic from search engines" and group these results, at least when reporting on referring domains. The problem with this is that not all traffic from these sites is simply search results. This traffic could be from banner ads, paid search inclusion, partnerships, affiliate programs or any number of non-search activities. The lumping of search engines together results in a loss in granularity from these referring domains and should be avoided if possible.

The definition of a referrer should be as follows:

> *"A referrer to any Web site should be an undifferentiated and complete uniform resource locator (URL) describing the exact page on the referring Web site that contained the link to the site in question."*

When reporting on referring URLs, all necessary components to reconstruct the referring page should be included (that is, the URI and query string). When reporting on referring domains, domains should be reported individually and without grouping or categorization. Any requests that do not contain referring source information should either be reported as "unknown referrer" or not displayed in a referrer report at all. Because referring source information is critical to measuring reach and acquisition (Chapters 11 and 12) this information should be reported as accurately and without bias as possible.

A Medium-Sized Group of Truly Useful Terms

This final group includes terms that are extremely important to Web analytics measurement, but are often either overlooked or are just now coming into common usage. This group includes terms like "conversion rate," "abandonment rate," "attrition," "loyalty," "recency" and "frequency."

Conversion Rate

Conversion rate is likely the most used and well understood of all these terms. Whereas in the past most traffic analysis focused on hits or page views, nearly all advocates of Web analytics encourage online businesses to measure and improve their conversion rate(s). Simply put:

> *"A conversion rate is the number of 'completers' divided by the number of 'starters' for any online activity that is more than one logical step in length."*

As you can see, this definition is devoid of units of measurement and any notes about where an activity begins and where it ends. The definition is devoid of units because conversion rate can be measured using views, visits or visitors (although you should not use views unless no other metric is available, and even then it is not a good idea). The definition does not suggest that conversion rate needs to be measured from the home page, or any page, as there are likely *many* different conversion rates one can measure on any Web site.

Conversion rates will be discussed at length in Chapter 13, describing the need for tools to measure multi-step processes online.

Abandonment Rate

Related to conversion rate, the abandonment rate is a measurement within any multi-step process describing the number of units that don't make it from "step n" to "step n + 1." Simply put:

> *The abandonment rate for any step in a multi-step process is one minus the number of units that make it to "step n + 1" divided by those at "step n" (1 —((n+1)/n))."*

"Again, this number can be measured using whatever metrics are available to you at the time (views, visits, visitors). You should see that for any multi-step process there are one fewer abandonment rates than there are steps in the process, e.g., a five step process will have four abandonment rates (Figure 3).

You may have seen the term "leakage" used in a similar context as abandonment. Leakage is a term that other authors use to describe the abandonment or loss experienced prior to a visitor actually engaging in a conversion activity. While there is a case to be made for differentiating leakage and abandonment, this separation is artificial and both terms are describing the same thing measured at different points in a process.

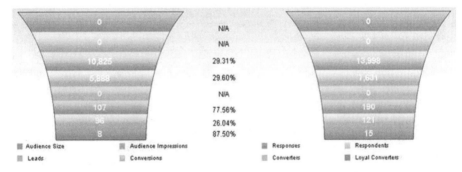

Figure 3: Example of how abandonment and conversion are often measured using some type of conversion funnel or process measurement tool.

Attrition

Once you have successfully been able to measure how many visitors convert after coming to your Web site, you will want to keep track of the number of these people that continue to come back and convert again. If your particular business model depends on acquiring visitors who convert and having them return to convert repeatedly, attrition is the measure of the number of repeaters that you lose. Put another way:

> *"Attrition is a measurement of the number of people you have been able to successfully convert once but are unable to retain to convert again."*

Here you can see that we apply a unit, people, since regardless of how you measure conversion and abandonment, it should be recognized that it is human beings that are doing the converting and abandoning.

Two important considerations when measuring attrition is A) do you expect people to return and convert a second time and B) how often do you expect this? If you are measuring the conversion rate for people downloading a white paper or application, one would expect your attrition rate to be nearly 100 percent since they very likely do not need to download that same item again. Conversely, if you are selling products over the Internet one would hope that any visitor you could successfully convert into a customer will return to purchase again and again. If the latter is true, being able to measure the average frequency of purchase will help you better measure your attrition rate, as you don't want to measure attrition over too short or too long a period of time.

Loyalty, Frequency and Recency

If it is a goal to have people visit your Web site more than once, which is nearly always the objective, it is a good idea to measure loyalty, frequency and recency. Each of these terms help the Web site owner quantify how well they are doing at retaining traffic.

Loyalty is the measure of the number of times a visitor can be expected to return. Simply put:

> *"Loyalty is a measure of the number of visits any visitor is likely to make over their lifetime as a visitor. It should be measured as the raw number of visits all visitors have made since measurement was initiated, and the number of visits should be de-duplicated."*

One should be able to quickly see that loyalty is a moving target, a measurement whose characteristics will change over time. If you measure loyalty the first week you turn your Web site on you are likely to be sorely disappointed, as most visitors will have only visited once. But if you measure loyalty over time you will be able to use this information to build a gross profile of your visitors.

Loyalty should be reported as the number of raw visits per visitor, for example, "100 visitors made 3 visits, 87 visitors made 4 visits," and so on. These numbers should be de-duplicated—if a person were to visit for the third time she should be counted in the "3 visits" column until she visits for her fourth time, at which time the "3 visits" column should be decremented and the "4 visits" column increased. Failure to do this will artificially increase the number of visitors to low visit groups and skew the profile one is able to build.

Frequency is the measure of the relative amount of time between visits, and is often reported in categories such as "once a day," "once a month," and so on, although reporting the actual number of average days between visits and the distribution of return visitors in each group is more useful. Frequency is defined much like loyalty:

> *"Frequency is a measure of the activity a visitor generates on your Web site in terms of average time between return visits. It is likely measured in logical groups or as discreet numbers of days between visits. Regardless of presentation, the data should be de-duplicated."*

Recency is related to loyalty and frequency, but is usually reported in the context of online purchasing as the number of days since the last purchase. It can, however, be extended to non-commerce activity. Simply put:

> *"Recency is the number of days since the last visit (or purchase) and should be reported as the number of visitors who returned after "n" days."*

Again, the reader should recognize that recency is a moving target and will evolve over time depending on the makeup and activity of the audience.

The Pyramid Model of Web Analytics Data

Within Web analytics there are many different sources and types of data. Thus far we've described a number of different data sources, drilling down into specific data sources for traffic analysis data, namely Web-server log files and client-side data collection. There are also different "types" of data inherent to each of these data sources, and these data types provide different kinds of information.

Specific to traffic analysis, there is a "pyramid" model of data, describing a continuum of data in terms of both volume and value. At the bottom of the pyramid are "hits"— data that has already been described as both voluminous and mostly useless. At the top of the pyramid are "identified unique visitors"—data that is likely difficult to collect in large numbers but is potentially very valuable to one's Web analytics program. Figure 4 describes the pyramid model, from bottom to top.

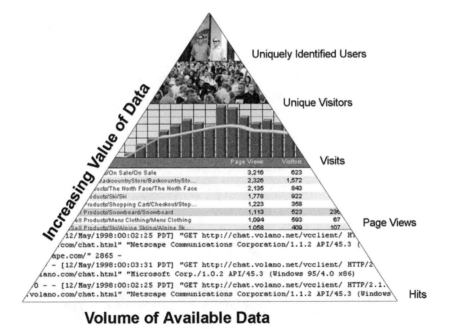

Figure 4: The pyramid model of Web analytics data.

Hits

Hits are useless as a Web analytics data type for the most part; data most commonly used by Network Administrators to determine the load on a single Web server within a server farm. It would not be unusual for a single day's analysis of a small Web site to report that "100,000,000 hits were received today" which unfortunately tells you nothing about actual human activity.

Here is some more about what WebTrends/NetIQ has to say about hits:

```
"Each file requested by a visitor registers as hit. There can be
several hits on each page. While the volume of hits reflects the
amount of server traffic, it is not an accurate reflection of the
number of pages viewed."
```

Without a doubt, the term "hit" is a remnant from the days when Web server log files were nothing more than a tool to monitor the activity of the server application, a term which should no longer be used by business and marketing professionals.

Page Views

Moving up in the data value continuum we have page views. Page views are the foundation for any Web analytics program. The measurement of overall activity on a Web site is measured in views, as is the popularity of any given page or section of a site. Keeping in mind the definition of a page view given previously, views are key to helping measure reach and acquisition (discussed in Chapters 11 and 12).

Page views are not a good basis for measuring rates, especially conversion and abandonment rates. The problem with using views for these measurements is that a view is recorded every time a page loads. Consider the following scenarios describing simple three-step activities:

1. Ten visitors view page one 10 times; five move on to page two and view page two five times; one moves on to page three and views that page once.
2. Ten visitors view page one 20 times, reloading the page twice on average; five move on to page two and view page two five times; one moves on to page three and views that page three times.

In the first example, based on the number of page views, the step one-to-step-three conversion rate is 10 percent, with 50 percent abandonment between step one and step two. In the second example, even though the same number of visitors move through the process, the step-one-to-step-three conversion rate is 15 percent $(3/20 = 0.15)$ with 75 percent abandonment between step one and step two. Although the two conversion rates only differ by 5 percent, one can imagine how these differences could be further aggravated with larger numbers.

Views should also not be used to determine the number of actual visits or visitors coming to a Web site. For this information one needs to move further up the pyramid.

Visits

Visits are the first level of measuring activity roughly in terms of human behavior. While it is impossible to learn much about interaction with a Web site from page views other than the popularity of individual pages and content, visits allow us to stitch together actual patterns of usage. Nearly all Web Analysis applications report navigation paths in terms of visits. Any tool that facilitates the measurement of a multi-step process should do so using visits (see Chapter 6).

Visits also provide us information about where visitors enter and exit the Web site, as well as the volume of traffic from any referring source.

Unique Visitors

Unique visitors are near the top of the pyramid, providing details regarding the number of people coming to the Web site in a given timeframe. While this metric is somewhat limited by the accuracy of collection, it is better than any type of data lower on the pyramid for determining the number of human beings visiting a Web site, especially if one has no way of uniquely identifying visitors—that is, actually being able to identify each visitor who comes to your site (see below).

Visitors are good for helping understand the global distribution of one's Web traffic, retention metrics such as loyalty, frequency and recency, whether someone has been to the Web site previously and the technographic breakdown of browsers used to access one's Web site.

Unique Identified Visitors

One thing that a unique visitor measurement is not good for is determining exactly who is visiting the Web site. For this one needs to have some way to uniquely identify a visitor in such a way that this identification can be tied back to a database of names, and so on. This identifier is often referred to as the "unique user identifier" or UUID. Depending on how your Web analytics package supports the UUID, one can use this data type to drill very deeply into one's understanding of the visitor. The UUID can enable one-to-one marketing and other "holy grails" of Web analytics.

Not all Web analytics packages support the UUID, and those that do may require a great deal of setup to take advantage of the data. That being said, depending on your overall goals for your Web site, finding a vendor that provides easy access and reporting based on the UUID may be critical to the success of your Web analytics program.

CHAPTER 5
CONTENT
ORGANIZATION TOOLS

"People won't use your Web site if they can't find their way around it."
Steve Krug in *Don't Make Me Think*

Every Web site has some kind of organization associated with it, either explicit or implied. In the best case, this organization is reflective of the site's information architecture or navigation schema. An example would be a site that has "product information," "company information" and "investor information." Theoretically every page on the Web site would fit cleanly into one of those categories, perhaps with the exception of the home page. Perhaps even the Web designers, when assembling the site, created three directories reflective of this schema:

```
/product_information
/company_information
/investor_information
homepage.html
```

If this were the case, when one is examining a report describing the activity to specific pages ("Top Pages" or "Most Requested Pages") there would be enough descriptive information to let you know what page and what part of the site was being accessed. This is fine, in theory, but problems arise when one considers the following confounding influences:

1. Poorly architected (or heavily appended) Web sites
2. Dynamically generated Web sites
3. Web sites derived from content management platforms

In the first case, imagine the same situation above except the pages and directories are now:

```
/p2002
/ci
/invtinfo
default.html
```

When analyzing content reports, you may be informed enough about the Web site to know that "p2002" was in fact "product information," that "ci" was "company information" and "invtinfo" was "investor information" but it is equally likely that you will have no idea. You also may or may not be aware that "default.html" is a common name for a home page. As you can see, this nomenclature, while not insurmountable, can cloud the process of reading Web analytics data, forcing a translation step that often times slows the analytics process.

Name	Date
..	
email	20031127 12:27
images	20031231 20:23
sample	20040129 12:58
stanford	20031113 19:55
sterne	20040130 17:02
robots.txt	20031231 13:53
wad.css	20031231 13:53
email_error.asp	20031231 13:53
index_traffic.asp	20031231 13:53
index_website.asp	20031231 13:53
index_logfiles.asp	20031231 13:53
free_preview.asp	20031231 13:53
index.asp	20031231 13:54

Figure 5: Sample content groups and page names from the author's Web site, www.webanalyticsdemystified.com.

In the second case, imagine a dynamically generated Web site that was built around a single page. The template presents different information to the visitor depending on the values passed into the template via the URL query string. Examples of this could be:

```
page.asp?pid=1234&cid=8&vid=41A
page.asp?pid=1234&cid=3&vid=41A
page.asp?pid=1234&cid=8&vid=42B
```

In order to translate this information meaningfully several things need to happen. There needs to be some way to determine exactly what information is being generated and map that back to a meaningful content grouping. For the sake of this discussion imagine that all three pages display information about a pair of shoes but that the first URL provides information about availability, the second URL information about pricing and the third URL compares these shoes to another pair. In this the case, reasonable content groups for these three URLs may be:

```
/shoes/availability
/shoes/pricing
/shoes/compare
```

The second list is clearly easier to read than the first, at least in common terms. The same kinds of problems arise in Web sites rendered from content management platforms. This demonstrates a key requirement for the content measurement tools that your Web analytics application provides:

Any robust and useful Web Analytics application will provide the tools necessary to translate meaningless or confusing content descriptions into meaningful and useful content groupings. These content groupings should be flexible, defined by the online business based on their needs and requirements, not by the limitations imposed by the application.

The ability to define content groups "manually," rather than being stuck with either the groups provided by your Webmaster or a flat, meaningless structure, should be required for the following reason: The easier the information is to read and share, the greater the likelihood that the information will be acted upon. Imagine that every time you generate a content usage report, one that provides critical information about how visitors interact with the information or products that you provide, sharing this information is met with replies of, "What does this line mean?" and, "Can you explain this report?" because people don't know how to translate the information into meaningful terms.

When people don't understand the information they're given, the tendency is to ignore or defer. By requiring reports that are readable and logically organized this common hurdle can be overcome, increasing the likelihood of success for your Web analytics program.

Metrics Content Organization Tools Should Provide

The minimum requirement for the kinds of metrics that can be measured using content organization tools is that you should be able to see how many page views were generated for any content or sub-content for whatever timeframe you are focusing on. Page views are the default measurement for popularity, so more popular or interesting content will usually receive a greater number of page views. Beyond page views, it would be nice to have the following information for any content group on your Web site:

- Number of visits
- Number of unique visitors, broken down by at least day and month (an option for custom timeframe is desirable as well)
- Average time spent viewing this content group
- Some type of content usage analysis, such as what content groups led visitors to this particular group, and what content groups they were likely to visit after this group

Occasionally it is also very useful to be able to assign a single page or group of pages to more than one content group. Imagine an online store that has products normally available but also makes some products available as "featured products." The Web analytics team may want to ask the question "how often are these products viewed, and how often are they viewed as part of the featured products section?" Being able to assign these products to their normal group ("/products") but to *also* assign them to a featured products group ("/featured products"), when they are viewed as such, would provide the answer to that question.

Examples of Different Content Organization Strategies

There are two very common content organization strategies and one that is less common, but arguably more powerful. These are commonly referred to as "directory structure," "information architecture" and "business objective" models of organization. The former is generally more IT or Webmaster-centric, reflecting the actual distribution of documents on your Web server. The latter is very business-centric, reflecting a natural language expression of your goals and reasons for having a Web site and how each Web document contributes to those expressed goals.

Directory Structure Content Organization

If you were to simply install your traffic analysis application and begin collecting data, either by parsing your Web-server log files or by dropping default code on your pages, you would very likely be looking at your data organized by directory structure. As companies first begin to establish Web analytics programs internally, a directory structure-based organization is often employed, if for no other reason than it is usually easy to set up. Every Web site has a directory structure of some kind—some very deep, some very flat—but the nature of HTML dictates some type of content structure by default. Some examples:

- **www.csd.toshiba.com/cgi-bin/tais/su/su_sc_home.jsp**—the document "su_sc_home.jsp" is organized into a hierarchical structure "cgi-bin/tais/su," which at least superficially suggests that the document is dynamic in nature (the "cgi-bin" is common to dynamically generated pages.)
- **www.cnn.com/2003/US/01/18/sproject.irq.us.protests/index.html**— the document "index.html" is organized into a hierarchical structure "2003/US/01/18/sproject.irq.us.protests" which appears to reflect the date this document was published and its general topic.
- **www.apple.com/switch/questions**—the default document is organized into a hierarchical structure "switch/questions," which is also a reflection of the information architecture on this site.
- **www.broadvision.com/OneToOne/SessionMgr/home_page.jsp**—the default document "home_page.jsp" is organized into an application structure "OneToOne/SessionMgr," which is common to nearly every "page" on this Web site.

Nearly every Web site has one of these four types of organization. The first and last examples presented above (from the Toshiba and BroadVision Web sites) present a common problem associated with this type of content organization. In dynamic environments content structures are often very "flat" owing to the fact that a single or small number of scripts are designed to deliver a large number of different pieces of content from a database or data structure.

Information Architecture Content Organization

A Web site's information architecture describes the relationship between content and navigation. Louis Rosenfeld, in a keynote presentation at the American Society for Information Science and Technology summit, said:

> "Information architecture involves the design of organization, labeling, navigation and searching systems to help people find and manage information more successfully."

You can see the information architecture for any Web site simply by examining the navigation system presented on any given page. A few examples:

- **www.circuitcity.com** —the primary navigation along the top of the Circuit City home page includes "Electronics," "Games," "Movies" and "Music." We can easily infer that Circuit City has made a decision to organize their content around broad product lines (Figure 6).

- **www.ebay.com** —the primary navigation for eBay users includes "Browse," "Search," "Sell," "My eBay" and access to the eBay "Community," as well as several secondary areas ("pay," "register," and so on) (Figure 7).
- **www.hotels.com** —the top line navigation for Hotels.com visitors includes "Hotels," "Suites & Vacation Rentals," "Vacation Packages," "Deals & Specials" and "Destinations & Interests" (Figure 8).

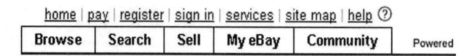

Figure 6: Example of top-line navigation on Circuit City Web site (www.circuitcity.com).

Figure 7: Example of top-line navigation on eBay site (www.eBay.com).

Figure 8: Example of top-line navigation on Hotels.com site (www.hotels.com).

The goal of information architecture is to assist visitors in more quickly finding the information that they have come to the Web site seeking or that they may be interested in. This same goal is easily extended to the concept of content organization within your Web analytics package.

Using the Circuit City Web site as an example, if you were to click from the home page to "Computers, Printers and PDAs," select "Desktop Computers" from the list and click a link to any of the desktop computers available you would theoretically be in an information group defined as:

```
Home > Computers Printers and PDAs > Desktop Computers
```

This information group can easily be translated into a content group to help Circuit City understand the flow of visitor traffic to pages in exactly the same way they have chosen to present those pages. Even though content on the site is dynamically rendered, and so is entirely flat, containing no information about "Computers" or "Desktop Computers" in the URL proper, most Web analytics application provide tools to translate the informative part of a URL into a logical and useful content group. In this example, if Circuit City were to opt for an information architecture-based content organization strategy, we would hope that their Web analytics application would support the creation of a content group that is roughly:

```
/Home/Computers Printers and PDAs/Desktop Computers/Product
Views
```

From this, Circuit City would be able to see how many visitors and views each level in this hierarchy ad from top to bottom, how much time visitors spent at each level, and so on.

As online businesses' understanding of Web analytics matures, the information architecture view of content becomes the most common type of content organization employed. This view is much more useful than the directory structure view in that it better ties Web analytics data back to the Web site using business-relevant language and structures.

Business Objective Content Organization

A content organization strategy that is emerging in popularity is that of "business objective" organization. Very few companies have Web sites just for the fun of having one. Most, if not all, companies build Web sites and Web-based applications to accomplish specific goals and objectives. At a high level, these business objectives are typically fairly straightforward. For example:

1. Sell products and/or services
2. Gather qualified leads for marketing
3. Decrease internal costs by servicing customers via less expensive channels
4. Attract loyal and frequent visitors (to increase advertising revenue)
5. Facilitate the visitors search for information

As you can see, each of these objectives is really "make more money" (in the case of items 1, 2 and 4) or "make money by saving money" (in the case of items 3 and 5). Each of these high-level goals can be described in abstract terms by specific online activities in which visitors can engage. Examples of such activities, for item 1, selling more products and/or services, are:

1. Find products or services
2. Research and compare products or services
3. Request more information about products or services
4. Purchase products or services

Now consider each of these activities in more concrete terms, thinking of them as a container for Web pages. Each will likely have an exclusive, or nearly so, set of Web pages that defines each activity. For item 1, find products or services, you would include the pages that have lists of products available for purchase online, perhaps including your home page. For item 2, research and compare, you would have pages with specific information about said products or services. For items 3 and 4 there are likely a small number of pages and forms that facilitate the visitors' request for information and purchase processes.

The concepts presented here regarding a business objective organization for your Web site are closely related to the practice of using "personas" to ensure that your Web site is built with a specific set of users in mind. Personas, first presented by Alan Cooper in *The Inmates Are Running The Asylum* in 1999, have become more and more popular among high-end design firms. When incorporated into application design processes, personas are a powerful tool to help focus design efforts and ensure that application flow is consistent with primary user needs. The relationship between business objective content organization and personas is simply this: If you use personas to design your Web site or application you should be absolutely sure that the goals of your key persona(s) are in line with your business objectives. If this is not the case then either A) you have misidentified key personas or B) you have misidentified your business objectives. Additional information about the relationship between personas and business objectives is presented in Chapter 16.

Consider the example of BackcountryStore.com, which exists online primarily to sell high-quality outdoor gear for the serious enthusiast, but is also interested in improving the customer experience through search features, online communities and education. BackcountryStore.com has used HitBox Enterprise to organize their content groupings around six major business objectives:

1. Selling products online
2. Facilitate searching for the products they sell
3. Introduce BackcountryStore.com to new visitors
4. Grow their online community
5. Educate their customers and potential customers
6. Gather leads for their online marketing group

Every page on the Web site can be categorized as belonging to one of these six main objectives, allowing management to easily see which pages and sub-content groups contribute most to the success of each business objective.

Content	Content Page Views	Content Daily Uniques
2. /Sell Products	34,704	4,282
3. /Facilitate Search	2,218	556
4. /Introduce BackcountryStore	1,396	829
5. /Grow Community	239	109
6. /Educate Customers	153	84
7. /Gather Leads	126	90

Figure 9: Business objective content groupings for BackcountryStore.com.

If the owners of BackcountryStore.com want to know how likely "men's ski jackets" are to contribute to the overall goal of selling products online they can simply drill-down into the "Sell Products" content group until they find "Men's Ski Jackets".

```
/Sell Products/Men's Clothing/Men's Winter Clothing/Men's Ski
Jackets
```

Content	Content Page Views	Content Daily Uniques
(parent directory)		
2. Mens Ski Jackets	888	220
3. Mens Fleece Jackets	745	213
4. Mens Down Jackets	508	152
5. Mens Soft Shell	492	112

Figure 10: Drill-down to "Men's Ski Jackets" in "Sell Products" on BackcountryStore.com.

As you can see in Figure 10, for the timeframe under examination 220 daily unique visitors generated 888 page views of Men's Ski Jackets, nearly four views per unique visitor. In this type of content organization view, the owners of BackcountryStore.com can easily see which product lines are most popular—and thus most likely to be purchased through their Web site.

Organizing content around a business objective model allows you to both measure the attraction of pages on your Web site as part of logical groups and *see how visitors' use of those pages contributes to your overall business success.*

This model immediately informs everyone responsible for Web site success about the number of visitors who were in the pool of candidates to purchase products, generate leads, and so on. After strategic changes are made these numbers can be compared to earlier numbers from the same content group to quickly measure the effect of these changes. This model allows managers to determine the success or failure of changes to specific activities online, providing easily understood data to answer questions such as, "Do more people move from 'research products' to 'purchase products' activities if a different color or layout is used on product description pages?" and, "Which are our most popular products or product lines?"

As more and more businesses accept that their Web site is simply a channel to support existing business goals, the business objective model for content organization will become more widely used. To take advantage of this model one must truly view the Web site as an integral—and integrated—part of the overall business and be prepared to deal with it as such. Many businesses that are serious about succeeding online see the value in the business objective model for content organization and are already implementing it successfully.

Risks Associated With Content Organization

The major risks associated with content organization are a lack of flexibility on the part of your reporting application and differing opinions about how content should be organized within your organization. In terms of lack of flexibility, it is not uncommon for Web analytics applications to impose rules on how content groups are named or formed. Web-server log-file analysis applications are often limited in their abilities to dynamically name content groups, often requiring some kind of translation file or table to map information derived from URLs to clean, readable content groups. Client-side data collection applications are typically more flexible in terms of defining and setting up content groups but often do not allow you to go back and rename content groups after they have been named and data has been collected (although there are exceptions). Additionally, outsourced applications often require a single page to belong only to a single content group (again, there are exceptions).

None of these risks are showstoppers, nor should they be treated as such. In the first case, using a Web-server log-file analysis application, the analytics and/or information technology team will have to pay careful attention to the relationship between the Web site's directory structure and how internal users would like to see pages mapped into content groupings. If the groups responsible for each do not communicate clearly with each other, or if the Web site directory structure is significantly changed, there is always the possibility that content mappings will be wrong or simply dropped from an analysis.

In the second case—where once content groups are named and data has been collected applications do not allow you to go back and change their names or relationships—this usually only poses a problem if you redesign your Web site or information architecture. Consider the situation where you have organized your content data collection around your information architecture. If your business decides to change the information architecture, and you are unable to go back and rename content groups for historical data, you will be forced to decide between renaming the content groupings with the new architecture or maintain the content grouping "as is."

The third case—where a single page is only allowed to belong to a single content group—leads directly into the second major risk in content organization, differing opinions about how content should be organized. Imagine three sets of stakeholders trying to decide what content organization strategy should be applied to the Web site. The information technology team will likely prefer a model based on the Web site's directory structure because the data makes sense to them. The marketing team may prefer a model reflective of the information architecture on the site, which is different than the directory structure, so that they are able to quickly assess visitor interest in each major category of information the company presents online. The executive staff will hopefully prefer a "business objective" model of organization so that they are able to quickly determine how the Web site contributes to overall business success. In this situation, if your Web analytics package only supports a single content structure for your site, who decides which model is applied? Most likely the executive team will get their "business objective" model, with the other groups being asked to "make due."

If the Web analytics package your organization uses supports multiple content groups per page, either through inherent technology or the ability to track multiple accounts or profiles per page, these kinds of problems can be avoided. A major factor in the success of any Web analytics program is the ability to analyze data in a context that you are familiar with. If you are forced to constantly translate data from a format you are unfamiliar with, compounded by the fact that Web analytics in itself is not easy, you are likely to be less focused or less interested in the information contained therein and so less likely to act.

Web Analytics Tip: Why Are Content Groupings Important?

Many customers I've had the pleasure of working with in the past have treated content grouping as an afterthought when implementing their analytics reporting. Faced with the choice between taking the time to think out how their content should be organized and implementing around that, and simply using the default content implementation, many clients have opted for the latter. While this does let them rapidly implement their analytics solution and start collecting data, it is very common that they will come back to me later and complain that the data is not organized very well and is hard to use.

Hmmm, really?

Being the consummate professional I always fight the temptation to say, "I told you so," and giggle—nobody wants to hear their consultant talk smack. I usually provide them a gentle reminder that we'd discussed this at the time of implementation and that they made a tactical decision to choose rapidity over detail. Then we go back and formulate a plan to re-implement using either the information architecture or business objective content groupings described in this chapter.

The lesson here is to not attempt to cut corners when implementing your analytics solution, especially regarding your content structure. Most of the work involved is mental—sitting down as a team, thinking about the content you have and mapping pages to the content groupings that you'd like to see. Technically, translating this content mapping can be more or less difficult, depending on the application environment you have, how your pages are published, and so on, but once the map is created all that is left is busywork. The time and money you spend having someone in your organization implement useful and well thought out content groups will be returned many times when the data turns out to be easy to use and easy to understand.

CHAPTER 6
PROCESS MEASUREMENT TOOLS

> **"If you want a great site, you've got to test... Testing reminds you that not everyone thinks the way you do, knows what you know, uses the Web the way you do."**
>
> **Steve Krug on "Several true things about testing" in *Don't Make Me Think***

As briefly described in the section on business objective content organization, most business-class Web sites are simply a set of activities that users hopefully engage in to contribute to business success. Since more often than not these activities are ordered, multiple-step processes, the Web analytics package that you choose should provide tools to facilitate process (or scenario) measurement. These tools are referred to in a variety of ways by vendors—scenario analysis, conversion funnels, process analysis, funnel analysis or fall-out reporting—but regardless of the name, process analysis tools should allow you to measure step-by-step abandonment and overall conversion rates for any multi-step process.

The value in measuring and understanding user interaction with your activities and processes is simply this:

The most effective strategy for using Web Analytics applications and the data they provide to truly improve the top or bottom lines for your online business is making use of data provided by process measurement tools. Data provided by process measurement tools, in tandem with successful application of the continuous improvement process, can help you dramatically increase your conversion rates. Increasing your key conversion rates is the easiest path to making more money on the Internet.

Consider the most common multiple-step process that people focus on online, the purchase process. Most purchase processes begin with a shopping cart and flow into a checkout process that requires the visitor to provide a variety of information. In most cases this process is three or four steps long, including the shopping cart, but longer purchase processes are not unheard of. Typically a Web site will be able to attract a large number of visitors to view products and many of those visitors will place an item in the shopping cart. The unfortunate reality is that significantly fewer visitors will then click the "checkout" button and fewer still will complete the actual checkout process.

While most Web analytics packages will provide information about the number of visitors that place an item in the shopping cart and the number of visitors who complete the process, process analysis tools take multi-step analysis a step further. Process analysis tools should enable the measurement of loss between any two steps and the total loss from start to end. Knowing which steps have the highest abandonment will help your Web design team know where to focus effort. The ability to measure the effect of changes to any step by observing changes in the abandonment rate at that step helps to validate the value of changes. The reduction of loss at any step in a multi-step process will have a net positive effect on the overall conversion rate for the process unless loss is introduced at other steps in the process at the same time.

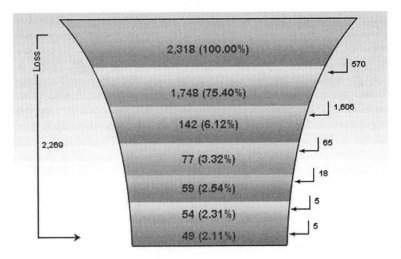

Figure 11: An example of how one vendor helps their customers visualize the abandonment and conversion through an online activity.

An Important Note about Process and Conversion Rates

Two important things to keep in mind are that A) the purchase process is by no means the only important multi-step process worth measuring and B) there are *many* different conversion rates that can be measured on any Web site. Regarding the first point, some example activities that can be measured with an eye towards overall improvement include:

- Forms used for lead generation
- Online purchase processes
- Search functions
- Navigation to support materials or information
- Downloads

Basically any activity that involves visitors viewing information on at least two successive pages can be measured as a process. That being said, the most valuable processes you should measure are those that collect some item of value from your visitors—those items that benefit your business.

Regarding the second point, any Web site has a number of different conversion rates. One rate is the number of visitors who visit the home page and then purchase. Another is the number of visitors who view a product or service description page and then place the item in a shopping cart. Another rate would be the number of visitors who click "checkout" and then complete the purchase process. Yet another would be the number of visitors who successfully find the customer support content they are looking for. The challenge of the business owner is figuring out which ones make the most sense to measure.

A complicating factor when calculating conversion rates is the disposition of your visitors at the time of their visit. If you calculate your "site" conversion rate as the number of total unique visitors divided by the number of actions (orders, leads, and so on) you are making the assumption that all of your unique visitors are potential converts. In many instances this is not the case—customers who have previously purchased may simply be looking for technical support, visitors who have previously submitted personal information may be simply double checking something they read, your competitors may be doing competitive analysis on your Web site, and so on. While it is impossible to truly know an anonymous visitor's intentions, you need to keep this complicating factor in mind and attempt to minimize the effect when calculating conversion rates.

Finally, conversion rates are numbers that are very frequently bantered about, often incorrectly. Many studies have been published detailing average conversion rates for online businesses and often companies try and compare their rate to these published rates. Problems associated with making this type of comparison include:

- Method of measurement—if the published rates were collected from Web-server log-file data but your business uses page-tagging technology the data is similar, but not same.
- Definition of activity—if the published rates are the measure of visitors to the home page who then successfully purchase but you are only able to measure visitors who place an item in a shopping cart who purchase, the conversion rates are apples and oranges and not valid for comparison.
- Statistic used to calculate rates—if the published rates are based on the data generated from page views but you are able to collect data based on visits or unique visitors, the data is not valid for comparison. The author's suspicion is that many groups publishing reports comparing conversion rates simply ask businesses for said rates, not the statistics used to calculate the rates.

In general it is best to simply ensure that you A) have an accurate method for measuring abandonment and conversion in multiple-step activities and B) compare your Web site only to previous data collected on your Web site using the continuous improvement process described in Chapter 1 of this book.

Metrics Provided by Process Measurement Tools

Regardless of the application you choose to facilitate your Web analytics program, the process measurement tools the application provides should allow you to do the following:

- Define multiple-step processes in terms of steps in the process
- Assign Web pages to a given step or steps
- Track the flow of visitors from step to step, measuring abandonment between steps
- Track conversion, that is, information about visitors who complete a process "as designed"

- Learn as much as possible about activity at each step, including average time spent on the step, pages leading to the step, pages leading from the step and links that visitors use to leave the process entirely

At a bare minimum, for any step in the process you should be able to see:

- Number of visits or unique visitors, but visits is preferred
- Number of page views to pages in the step, both as an aggregate and individually
- Average time spent as an aggregate for the step
- Links most likely to be clicked leading to abandonment from the step

These data are enough to create a very complete understanding of activity through any online funnel or process. Some "nice to have" features would be:

- Side-by-side process visualization tools, or the ability to compare two days, weeks or months graphically without having to open two applications or browser windows.
- Notes, allowing for easy sharing of information regarding changes that had been made to the process regarding when and why any modifications were made.
- Measurements of visits, page views *and* unique visitors, allowing greater flexibility for comparison to legacy processes for measuring process abandonment and conversion. Having these data also allows you to calculate the number of times the average unique visitor is likely to engage in the process (visits divided by unique visitors = visits per visitor per timeframe, see Chapter 12).

As long as the application you choose provides for the bare minimum measurements you will be set to measure and improve the flow through any multi-step process your Web site may have.

Example Uses for Process Measurement Tools

As described above, process measurement tools can be used in a number of common situations online to better understand where visitors *are not* successful. If you think you have an activity on your Web site that is a good candidate for measurement using these types of tools, but you are not sure, ask yourself this question:

If I can get more visitors to complete this activity, will I be more successful online?

If the answer to the question is "yes" then the activity should definitely be measured. The most common online activities that businesses are measuring include:

- Purchase processes, to understand where potential customers drop out of the process and monitor changes in abandonment and conversion rates;
- Registration processes, especially those that are many steps long, to start to understand what questions you may be asking potential registrants that are driving them away;

- Demonstrations of products or services that are many steps long, to ensure that prospects are seeing the entire length of the demo and not just getting part of the picture;

- On-site search tools, especially those designed to lead visitors either to product purchases or support content and information, to ensure that visitors are successfully able to use your search tools;

- The use of any online application that you may have built specifically for customer use to ensure that customers are getting full value out of the tools you have built.

One of the best examples of how process management tools are effectively used is demonstrated by BackcountryStore.com and its efforts to improve their site-wide conversion rate. In early 2002, the checkout process on BackcountryStore.com included a required registration step for every visitor who wanted to make a purchase. When anyone clicked the "Checkout Now" button they were not taken to the first step in the checkout process, where they would provide shipping and billing information. Rather they were taken to a page very similar to the one presented in Figure 12.

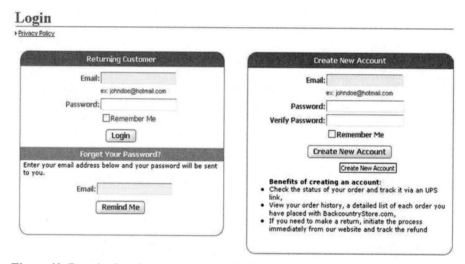

Figure 12: Required registration step on BackcountryStore.com from early 2002.

While requiring registration is not always a bad idea, when BackcountryStore.com applied process measurement tools it was able to see significant abandonment at the registration step (Figure 13).

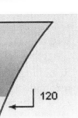

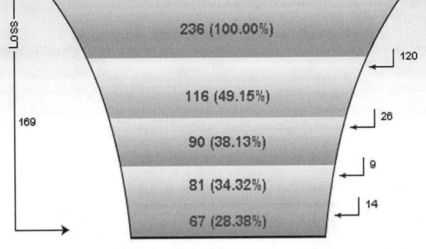

Figure 13: Process measurement tools employed by BackcountryStore.com.

To make a long story short, BackcountryStore.com made the decision to remove this step and provide customers a different path to register and log in if they were inclined (Figure 14). The end result of making this change, combined with a small handful of usability improvements that were also identified using Web analytics tools, resulted in a *20 percent increase in the site-wide conversion rate*. What is more interesting is that, during BackcountryStore.com's twice-yearly sales, the lift in conversion rate is estimated to *go up by as much as 30 percent when compared to pre-change numbers*.

Figure 14: New method for logging in as a registered user on BackcountryStore.com.

While not every online business employing process measurement tools will be as successful as BackcountryStore.com, you can be assured that some will be much, much more successful increasing conversion rates, depending on the scope of the problem the visitors are experiencing.

Web Analytics Tip: When to Require Registration

Regarding the BackcountryStore.com example, clients will often ask me whether I recommend required registration in online purchase processes. The catalyst behind requiring registration appears to be a combination of factors:

- Marketing people want to have the registration information for a variety of reasons (opt-in mailing, database marketing, and so on).
- The commerce application used to drive the purchase process requires this information.
- Amazon.com does it so it must be the right thing to do…

Consider these factors in order—of course marketing people want to have this information, marketing people *live for information that will let them know their customers better.* Unfortunately the potential customer has learned to be wary of marketers thanks to a constant deluge of mail spam, phone spam and email spam, as well as the recent emergence of identity theft. The funny thing is that the potential customer will likely end up giving you most, if not all, of the information you are trying to elicit in the course of the checkout process if you just let them get there.

Concerning commerce applications that have hard and fast rules about how the purchase process works—software is code and code can be changed. Rather than run the risk of alienating some percentage of people who are actively engaged in the process of trying to give you money, and so help you grow and maintain your business, you should seriously consider modifying the code that drives your purchase process, or implementing new code that provides you more flexibility. Successful online businesses *never* let themselves be held hostage by code or the programmers who create code.

Regarding the "Amazon.com does it" phenomenon, authors and analysts like me are guilty of perpetuating this problem to some extent. Because Amazon.com has been so phenomenally successful on the Internet, everyone has a tendency to look to them and see what they are doing. The problem is that Amazon.com has spent what are likely millions of dollars perfecting processes that are the best for *their customers*, not necessarily yours. Amazon.com has created a one-stop-shop for all kinds of purchases and thusly has developed an audience that is likely to return and purchase quite frequently. It is this frequency of purchase that drives the registration requirement online, not the desire to have information.

In general if you are debating whether to require registration or not you should ask yourselves the following questions:

- How often do our customers make online purchases? If the answer to this question is "hmmm, we don't know" or "less than three times a year" then *do not* require registration.
- Can we collect the same information in the course of the purchase process and then automatically register the customer? If the answer to this question is "yes" then *do not* require registration. If the answer is "no, we cannot" you should let the answer to question 1 drive your decision.

- Can we offer our customers any monetary incentive to register in the purchase process, such as free shipping or a discount on the total order? If the answer is "no" to this question then *do not* require registration.

In summary, nine times out of ten when someone asks me if I recommend registration in purchase processes I answer "no"; fortunately, in nearly all instances when clients have followed my advice and removed registration the results have been positive.

Risks Associated with Process Measurement Tools

The biggest risks associated with process measurement tools are A) the tools you have chosen are not able to provide accurate, useful data and B) even though you have the data you are not entirely sure what it is telling you. In the case of the former, your business *should not* invest in a Web analytics package that provides process measurement *solely* based on "page view" metrics. There are multiple inherent dangers in this type of process measurement, most notably the effect of reloads and multiple page views and, fundamentally, if a vendor is telling you that "page views are a fine way to measure process abandonment" they are also telling you "we have no idea what we're talking about."

Process measurement statistics should always be based on "visits" or "unique visitors," with visits being the preferred metric. Visits are preferable to unique visitors because unique statistics are always tied to a timeframe, such as a day, and if a visitor attempts to repeat the process more than one time in a day this information is potentially lost. Visits are the single most accurate statistic for measuring process abandonment because the visit captures information about both multiple visits in a single day/week/month and also the visit has a timeout that lets us understand how often a visitor is attempting a process. You are encouraged to revisit Chapter 4 for more on the differences between a visit and a visitor.

Regarding not knowing what the data is telling you, this is the Web analytics "catch-22." While you can be assured that if you are *not collecting* Web analytics data regarding activities on your Web site then you have no chance of knowing how or where improvements can be made, the author has no way to ensure that if you are collecting this type of data that it will be easy to use. Process measurement tools are designed to help you generate baseline data regarding visitor success while they move through designed activities. This data will easily identify the steps in an activity that visitors have the most trouble with but not necessarily tell you *why* these visitors have trouble.

Fortunately you have already read about the continuous improvement methodology in Chapter 2 of this book. By following a "measure > change > measure" strategy you will be able to identify the high abandonment steps in a multiple-step process, hypothesize about possible reasons for abandonment ("Visitors don't want to be asked their mother's maiden name," "Our next button appears below the fold and many visitors do not even see it"), make changes based on well thought-out hypotheses and then test the effects of those changes. By following this strategy you will very likely be able to iteratively identify the problems visitors are having and remove them from your process.

Two bits of advice:

- Try and let go of pre-conceived notions of "how your visitors behave." Most often these assumptions are false and will often limit your ability to hone in on the changes that will yield the biggest gains.
- Don't expect miracles. Nobody has 0 percent abandonment from step-to-step and a 100 percent conversion rate, nobody. The work you are doing using process measurement tools is attempting to *minimize loss* not *maximize flow*. It is a subtle but important difference.

About A/B Testing

One of the most frequent uses for process measurement tools is to conduct A/B tests to determine whether changes actually have a positive and measurable effect. If you make a small number of changes to pages or content in a known multiple-step conversion path that you can send some percentage of your traffic through, you can measure the difference on the changed, or "B," path, compared to the original process. This strategy is often favored because you are able to maintain your current conversion rate for at least part of your traffic, just in case the changes are detrimental. If you are planning on running A/B tests on your critical conversion processes, here are a few tips that can help ensure that you get meaningful, measurable results:

Only Change One Variable at a Time

Web designers often forget that if you change more than a single variable in an analysis like this you will be unable to determine whether the changes are due to "change 1" or "change 2" or the combination of "changes 1 and 2." Apply the scientific method in these instances and make sure that you can isolate the source of any measured differences. Please see Chapter 2 and the section on continuous improvement for additional guidance about making and testing changes.

Understand the Process for Diverting Traffic

A common mistake for those running the test is that they do not fully understand the mechanism for diverting traffic and so are not getting accurate counts of traffic volume. There are many strategies for diverting traffic (application layer, load balancers, scripts on pages) but a common problem with A/B testing is that these are not well understood. The essential goal of the traffic diversion mechanism is to be able to redirect a known percentage of visitors through this modified process. Ideally, the percentage of traffic redirected is easily changed without having to radically modify pages.

Determine Accurate Measures of Volume

If you are able to get a "visitors per page" count from your Web analytics package it is highly recommended that you do so for the first step in the test. Having this number allows you to ensure that you are actually getting the percentage of traffic moving through the funnel that you expect. If you are flowing 50/50 through "A" and "B" you should see near equal numbers of visitors to the first page in the process, running the test until the numbers have converged to almost exactly 50 percent through each path.

Analyze Carefully

This is very important! Hopefully you have robust process measurement tools at your disposal and you are able to measure abandonment at each step in your multiple-step process. If you see a difference in the conversion rate for the "B" test you need to ensure that this difference can be attributed to the *step that you changed* in the process. If you are getting small differences from many different steps then you are not testing anything; all you are seeing is variation in the quality of visitors flowing through the "A" and "B" tests ("noise"). You need to run your test until all of the change can be attributed to the exact step that you modified in the process, or until you are confident there is no change.

Run a "Null Test"

Once you have set everything up and are ready to test, take the time to flow 50/50 traffic through the exact same pages. Doing so will let you verify that you get the same conversion and abandonment rates and that the measurement tools are correctly set up. If you are not getting nearly exactly the same rates (within 5 percent) for both tests then something is wrong and any data you get from an actual test will be invalid. If this kind of problem is happening you should check that A) you are sending people into the tests *exactly* the same way (so you are not pre-selecting participants and sending more qualified people down one path or the other) and B) you are sending enough people into the test. You will see differences in rates until you have a reasonable sample. Depending on the volume of traffic your Web site receives, attaining a reasonable sample can take some time. Believe that this is time well spent and run a proper null test prior to making changes; if you do you will be more confident in the resulting data.

Run Your Test Until You Are Sure the Results Are Real

A common mistake in A/B testing is not running the test for long enough to determine actual differences. Often Web designers will take the time to set up an A/B test only to run it for just a few hours because they see differences and declare "B the winner!" This is dangerous because until you have a representative sample you cannot be entirely sure that "B" really does increase or decrease your conversion rate. It is not uncommon for a rate to be higher or lower at the onset of a test and then have that number drift back towards the original rate as the sample grows larger. For information on what constitutes a "statistically relevant sample" consult the college statistics textbook you have kept on your bookshelf all these years for exactly this reason.

Consider Segmenting Test Subjects

Depending on the segmentation tools that your application provides, segmenting test subjects will allow you to monitor the activity of test subjects when they return to your Web site. While these visitors may behave no differently than non-test subjects, you won't know unless you "tag" them. A reasonable question that could be answered is "what percentage of visitors that went through the "B" test returned to the Web site within three months?" Having this information, and being able to compare it to your site-wide loyalty metrics, will let you better understand the long-term effects of the A/B test.

If you follow these simple guidelines you will be able to take advantage of one of the more complex applications of the continuous improvement process. The upside of A/B testing is that if your changes are detrimental you will not alienate *all* of the visitors moving through the process as you would if you simply changed the process for everyone and then watched the effect. The downside is that A/B tests are not always easy to set up properly and do require some additional thought during the analysis phase.

Web analytics vendors are moving towards providing tools that support A/B testing such as multiple-timeframe views and side-by-side funnels for viewing data. While these visualization tools are great, keep in mind that they are only that, visualization tools and not a substitute for careful design and set-up as described above. Any Web analytics application will allow you to conduct A/B tests, even if the application does not support process measurement tools, although the testing becomes much trickier.

CHAPTER 7
VISITOR SEGMENTATION TOOLS

"Retailers, on average, generated $7 in revenue for every dollar invested in acquisition and $25 for every dollar spent on retention, nearly double the previous year's averages of $4 and $13, respectively."
Boston Consulting Group report on *Retailing Online: Coming of Age*

Every online business has many different visitor value groups, or visitor segments, making use of their Web site every day. Some visitors are simply browsing the Web site, trying to form an opinion of what the business does. Others have actively engaged with the Web site by providing some type of personal information. Still others are committed to the Web site, having made a purchase or downloaded a document. It is a mistake to lump all visitor value groups together and use that information to try and understand how to best serve the groups providing the highest value—thus the need for visitor segmentation tools.

Visitor segmentation tools are a general term for some technology that allows Web analytics teams to say, "Based on some behavior, I want to track this visitor as a member of a specific segment or group of segments." Some Web analytics application vendors provide this functionality by allowing you to place visitors in a segment at the time they perform a specific activity. Others allow you to mine data already collected and place visitors in a segment based on past activity or visit data.

Regardless of the strategy used by the Web analytics package you employ it is important to have the ability to segment visitors. Visitor segmentation allows you to answer important questions like:

- Do different segments of visitors behave differently in terms of the pages or products that they view?
- Do different segments of visitors spend more time on your Web site or return more or less frequently than others?
- Are different segments of visitors converting at higher or lower rates than others?
- How long does it take, on average, to move a visitor from a lower value group to a higher-value group and can that time be influenced by making changes to the Web site?

The fundamental use for visitor segmentation tools is to better understand how your most valuable visitors interact with your Web site. This information will allow you to ensure that any changes you make will not negatively impact these visitors. You can also use this type of information to give preference to content that higher-value groups are interested in, hopefully attracting more members of these higher-value groups.

Metrics Provided by Visitor Segmentation Tools

In a perfect world Web analytics vendors would collect data on all available metrics for visitor segments, providing complete coverage for all segments as well as the larger group of visitors as a whole. Because this is not a perfect world, likely you will be required to settle for fewer metrics than you would like. In fact, many Web analytics vendors do not support visitor segmentation at all. You don't necessarily need to avoid these vendors but the author does recommend questioning them very carefully about their future plans to support segmentation prior to signing any contract.

With that in mind, the following are metrics that are useful in understanding the activity of segmented groups of visitors:

- Traffic statistics such as page views and visits
- Daily and monthly unique visitors
- Pages and contents viewed
- Time spent on site and content distributions
- Referring source information (if present)
- Campaign source information (if present)
- Process conversion information (starters, converters, if applicable)
- Commerce information (if applicable)
- Segment information, such as segment conversion and new vs. returning members of the segment

Each of these measurements contributes to building a more detailed picture of how different value groups interact with your Web site. Knowing which pages and content different visitor segments view most often will help you better target members—and potential members—of that group. Campaign and referring source information will let you know how best to reach members of a group. Process measurement information will let you identify which segments are likely to begin an activity but not complete it, and which segments are most likely to complete business-critical activities.

Again, no vendor known to the author at the time of writing supplies all of the data points listed above. These recommendations are a guide to help you make better decisions when choosing an analytics package and are provided in hopes that eventually all vendors will support robust visitor segmentation tools.

Examples of Uses for Visitor Segmentation Tools

The two best uses for visitor segmentation tools are identifying higher-value visitor preferences and understanding visitor flow over time from lower- to higher-value groups. Some examples of each type of usage include:

- Segmenting visitors into "browsers" and "buyers" based on whether they have made a past purchase. Doing so would allow you to identify pages and content preferred by the "buyers" (more valuable) group, enabling you to draw greater attention to those pages and content. By highlighting valuable pages and simplifying the navigation to these pages you effectively improve the overall customer experience.

- Segmenting visitors into "interested" and "committed" based on the total number of pages they have viewed during previous visits to the Web site. Doing so would again allow you to identify content deemed more important by the "committed" group.
- Measuring the time to conversion from lower-value groups such as "unregistered visitors" to higher-value groups, such as "registered users" and "customers" in order to form more clear expectations of how long it takes to truly acquire a "customer."
- Tracking referring domains and/or campaigns that bring higher-value visitors like "customers" to the Web site. Doing so will help you identify online business partners more likely to contribute to your ongoing success.
- Mining previously collected data to identify the referring sources for visitors who browsed a specific combination of pages in order to again identify best online business partners.

The list goes on and on. Visitor segmentation tools will play an increasingly important role in improving online marketing in the future.

Perhaps a more concrete example of visitor segmentation in action, especially segment conversion, is how BackcountryStore.com went about determining whether visitors prefer registering prior to purchasing or purchasing anonymously. Similar to the example given in Chapter 6, BackcountryStore.com was concerned that its required registration prior to checkout was driving some visitors to abandon their shopping carts. To test this, BackcountryStore.com created a handful of visitor segments including "unregistered," "registered" and "customer" (Figure 15).

Segment Name	Entries
⇒Unregistered	2,937
⇒Searcher	324
⇒Sale Items	166
⇒Customer	44
⇒Registered	17
⇒from Epinions	3
⇒from Bizrate	2
⇒from Dealtime	1

Figure 15: Visitor segments being tracked by BackcountryStore.com.

Whenever a visitor used the "anonymous checkout" option on BackcountryStore.com they were put in the "unregistered" segment. When they registered they were segmented as such. Then when either segment completed a purchase they were "segment converted" to the "customer" segment. Thanks to segment conversion, BackcountryStore.com was able to see a strong visitor preference for anonymous checkout, additional data that supported removing required registration, as described in Chapter 6 (Figure 16).

	Segment Name	Avg Visits	Avg Time Spent	Segment Conversions
1.	Unregistered⇒Customer	1.01	0:20:52:44	78
2.	Unregistered⇒Registered	0.97	1:02:46:54	28
3.	Searcher⇒Customer	1.15	2:03:55:53	23
4.	Sale Items⇒Customer	1.36	3:11:14:43	18
5.	Registered⇒Customer	0.67	0:13:57:46	7

Figure 16: Visitor segment conversion observed by BackcountryStore.com to support a streamlined checkout process.

Although you can see that registered visitors were making purchases faster, as evidenced by a lower number of average visits before conversion and a shorter average amount of time spent before conversion, more than 10 times as many anonymous visitors made purchases ("Unregistered => Customer") compared to registered visitors ("Registered => Customer"). In the end the data pointed out that visitors preferred anonymous checkout and BackcountryStore.com implemented this to great success (see "Examples" in Chapter 6).

Risks Associated with Visitor Segmentation Tools

The major risk associated with visitor segmentation is that segmentation tools currently provided by the major Web analytics vendors are limited in their abilities. Some vendors only allow for "move forward" segmentation and are unable to create segments by mining previously collected data. Other vendors only allow for data mining segmentation and are limited in their ability to "permanently" identify a visitor as a member of a group. Still other vendors do not support visitor segmentation at all.

An associated risk is the number and type of measurements available in visitor segmentation toolsets. While some vendors provide limited numbers of statistics associated with visitor segments, none known to this author provide truly *complete* sets of statistics. The limitations imposed are often due to volume or type of data, or to presentation limitations. Regardless, truly useful Web analytics packages in the future should support flexible definition of segments and complete statistics packages for those segments.

Web Analytics Tip: Use Segments to Collect Demographic Data

Many of the customers that I work with have some type of registration process on their Web site. Often these registration processes ask moderately benign questions, such as, "What year were you born?" and, "Which gender are you?"—questions with answers that can be used to segment visitors based on demographics. Whenever you can determine the year someone was born, their gender, their marital status or household income you should consider translating this information and tracking these visitors as large demographic aggregates.

Imagine that you ask for year of birth and gender. From this information you can create seven demographic segments —two for gender and five for age brackets.

Gender	Age Group
Male	Under 18
Female	18 to 25
	26 to 31
	31 to 40
	Over 40

Then, depending on the answers a visitor provided on the registration form, you would add that visitor to either segment 1 or 2 and one of the segments 3 through 7. As an example, if I indicated that I was a male born in 1970 I would be added to segments 1 and 6.

Doing so will allow you to do several things. First and foremost you'll be able to determine through sampling how your Web audience breaks down along demographic lines, by counting page views, visits and unique visitors. Second, depending on which metrics your Web analytics application provides, you'll be able to see what pages and content each demographic group finds most interesting. This information can be leveraged a number of different ways—by your marketing group to better speak to your most important demographic, by your advertising sales group to help sell advertising space to advertisers seeking specific demographics, by your product design group to help ensure that you've created the right personas for your usability and design testing.

The nice thing about this type of segmentation is that it is done in aggregate and so provides anonymity to your visitors. Nobody has to worry about individuals being identified by age or gender because—hopefully—you can get large numbers of visitors segmented using this strategy. A potential pitfall and something that should be watched very closely, however, is whether you're able to segment enough visitors using this strategy to provide a statistically relevant population. Consult your college statistics book for more information about what constitutes "statistically relevant," but be cautious of making business decisions based on small samples.

CHAPTER **8**
CAMPAIGN ANALYSIS
TOOLS

"Potential customers make a decision to visit, and in doing so, are broadcasting their needs, which they look to the Web site to meet."
Bryan Eisenberg in *Converting Search Engine Traffic*

Building a Web site without advertising and marketing the products or services you provide is like building a house that no one ever lives in. You certainly could do it, by why would you? Assuming you agree with that statement you will immediately see the need for tools to help measure the effectiveness of drawing people to your Web site.

Likely you are using common marketing techniques to let people know that you are out there and have the products, services or information that they're looking for. You may be purchasing pay-per-click advertising, such as that offered by Overture or Google in their keyword buying programs. Perhaps you are sending email to opted-in or unknown recipients; perhaps you are buying banner ads on large portals sites. Perhaps you have a business partnership with a portal or a company like your own and you are trying to create synergy through common interests. Regardless of how you are trying to make people aware of your online business you need to track the quality of each message and medium.

Campaign analysis tools are designed to help you measure two things at minimum: response and conversion. Response is the number of visitors, called "respondents" in this context, who actually click on the link you have embedded in your advertising. Conversion is the number of responders that complete a specific activity after they arrive at your Web site. Being able to measure response and conversion is key to designing campaigns that contribute positively to your online business. Without these metrics you are only guessing that your marketing efforts are working.

Name	Responses	Conversions	Conversion Rate	Campaign Value
web analytics	113	4	3.53%	$415.27
traffic analysis	116	4	3.44%	$606.75
online marketing analysis	141	4	2.83%	$294.69
web traffic analysis	163	4	2.45%	$425.03
web traffic	187	4	2.13%	$282.70

Figure 17: Example of how one vendor helps their customers measure response, conversion, conversion rates and campaign values for pay-per-click advertising online.

One important thing to keep in mind: If you are not measuring some type of conversion activity for your campaign respondents, and you are not simply a portal designed to sell advertising and little more, you are likely wasting your time advertising online. You should *not* be spending money or taking time establishing marketing channels that simply bring people to your Web site—you should be bringing them to your Web site with a specific goal in mind (serving Web pages is not a goal, it is a means to an end). Make sure that you have specific goals in mind for the visitors you are trying to reach—purchase something, submit information, download a document, and so on—before you try and attract visitors to your Web site.

This opinion contrasts that of those online marketers who insist that bringing visitors to your site, regardless of their likelihood to complete a conversion activity, is helping you build and establish "brand identity." While this is likely true, that the more people who see your advertising the more well known you become, very few businesses have flourished simply for being "well known." There is nothing wrong with building brand identity as long as you are also working to create a more personal relationship with visitors at the same time, learning more about the visitor or providing them something that they desire.

Metrics Provided by Campaign Analysis Tools

The fundamental metrics that you need from a campaign analysis tool are the number of respondents and number of respondents converted for any given campaign. From these, providing you know roughly how many times the ad or message was viewed, you can calculate the three most important metrics in online advertising:

- Response rate (respondents divided by total impressions served)
- Total respondents
- Conversion rate

Consider the discussion on conversion rates in Chapter 6. Well-designed campaigns are simply a process like any other, only one that is tied to a specific referring source. Metrics for measuring campaign success are exactly the same, except you are likely measuring abandonment for many pages as a group rather than discreet steps.

In addition to response and conversion there a number of useful functions and metrics when measuring campaigns. Additional functionality includes:

- The ability to measure multiple, sequential goals over a period of time, such as a campaign designed to attract visitors and have them register (conversion activity 1) then later purchase (conversion activity 2). This type of information is useful for tracking multiple abandonment points if you have complex conversion goals.
- The ability to organize campaigns into flexible groups. More often than not businesses are running hundreds of campaigns at any given time. Given this, it is powerful to be able to group these campaigns using flexible criteria such as "type of campaign," "site(s) campaigns are running on," "active dates," "message," "placement," "creative," and so on. Having the ability to aggregate and roll-up the response and conversion for flexible groupings allows online marketers to easily see where their money is best spent.
- The ability to easily create campaigns or create them "on the fly." Some Web analytics packages require a campaign setup that, while not particularly difficult, is cumbersome, especially when running hundreds or thousands of

campaigns. Being able to dynamically create campaigns and then modify their properties after the fact simplifies the process of collecting data.

- The ability to assign flexible costs and values to campaigns in order to build return on investment (ROI) models for campaigns. While being able to calculate response and conversion rates are the minimum for campaign analysis, new tools are emerging that allow online marketers to input cost information for campaigns ("total cost of campaign," "cost per click" or "cost per acquisition," and so on), as well as the real value of a conversion (lifetime value of a customer, value of products purchased, and so on). This information enables Web analytics applications to calculate ROI, helping business people to better predict when a campaign will pay for itself, as well as the likely positive value of a campaign.

Useful metrics for measuring campaign analysis (in addition to the functionality described above) include:

- Campaign respondents
- Campaign conversions and conversion rate
- Campaign entry pages (assuming multiple entry points)
- Campaign goal pages (assuming multiple goal pages)
- Paths to conversion
- Referring domains (assuming the campaign is running on more than one Web site)
- Commerce statistics (including "products purchased" and more. This topic is discussed in Chapter 9, Commerce Measurement Tools.)

Again, keep in mind that the minimum functionality for campaign analysis is the ability to measure the number of people who click on a link and successfully arrive at your Web site, as well as the number of those people who complete an activity that has some value to your online business. If the Web analytics package that you have supports this, you are in business.

An Important Note about Response Rates

A very common problem that businesses have trouble understanding is the "drop-off" between clicks and response in online campaigning. The basic scenario is this: Your pay-per-click (PPC) advertising engine is telling you that a particular campaign has recorded 1,000 unique "clicks" for the month. They report this to you because you pay them some amount for each click generated. The problem arises when you then consult your campaign analysis tools in which you have coded and measured the response to your PPC advertising and you notice that you only had 800 respondents for the same timeframe. What happened to the other 200 respondents?

What happened, most likely, is that people "dropped off" between the time it took to click and the time it took to get to your Web site, that is they clicked the link but never arrived. Why would people do that, you ask? The single most common reason for this type of abandonment is slow response.

If you are purchasing keywords on Google, which is notoriously fast to respond, but your Web site is "bloated" with code and images, visitors are very likely clicking your link and then backing up when your Web site does not immediately load in their browser. While it is very important for online businesses to look good and have "sexy" Web sites, online business owners need to recognize that your potential visitors want the information they are looking for right away. See the discussion under Web Server Performance Data, in Chapter 2, for more information.

If visitors are searching for information on a very responsive search engine they are having a particular type of experience. Imagine now that they search for a keyword that you and your competitors have purchased, and your PPC ad is one of many in a list on the search results page. If the visitor clicks on your link after having been moving quickly through search results pages and has to wait more than a few seconds for your Web site to respond it is very likely will hit the "back" button and click on one of your competitor's links.

Now imagine the same scenario on a 28.8 modem connection.

In general when you are paying anyone to help you generate visiting traffic it is important to keep the following "best practices" in mind:

- Be mindful of page weight in terms of total kilobytes and load time. If you have to have an "image rich" page consider using a delivery optimization service such as Akamai or Speedera to speed the delivery of images.
- Design landing pages that are targeting the type of visitors you are trying to attract with the particular campaign you are running. If you are attempting to pull traffic from a large portal, such as America Online, be sure that the language and look and feel of the landing page reflects the demographic you are likely to attract.
- Make sure the message on the landing page closely matches the message in your advertising. Don't run a banner ad promising "free service for a month" and then *not* have a big, obvious link on the landing page describing how they can get this free service. Visitors have little patience for having to search for information they think should be readily available.
- Similarly, be sure that the action item is completely obvious to the respondent as soon as they arrive. If your ad stated "free shipping with any purchase" then the landing page should have language describing the free shipping offer and a big, bold button that tells them to "start shopping now!"
- If possible, have as few links as necessary on the landing page to make the respondent comfortable, as well as to push them towards the conversion activity. Having too many links on your landing pages simply provides increased opportunity for distraction. Of course you should give visitors a link to your "normal" Web site but don't push them towards it.

Example Uses for Campaign Analysis Tools

Besides the obvious use of quantifying how each and every one of your online campaigns contributes to your overall business success, some companies have also used campaign analysis tools to measure internal usability. Imagine the scenario where you have three different links from you home page that lead to a particular product you are trying to sell. A commonly asked question is, "Which of these three links leads to the most purchases?"

In most Web analytics packages known to this author it would be trivial to code each of the links with a unique campaign ID (usually by appending the campaign ID to the URL's query string). Then A) every time a visitor clicked one of the "tagged" links, that link would be counted as a "response" to the specific link's campaign and B) when visitors completed the purchase process the link would be credited with the conversion. Then, at the end of the day, it would be simple to assess the contribution each link made to the overall business success.

Another important thing to keep in mind regarding campaign analysis is that there is no reason to limit your measurement to only online campaigns. For many successful businesses of reasonable size, online advertising is only part of the total marketing program. If you also run television spots, radio ads, print ads or create and distribute brochures you can make a reasonable attempt at quantifying the effect each have at driving visitors to your Web site by creating unique, branded landing pages.

Imagine, for example, that a multi-channel retailer like Circuit City had a unique landing page at http://www.circuitcity.com/tv. This page redirected anyone typing that URL into their browser directly to the television section of their Web site and told the visitor that not only did Circuit City have the greatest selection of TVs on the Internet but they also offered free shipping and also no interest financing until January 2005. This is a nearly perfect example of a landing page and how to measure the effect of offline campaigning.

Now imagine that Circuit City was running ads in the Sunday circular in your local paper, telling you that you could "purchase from the best selection of televisions online, have your new TV delivered to your front door and get no-interest financing until January 2005, simply by going to your computer and typing in http://www.circuitcity.com/tv." If you were to do that, and they were to associate any visitor that came to that page with a unique campaign ID, Circuit City would easily be able to quantify the effect the ad in the Sunday circular had on their business. (Please note that this is a made-up example, and does not reflect any current content or special that Circuit City may or may not have on their site.)

One important caveat to this is that, in general, people are lazy. While 10,000 visitors may have been added to the "offline television" campaign because they followed instructions and included the "/tv" portion of the URL, it is likely that many others simply went to www.circuitcity.com and looked around for televisions in the navigation system. This is fine, nobody can change human nature, so it is simply important to remember that the response you measure using this strategy is likely lower than the total number of responses and conversions you can attribute to the campaign. This does not discount the value of measuring offline campaigns at all—the "lazy visitor" factor is probably even across all similar campaigns and therefore can be factored out *as long as* you are careful when designing these landing page URLs.

Designing landing page URLs carefully for offline campaigns simply means that www.circuitcity.com/tv or tv.circuitcity.com is better than www.circuitcity.com/television_ad_2004 or www.circuitcity.com/departments.jsp? c=1&b=g&department=Televisions. You want to design unique landing page URLs that are short, sweet and easy to remember. Consider adding "/tv" or "/radio" or "/august" to the end of your domain URL and using redirect scripts on those pages to add your campaign ID and pass the visitor along. You should also consider mentioning to your audience that they need to use this "special URL" to take full advantage of your offer to try and create a little more urgency to remember the vanity URL.

Another example of the use of campaign analysis tools is the work that this author does in buying keywords on pay-per-click engines like Google and Overture. Because the author is working from a budget to spread the word about demystifying Web analytics, he needs to be careful to spend money only on words that successfully attract book buyers. One of the tools used to keep track of this are the campaign analysis tools provided by his Web analytics provider.

Free Web Analytics Book
Learn more about Web Analysis and
how it can help your Web business
www.webanalyticsdemystified.com
Interest: ▬▬▬

Figure 18: Example of how the author's pay-per-click terms show up in Google AdWords search results.

In Figure 18 we can see what would appear in the right-hand column on Google if you were to search for "web analytics demystified" or some derivative thereof. The click-through URLs in the Google engine are tagged with a name-value pair that identifies that click as having come from the keyword buy at Google. Because of this identifier and the Web analytics package that the author uses, as soon as visitors start responding to this keyword campaign he can begin to see the response in real-time.

Name	Responses	Conversions	Conversion Rate	Campaign Value
web analytics	113	4	3.53%	$415.27
traffic analysis	116	4	3.44%	$606.75
online marketing analysis	141	4	2.83%	$294.69
web traffic analysis	163	4	2.45%	$425.03
web traffic	187	4	2.13%	$282.70

Figure 19: Responses, conversions, conversion rate and campaign value for a sample of keywords purchased at Google by this book's author.

As you can see in Figure 19, the author is able to easily determine both the rate at which he can expect people clicking on the paid link to make purchases and also the actual value of the campaign, to date, for each individual keyword purchased. This information can be easily compared to the cost information provided by Google to ensure that each keyword purchased is paying for itself and helping keep *Web Analytics Demystified* a profitable venture.

In addition to this granular information it is important to the author to keep track of how the entire Google "pay-per-click" campaign is performing relative to previous timeframes. Remember, Web analytics is not about numbers but how those numbers are changing (see Chapter 15 for more information on key performance indicators).

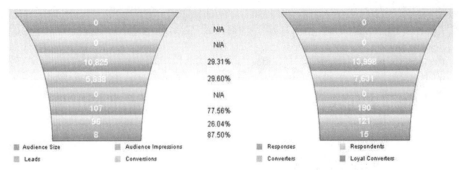

Figure 20: Campaign performance comparing two different timeframes.

As you can see in Figure 20, the news is mostly good for the author regarding the Google PPC campaign, as all of the raw response and conversion metrics are increasing while the campaign conversion rate stays the same.

Risks Associated with Campaign Analysis Tools

The major risks associated with campaign analysis tools are generally improper setup and campaign IDs overriding each other. In the former case, user error is surprisingly common when setting up campaign IDs for tracking, as most Web analytics packages currently available provide some interface or tool to create campaign IDs and a fairly regimented way to track said campaigns. It is likely that if one fails to properly define a campaign or tell the analytics package what to look for the data may be lost (although Web-server log-file analysis applications minimize this risk). The only real solution for this problem is to be careful when setting up campaigns and campaign tracking.

Regarding the latter risk, campaigns can override each other if you are tracking many different campaigns at one time. If a visitor gets an email from you and clicks the link you will count that visitor as a respondent to the email campaign. Imagine then that this visitor leaves your Web site without completing the conversion activity but a few days later sees a banner ad, is reminded that they intended to complete that activity and clicks the banner ad to return to your Web site. At this point you have counted the same visitor as a respondent twice, assuming you are tracking both the email and banner ad campaigns, which you should be. If the visitor then completes the conversion activity, it is likely that the conversion will be attributed to the banner ad campaign, not the email campaign. While making the assumption that the last campaign responded to should be given credit for the conversion is not a huge problem, it does increase the risk of drawing faulty conclusions.

A reasonable solution to this problem would be to credit *all* the campaigns the visitor responded to within a reasonable amount of time from the conversion. If your Web analytics package supports this option you should consider using it if you are interested in knowing the contribution that each campaign makes to the likelihood a visitor will convert. But if you are more interested in knowing only which message, method or medium is most likely to actually get the visitor to complete the action, only crediting the conversion to the *last* campaign the visitor responded makes sense.

Web Analytics Tip: Track Every Campaign You Run, Carefully

As the technology sector picks up again, as it appears to be doing in the first half of 2004, it is worthwhile to remind online businesses not to invest in online marketing with the same blind exuberance that was exhibited in the late 1990s. While there is surely temptation to invest heavily in customer acquisition, the smartest course is to invest carefully in marketing campaigns that demonstrate positive returns in both the short and long term.

To ensure that every campaign is tracked through to conversion, the best course of action is to encourage your marketing and marketing analytics groups to work together and make sure that they understand how to use the campaign analysis tools provided by your Web analytics application. Making sure that every campaign is coded correctly and goal pages are properly set will help ensure that the effect of each campaign can be accurately quantified.

Additionally, many clients I have worked with expressed the desire to track both internal and external campaigns—the former being elements designed to drive traffic towards a particular goal, such as internal banner ads, merchandising offers or specific applications on the site itself. While the aforementioned recommendation is to track everything, one must be cautious and ensure that your analytics package supports both internal and external tracking. If your application only has a single campaign set and is unable to differentiate internally and externally driven responses, tracking internal campaigns can cause data loss for external campaigns at the point of conversion.

Be sure when planning your campaigns that you consult with your analytics provider and ask them for their recommendations regarding campaign setup and tracking internal campaigns. They will likely have specific recommendations and be able to guide you towards the most efficient and accurate implementation.

CHAPTER 9
COMMERCE
MEASUREMENT TOOLS

> **"In 2002, US online retail grew to $76 billion. This represents a 48 percent increase over 2001. In 2003, online sales will grow by 26 percent over 2002, to $96 billion. Online sales will account for 4.5 percent of total retail sales in 2003, up 3.6 percent from 2002."**
> *The State of Retailing Online 6.0* from Shop.org/Forrester Research

Although most online commerce platforms provide reporting of some kind, from a Web analytics perspective there are a number reasons to employ additional commerce measurement tools—primarily for the ability to tie commerce activity directly back to the Internet, that is, the referring sources that sent visitors to the Web site in the first place. While any good commerce platform, regardless of its price and functionality, will provide information about which products, categories and brands you are selling, few are able to directly tie sales back to campaign activity and even fewer can connect to non-campaign referring sources. A good set of commerce tools provided by your Web analytics vendor should allow you to do this with ease.

A secondary reason to employ commerce measurement tools within your Web analytics application is to facilitate ease-of-use and ease-of-understanding. If all of the data about inbound campaigns, visiting traffic and online purchases are available in one place the data is likely more actionable. Imagine how much easier it is to have all of this valuable data in one place and not have to move between applications, setting date ranges and parameters in each, only then to have to move that data to a third-party application for summary reporting. You can definitely do it, but why spend the time if you can avoid it?

Robust commerce measurement tools within Web analytics applications should provide functionality to allow you to easily measure key processes such as shopping cart and checkout, visualize product abandonment, generate browse-to-buy ratios and filter customers based on common segments (new vs. returning, first visit vs. many previous visits, and so on). The greater the additional *useful* functionality a Web analytics commerce toolset can provide, the greater the likelihood that the information provided can help you increase online sales.

Functionally, commerce analysis tools should provide the "who, what, when, where and how" for your online purchasers:

- "Who" is making the purchase, granular to the person's name if your application and privacy policy support this
- "What" did they purchase?
- "When" did they make the purchase?

- "Where" did they come from?
- "How" did they purchase?

The answers to these questions allow the online business to make significantly better decisions regarding marketing and merchandising.

Finally, imagine the case where you have built your own commerce application from the ground up, a situation common to many smaller online businesses. In this case it is very likely that you only took the time to include the bare minimum of data reporting capabilities, just what you needed to do order fulfillment and inventory management. In this instance, implementing a Web analytics package that provides commerce tools can have significant benefits, often at a very reasonable cost. By simply identifying or tagging your order confirmation page to collect transaction data it is very likely that you will greatly increase your knowledge of the customer with little or no additional programming on your part.

Metrics Provided by Commerce Measurement Tools

As described above, your online commerce application likely provides a great deal of information about total products sold and the customers who purchased them, information that is important to your inventory and fulfillment groups. The metrics that are most useful to Web analytics users are those dealing with merchandising, sources of customer traffic and the online purchase process.

Merchandising

Metrics that are most valuable when measuring the effects of your online merchandising include:

- Products, categories and brands sold, especially if this data is available by placement or position so you can measure lift (that is, "featured product" vs. "category listing" vs. "search results")
- Product conversion rates (browse-to-buy ratio, shopping cart conversion)
- Internal searches leading to purchase, helping you understand better how your customers think about the products you sell and observe the effects of any cross-selling activities you engage in ("people searching for books are purchasing both books and shoes")
- Links leading to purchases and amount of revenue attributable to each. While it is not always clear how to attribute value to a link on a page, vendor attempts to do so have been met with great enthusiasm from merchandisers and thus any reasonable, well-explained algorithm for making this assignment is worth looking at.

Being able to determine the effect of different merchandising strategies allows you to optimize your product merchandising efforts. While there are relatively few unique ways to present products to online shoppers, available data suggests that different products and product categories have dramatically different purchase rates depending on how they are presented. With this in mind, successful online businesses work to understand the best method for presenting products to optimize the look-to-book ratio.

Referring Sources

Sources of customer traffic can be paid or unpaid. Metrics most valuable in helping to quantify the effects of referring traffic include:

- Referring domain and URL
- Search engine and search engine keyword or phrase
- Campaign measurement tools, as described in Chapter 8. It is especially important to be able to tie paid campaigns to real product purchases as well as the number of customers attracted, the number of orders placed and total revenue from the campaign. Ideally you are able to directly tie the campaign metrics previously described to all customer order activity generated via the campaign.
- Lifetime value of a customer from each type of referring source. It is very useful to know which of the different types of referring sources are sending you the most valuable traffic over time. The idea behind "lifetime value of a customer by source" is to keep track of all recurring purchases from a customer and credit them back to their original source. The value of this is delivered over time because, given this data, you will be able to not only determine which sources provide the greatest short-term gains but also which sources are sending you the most qualified traffic over time.

Search engine keywords are especially useful because this information provides insight into what customers were thinking about just before they found your Web site. Much like measuring the merchandising effects of internal searches, understanding how your "best visitors" find your Web site will help you optimize your site for these kinds of visitors.

Online Purchase Process

The online purchase process is simply a specialized process and is measured much like the processes described in Chapter 6. The key conversion rates and statistics useful to measure the online purchase process include:

- Shopping cart and checkout conversion rates. The shopping cart conversion rate is the ratio of completed shopping carts to "cart starts" (visitors adding at least one item to the cart). The checkout conversion rate is the ratio of completed shopping carts to the number of times a visitor clicked the "checkout" button.
- Product, category and brand cart and checkout conversion rates. For any product on you offer you should be able to see how many times this product was added to a shopping cart, checked out and ultimately purchased. It is desirable to be able to see this information for both category and brand, as well. A key metric is the ratio of times an item/category/brand is carted to the number of times that item/category/brand is actually purchased.
- Overall conversion metrics specific to the commerce process, including key averages (revenue per customer, revenue per visitor, items purchased per customer, items per order)

- Browse-to-buy ratios for products, categories and brands. The ability to see how often an item or group is looked at and quickly compare that to the number of times those items or groups are purchased provides valuable insight into which products and groups are currently "in favor" and should be considered for additional merchandising efforts.

Making these kinds of measurements for your purchase process will help you identify the areas where visitors struggle. Additionally, by measuring product, category and brand conversion rates you will be able to better merchandise on key pages by featuring items that are more likely to sell. Making simple but smart decisions like these are important to improving overall sales online, keeping in mind the four "Ps"— product, placement, price and promotion. These rates and ideas are discussed at length in Chapter 13.

Sessionizing/Identifying Information

In addition to merchandising, referring sources and online purchase processes, many companies may be able to derive value from tracking customers based on sessions. Some vendors provide the ability to segment based on individual visitor activities, including purchase history. This information potentially provides answers such as, "Customers who have made less than $100 in lifetime purchases are interested in these pages," "Customers who have purchased 'product A' and 'product B' come back to the Web site with "x" frequency" and, "Give me a list of all of the names and email addresses for visitors who have put 'product C' and 'product D' into their shopping carts but did not complete the purchase."

While the answers to the first two examples are interesting it can be less clear how to make these types of information actionable; for the larger analytics audience, attempting to obtain this type of information may simply result in increased costs without significant gains.

The third example, however, is potentially very useful to any Web analytics program; being able to tie specific online activities back to known individuals makes for much improved online marketing. While there is potential to anger visitors who have not specifically requested information and you may run afoul of privacy guidelines, being able to market directly to measured visitor interests is very likely a large part of the future of Web analytics.

Ideally, for all of the merchandising and referring source metrics listed above, your Web analytics application will provide access to identifying information for all customers. Even more useful is the ability to obtain this information for non-purchasers, visitors who put items in the shopping cart but do not purchase or people who look at a particular group of content but never put items in the cart. Whether this information is provided within the application via an interface or via a customer ID export for integration into your data warehouse is just a matter of preference, as both require some level of setup.

If you think your online business would be able to take advantage of this type of information it is worth asking your application provider how they are able to deliver this information. The easiest case should be that you provide a unique ID for each visitor you wish to track and the application allows you to use this to build relevant views of the data. Some applications take this a step further and give you the ability to import or integrate your own customer database to query information "inline." Again, where the information is made available is a matter of preference, as long as the information is available somewhere.

Example Uses of Commerce Analysis Tools

The most practical application of commerce analysis tools within a Web analytics application is the ability to tie purchasing activity back to referring sources. Some of the most significant wins in terms of return on investment into Web analytics occur when online businesses use these types of tools to quantify the effects of pay-per-click campaigning or business relationships.

The popularity of search engine keyword buying and the pay-per-click purchasing strategy has prompted many online businesses to begin bidding on words with wild abandon. While companies report great success tied to this relatively new channel for online marketing, others are discovering that, with alarming frequency, clicks are not translating into conversions, or if they are, not high-value conversions. The campaign analysis tools described in Chapter 8 are excellent for helping you to ensure that you are achieving a minimum conversion rate for any campaign that you are paying for. Commerce analysis tools are good at getting deeper into the data and helping you to ensure that the campaign is selling the "right" products and that the campaign itself has a good average order value.

Consider an example company bidding for a popular, generic keyword and having to pay $1.00 per click. Now imagine that they get 1,000 clicks from that word every day for a total cost of $1,000 per day or $7,000 per week. Most companies prefer to invest in marketing that will return 10 times, meaning that this company would need to make $70,000 per week from this campaign. If they measure their conversion rate from this word to be 3 percent, again not unheard of, then every day they would be converting roughly 30 respondents to customers. This keyword campaign would need to be selling products with a minimum average order value (AOV) of $333.00 to be hitting their return target. So:

$10,000 daily target / 30 customers converted = $333.33

So now imagine that the company is selling trading cards and their AOV is only $4.00 per order driven from the campaign.

$4.00 AOV from campaign * 30 customers converted = $120.00

Every day this campaign costs the company $880.00 (or has an ROI of 0.12—for every dollar spent the campaign returns $0.12).

When shown the math, most marketing managers would agree that this campaign is a dud and immediately pull the keyword from spending rotation; however many marketing managers never see this type of information. Even in this modern age companies are spending money without any tools to quantify the results, effectively wasting money. More information about quantifying the value and return for online campaigns is presented in Chapters 12 and 13.

Regarding the use of commerce analysis tools to quantify the quality of business relationships, consider the explosion of Web sites and the "you link to me I'll link to you" schemes that occurred in the late 1990s. Any number of Web sites may have approached you with promises of large volumes of high-quality traffic that they could send to *your* Web site, for a fee. In the absence of any Web analytics tools this type of relationship is a mistake—how do you know you are getting any of this traffic and that respondents are engaged in activities that provide your business value? The deployment of commerce analysis tools allows you to take relationships like this one step further and quantify the value you get from your "traffic partner."

An example of quantifying the value of a relationship between business partners can be seen at BackcountryStore.com which has relationships with a number of different Web sites to drive traffic their way. Using the Web analytics package it has standardized on, BackcountryStore.com is able to keep track of who is sending traffic that converts into customers and drill down into the products those visitors are purchasing.

	Domain	Orders▼	Revenue	Customers	Visits	B/B%	Items	Shipping
1.	⊙ ■ Bookmarks or directly referred URLs	240	$38,716.75	237	6,179	3.88%	378	$1,476.45
2.	⊙ ■ Search Engines	70	$7,761.86	69	--	--	111	$402.84
3.	⊙ ■ northface.com	22	$2,592.63	21	522	4.21%	39	$144.48
4.	⊙ ■ thenorthface.com	17	$2,599.58	17	685	2.48%	27	$146.26
5.	⊙ ■ marmot.com	4	$440.04	4	99	4.04%	6	$28.29
6.	⊙ ■ jansport.com	4	$205.64	4	94	4.26%	4	$23.46
7.	⊙ ■ epinions.com	4	$969.77	4	193	2.07%	5	$24.34
8.	⊙ ■	4	$474.83	4	173	2.31%	4	$0.00
9.	Cross Tabs	3	$293.32	3	134	2.24%	3	$28.85
10.	Acquisition ▶ .com	3	$151.57	3	417	0.72%	4	$14.27
11.	Conversion ▶	3	$363.75	3	39	7.69%	5	$34.60
12.	Merchandising ▶ Products	3	$727.68	3	11	27.27%	6	$15.98
13.	Demographics ▶ Categories	2	$115.17	2	42	4.76%	3	$5.08
14.	Drilldowns Brands	2	$179.86	2	152	1.32%	2	$14.26
15.	Trend SKUs	2	$247.12	2	13	15.38%	2	$13.30
16.	Export Customer IDs Custom 1	2	$151.92	2	19	10.53%	2	$18.80
17.	⊙ burton.com Custom 2	2	$759.85	2	72	2.78%	3	$16.28

Figure 21: Commerce data showing the distribution of orders, revenue, and so on, from referring traffic partners. Of note is the browse-to-buy ratio (B/B%), which is good for comparing the quality of traffic sent by each partner.

As you can see in Figure 21, BackcountryStore.com is able to learn a great deal about traffic sent to it from each online business partner, regardless of the type of partner. BackcountryStore.com is also able to drill down for any business partner and see exactly what products that partner is helping to sell (Figure 22).

	Product	Orders▼	Revenue	Customers	Items	ASP
1.	■ Salomon Tech Amphibian Shoe - Mens	2	$127.92	2	2	$63.96
2.	■ The North Face Paramount Convertible Pant - Womens	2	$77.94	2	2	$38.97
3.	■ The North Face Chilkats - Mens	2	$159.92	2	2	$79.96
4.	■ Oakley Heater M Frame Iridium Replacement Lenses	2	$139.90	2	2	$69.95
5.	■ The North Face Denali Jacket - Womens	2	$329.90	2	2	$164.95
6.	■ Gift Box	1	$6.95	1	1	$6.95
7.	■ Oakley M Frame Sweep Sunglasses - Iridium Lens	1	$144.95	1	1	$144.95
8.	■ The North Face Chilkats Zip - Womens	1	$75.96	1	1	$75.96
9.	■ Prana Sonora Shorts - Mens	1	$26.36	1	1	$26.36
10.	■ Nikwax Tech Wash	1	$15.90	1	2	$15.90
11.	The North Face Flight Sleeping ...ard - 2003 Model	1	$173.00	1	2	$173.00

Figure 22: Drill-down into the products that BizRate.com helped BackcountryStore.com sell in this example.

BackcountryStore.com can now take this information and mine it to learn which products each online partner is most likely to help sell. Having this information will allow them to refine the relationship they have with each company and work towards optimizing these relationships. Many smart marketing and commerce managers have used this kind of information to save their companies money, millions of dollars in some instances, simply by applying the right metrics to the problem. While you will not always endear yourself to the traffic partner, especially if you need to go back to them and end the relationship, this should be of no concern. The goal of every online business working to be successful should be to make and save money.

Risks Associated with Commerce Analysis Tools

The major risks associated with commerce analysis tools are expectations and accuracy. Often when managers hear that new tools are being implemented to track something they expect that these tools will track "everything." While it would be nice to be able to purchase one of the available Web analytics packages and have it collect and report on every measurement your business needs, this is, unfortunately, unrealistic. Of the available packages known to the author, some are very good at collecting information about individual customers but less good at summary reporting, others are very good at presenting information but only present a limited subset of what would be truly useful. The challenge to the commerce manager is to select the application that provides the best fit for their needs *now* and answers the questions that people have already been asking.

It is extremely common for companies, when selecting a Web analytics vendor, to create an extensive request for proposal (RFP) that lists every metric and feature the company needs, will need, may need or has ever heard of. When you are trying to select an analytics package the best advice you can get is to fight these temptations and not create a list so long and complex that no one vendor can hope to satisfy your requirements. RFPs like this do not help vendors and in most cases simply draw out the decision-making process, preventing anyone from getting any analytic work accomplished. By properly setting expectations about what commerce analysis tools will provide you will save yourself, and your co-workers, time and headaches.

Accuracy is a sticky subject for Web analytics practitioners, one that becomes even stickier when you are talking about commerce analysis. Consider the information provided about accuracy in Chapter 3. Each Web analytics data source has the potential to be more or less accurate than the other in regards to the number of page views, visits and visitors to your Web site. The same complication extends to commerce analysis but is further aggravated by the simple fact that *people expect any commerce or revenue reporting to be 100 percent accurate.* When customers are asked, "How accurate is accurate enough for Web traffic data?" most indicate that somewhere between 90 percent and 95 percent is pretty good. Ask the same question about commerce data and the answer is almost always 100 percent.

While 100 percent accuracy in commerce data is highly desired it is, unfortunately, an unreasonable expectation. Because the Internet is not perfect, and was not designed to be so, some information will occasionally be lost. While it may be a small percentage of traffic and commerce data, even a single transaction lost will prevent in-house numbers from matching those from a commerce analysis application. Rather than viewing this as a significant problem and picking up the phone to berate your application vendor, consider the following points about commerce analysis applications:

- Commerce analysis tools that are embedded in Web analytics applications are designed to help you understand where your best customers come from, what they respond to and where they have difficulty in your online purchasing process. They are not designed to be a replacement for the existing analytics and reporting tools that are part of your commerce engine.

- Even 95 percent accuracy is enough to make good use of commerce analysis tools. If you collect all but 5 percent of your transactions you will still be able to see the trends that you are looking for. Again, these trends are the "who, what, when, where and how" for your online purchasers.

- You should hold any vendor you choose responsible for data collection within 95 to 98 percent accuracy but not call them every time these numbers slip a bit. The "best practices" recommendation is to compare the numbers your commerce analysis tools report to your actual numbers once a week. If you see a downward (that is, less accurate) movement for more than two weeks, or of more than 2 or 3 percentage points in a single week, then consider picking up the phone. Look at both number of orders and revenue, as sometimes a great deal of revenue difference is due to a single lost order and this situation does not warrant an angry call to your Web analytics application vendor.

If you keep these simple guidelines in mind whenever you look at your commerce analysis data you are almost assured to have a better experience and be able to use the data "as designed" to great benefit for your organization.

Web Analytics Tip: Tie Internal Searches to Purchases

One of the great advantages of having a suite of commerce tools tied to your Web analytics package is the ability to measure how specific events or activities drive visitors to purchase. One of the most common events I recommend that my clients track is internal searches. The careful use of a session cookie can allow you to track the search words and phrases that visitors are entering into your internal search engine that result in a purchase in that same visit. The basic setup looks like this:

1. Your customer uses the internal search engine.
2. You tell your Web analytics application about the search term, ideally using a custom variable.
3. At the same time you write this search term to a session or visit cookie, one set to expire at the same time the visit ends.
4. If the visitor successfully completes a purchase in the same visit, you include the search term as part of the information you pass to your commerce toolset.

This strategy, of course, depends on your commerce toolset having the ability to accept custom order-level variables that can be tied to the products actually purchased. If you have that ability, following this strategy can create visibility into which search terms sell which products and how much each internal search is worth. Some variations on this theme include tracking *all* of the search terms entered during a visit, perhaps as a comma-separated list, or keeping track of search terms across multiple visits and crediting the search term when the purchase is finally made.

Clients I have worked with have used this strategy to calculate browse-to-buy ratios for individual internal search terms, information that can be leveraged in a number of different ways. I commonly recommend that Web business owners keep track of internal search terms to understand the visitor mindset—visitor intent is very difficult to determine but search-term analysis can provide valuable clues to what is on someone's mind when they visit your Web site. Tracking search terms to purchase takes this a step further and helps the business owner figure out which searches are the most valuable financially. With this information you can begin to move from understanding the intent of the average visitor to the intent of the average *customer*.

CHAPTER 10
AN INTRODUCTION TO THE CUSTOMER LIFE CYCLE

> "People come to your site, leave footprints and move on. But those footprints
> are merely an indication that they were there and tell you nothing about the
> people who made those marks. Unless you know who are casual callers and
> who are loyal devotees, you cannot tell if your promotion and conversion efforts
> are working to your benefit or not."
> Sterne and Cutler in *E-Metrics for the New Economy*

At this point you may be thinking, "Great, I understand what Web analytics can do for
me and the tools that will facilitate my goals but I still can't make heads or tails of the
actual data we've collected." Or you may be thinking, "I paid good money for this
book and the author has not taught me jack-squat that I can take to my boss…" While
the information presented in the previous chapters are an important background on
the subject, everything from this point forward is where the rubber hits the road—
practical Web analytics.

The framework for our discussion about which metrics you should be measuring and
what they mean to different business types is the customer life cycle—reach,
acquisition, conversion and retention. Any online business manager who has taken the
time to read this book has a business that needs to identify high-quality sources of
potential visitors, attract them to their Web site using a variety of marketing programs,
entice them to perform some activity or activities that are of value to the business and
then keep them coming back to perform these activities.

Some readers may now be thinking, "But that's not what I'm trying to do. I don't have
any conversion activities on my Web site," or, "We really only depend on getting
someone to the Web site one time." In the first case, all Web sites have conversion
activities of some kind, even yours. In the latter case, you should still understand
reach, acquisition and conversion even if you only want to convert visitors one time.
Every business spending money on marketing online can take advantage of developing
a Web analytics program around the customer life-cycle framework. The reasons for
this are two-fold:

The framework provides a business-centric model for understanding your Web site and
relating your successes to others. As more and more online businesses become critical
components of larger multi-channel organizations it becomes more important to have
a common language throughout. Data suggests that more companies are working to
integrate promotion and marketing in both on-and offline channels. By establishing
the same broad categories for success (reach, acquisition, and so on) managers from

different groups tasked with the same goals will be able to report back regarding success in the same terms.

Your Web analytics program will be entirely more successful if you apply a framework to it, and the customer life cycle is better than most. Many Web managers in the past have attempted to simply collect data and then relate it back to the business. This model resulted in many reports that stated, "We have 20 percent more hits this month than last" to which most people responded, "Great! What does that tell us?" The customer life cycle as a framework allows Web managers to generate reports that let the company know that "Our online marketing activities have helped us to acquire 20 percent more visitors, month-over-month, and these visitors are completing our key activities at a rate of 4 percent." The difference is subtle but powerful.

So assuming the reader is at least intrigued about applying this framework to their measurement, the following definitions of reach, acquisition, conversion and retention will clarify the types of metrics we'll be looking at starting in Chapter 11.

Reach

Reach, in advertising terms, is the likelihood or potential that you will be able to gain a prospective visitor's attention. Depending on the vehicle you use for advertising, this can be quantified in a number of different ways:

- The number of people who see banner impressions served on a Web site
- The number of people who search for a keyword that you bid on
- The number of people who see an article written about your company or products
- The number of subscribers to a newsletter you sponsor or advertise in
- The number of readers who subscribe to a newspaper or magazine you advertise in
- The number of drivers who see a billboard advertising your business or products
- The number of viewers who watch a commercial you run on television
- The number of recipients who receive a piece of direct mail you send

As you can see, each metric is both easy *and* impossible to accurately quantify. They are easy to quantify in that any banner network can tell you how many banner impressions were served or search terms searched for, any magazine or newsletter can tell you how many readers they have and any marketing manager can tell you how many valid addresses your direct mailing was shipped to. But they are impossible to accurately quantify in that you have no way to know exactly how many people *actually read* your message.

Herein lies the difficulty in measuring reach within your Web analytics program. Few applications have the ability to automatically measure impressions served across multiple marketing channels. While Web-server log-file analyzers are often able to measure the number of impressions served for banners, images and media files, this same ability does not extend to offline channels. Page tagging applications, at least those known to the author, do not have the same ability but often are able to measure impressions within some types of email and rich banner advertising. Regardless of what your application *can* measure, it most assuredly cannot measure the number of people who actually read and think about your marketing message.

Because of this, reach is often tied closely to acquisition; while we cannot measure the number of people who read a message we can infer this value from the percentage of people you are able to acquire. Practically speaking, most of the measurements of reach discussed in this book are those tied to the actual acquisition of visitors.

Acquisition

If reach is a measure of the likelihood to gain a prospective visitor's attention, acquisition is the measurement how successful you are in driving them to action; the number of people who click on a link or type a URL into their browser and arrive successfully at your site. While some may argue that acquisition is better measured in terms of a visitor arriving *and* at least starting some activity of value, it is the author's opinion that A) any visitor who arrives at your site after responding to some type of advertising has the potential to complete an activity of value and B) sometimes simple metrics are more powerful and in most instances it is much simpler to measure the act of arrival or response.

Statistics used to measure acquisition are primarily focused on the source of traffic—what referring domains, search engines, search keywords, and so on—are bringing visitors to you. Campaign analysis tools extend this measurement and allow for the qualification of visitors—and in the process bleeds over into the measurement of conversion.

Conversion

Conversion and activities leading to conversion are the reason that you have your Web site; the successful completion of specific activities by visitors that somehow contributes positively to your online business. Conversion can be measured a number of different ways for a variety of different activities, many of which were discussed in Chapter 6. As a reminder, a successful conversion does not have to be an online purchase, it can be:

- Starting a download of a document or application
- Submitting information—lead generation
- Locating information, such as a support document or FAQ
- Navigating from more general to more specific information
- Spending a defined amount of time or viewing a specific number of pages
- Viewing key pages, such as a pricing page or service agreement

The list goes on and on. Depending on the multiple goal page flexibility provided by your Web analytics application you can develop a very complex model for understanding how changes to your Web site and marketing program have an impact on your visitor's ability to complete goals.

Another important piece of information to remember from Chapter 6 is that there are many different "conversion rates" for any Web site. While it is very important to measure conversion rates it is equally important to not get too hung up on one rate or the other, especially when it comes to comparison. As previously discussed, research firms have put out studies talking about "conversion rates online" and "conversion rates by business type or category." While this information is interesting, especially when you are able to know the conversion rate for a particular Web site that you can then go and visit, one should be careful to not put too much value on reported numbers. With few exceptions these numbers are derived from different types of data and so are, in this author's opinion, not valid for comparison. One recently published report from the Forrester Group's Shop.ORG project cites a slight increase in overall conversion rates for multi-channel retailers from 2001 to 2002 (from 3.1 percent to 3.2 percent). This increase is much larger for Web-based companies, with an average increase from 3.2 percent to 5.8 percent. While this report does define their measurement of conversion to be "site visitors divided by total orders" it does not tell us how site visitors are calculated (which data source was used for the analysis) and so creates potential "apples and oranges" comparisons of these rates to your own data.

When it comes to conversion rates and comparing yourself to others, you should do three things:

- Develop your Web analytics program in such a way that you are able to measure three or four "key" conversion rates and watch these religiously. These will differ depending on your business model but every business model has three or four key rates that should be watched and added to your own regular key performance indication program.
- Do not compare your rate to published rates, even if they are for your direct competitors. Because, by virtue of having read this book, you will have a very well-developed understanding of conversion rates and how to measure them you will likely get little value out of comparing yourself to other Web sites. Additionally, the audience you reach and acquire is not necessarily that of any other site—you should make changes to your site that will improve the customer experience for *your* customers.
- Use conversion rates to drive action in your Web analytics program. Conversion rates are an easy-to-understand metric telling you if changes you have made are successful or not. If your rate goes up, they were successful; if your rate goes down, they were not and you should back out the changes. Obviously Web analytics is more complex than this, but if you learn to live and die by your conversion rate you are doing most of the hard work.

Additionally, guard your conversion rate as if it were one of your trade secrets. Don't brag about how great your rate is, don't tell the press or analysts unless you are extremely sure they will protect your identity when reporting rates, and by all means don't tell your competitors. All anyone needs to know a tremendous amount about the success of your business is an estimate of your monthly traffic—which is available for purchase through services like ComScore—and your conversion rate. Roll in your average order value and any competitor can know how much revenue you are bringing in every month.

Retention

Even after you have spent the time and money necessary to reach, acquire and convert visitors you still need to work to keep them coming back. It is very easy to find studies talking about how much more valuable repeat customers are than first time customers, how they spend more money, how they tell their friends about you, and so on. The hard thing is to actually get customers to repeat, perhaps because there is very little loyalty on the Internet. If you are selling something this week, next week a competitor may have it cheaper. If you are providing a service, someone else may be able to deliver it more quickly. Unless you are selling a brand or providing a service that nobody else can deliver you will always have to deal with churn. Even if you have the luxury of selling your own items you may still have to work to compete with your channel—or rather, work to not compete with your channel.

Retention is the measurement of the activities of your repeat visitors, whether they are back for support information, back to purchase again or just back to do additional research. Being able to segregate these visitors such that you can better understand their behaviors and habits will allow you to better respond to their needs and market additional products and services to them. Visitor segmentation tools are critical to understanding different classes of repeat visitors.

A Note about the "Average" Visitor

Throughout the following chapters of *Web Analytics Demystified* the concept of the "average" visitor or the "average" visit will be used and this abstract concept merits some discussion. The fact that most Web analytics applications, at least in their default implementations, treat Web visitors as anonymous entities often creates issues for marketing folks who are constantly striving to "understand the visitor better." Unfortunately it is difficult to understand something that is essentially unknowable because of its anonymous nature or the sheer size of the population.

To compensate it is recommended that you become comfortable with the concept of the "average visitor" and the types of things the "average visitor" may do on your Web site. In future chapters you will read about metrics that help you to understand the average visitor's frequency of visit, the average number of pages that visitor sees in an average visit and other useful but not particularly detailed data. While it would be more interesting to be able to say "Eric T. Peterson, the author of *Web Analytics Demystified*, came to our Web site 5 times in August and viewed 37 pages on his first visit, 12 on his second, and so on …" this is A) not practical for most online businesses and B) not available in most Web analytics applications.

Trust in the fact that the "average visitor" is not a bad person and that they too want to contribute towards your success online, provided you are using the continuous improvement process to make sure your Web site is easy to use. But be cautious of the "average visitor"—make sure that "he or she" is an average of enough real visitors to provide a statistically valid distribution. One of the most common mistakes people make when using averages is to not ensure that their population is large enough. Think back to your college statistics courses and make sure that you have a large enough population to generate a normal distribution— the bell curve. A good rule of thumb is to not start working from averages until you have at least 1,000 data points to support the average. Fortunately, for many Web sites, 1,000 data points come very easily, as the "average visitor" spends quite a bit of time online.

CHAPTER 11
MEASURING REACH

"(Although) you might have developed the best communication material on the market, if your Web site does not deliver on the promise made in this material you will experience large dropout volumes. Reach techniques must reflect the purpose and capability of Web sites—because anything else misleads people as to the content of the site."

Hurol Inan in *Measuring the Success of your Web site*

On the Internet reach is very difficult to quantify; our best estimates of reach are built from demographic surveys and estimates of the number of people who will pause long enough while browsing some other message to consider what you have to offer. Marketing professionals attempt to buy advertising in such a way that they will reach the greatest number of people they believe are likely to respond to their message and show them that message with the "right" frequency—the idea being that if you show "qualified" individuals the right message the right number of times they will respond favorably.

The problem with translating buying advertising in more traditional media to the Internet is that offline people are buying media impressions and online they are buying "ad" impressions. The offline metric is typically easy to quantify—the number and demographic of subscribers to a magazine, the Nielsen ratings for a television program, the number newspaper sales within specific zip codes, and so on. But because the Internet is anonymous by design, the same level of accuracy in numbers is difficult to attain. Often advertisers are hard pressed to provide meaningful and accurate numbers to media buyers regarding the number of unique visitors they reach and the frequency with which they reach them. And frequently media buyers are distrustful of the numbers that are reported.

General Metrics to Help Measure Reach

The following metrics are recommended to help you understand the effect of marketing programs designed to reach new visitors in an effort to attract them to your Web site.

Overall Traffic Volumes

Because reach and frequency are very difficult to measure accurately online, Web analysts often look towards "proxy" measurements to help them understand how well they are reaching people. Examining the overall traffic volume coming to one's Web site is an effective proxy for reach in that you cannot attract people that you do not reach in some way or another. Put another way, if you are doing anything online or offline to let people know you exist then you are attempting to reach them and attract them to your Web site. Overall traffic volumes are a moderately useful key performance indicator, depending on your overall business goals.

How to Calculate

In most cases some measure of overall traffic volume is reported directly, likely in a "page views" or "total page views" metric broken down by the hour in a day view, the day in a week or month view and the month in a year view. Some Web analytics applications provide averages and forecasting with this metric, which can be helpful if for no other reason that it provides additional visual clues as to how your traffic volumes are changing over time.

Dependence

If you are looking at a "page view" metric, keep in mind the pyramid model of Web analytics data (Chapter 4). There are visitors coming to your Web site generating these page views. It is important to *not* assume that a large spike in page view traffic is directly correlated to a similar increase in the number of visitors. Especially if you are using Web-server log files as a data source, automated agents could potentially cause spikes in page view traffic. When you observe spikes in page view traffic be careful to look at visit and visitor metrics to validate that this increase in traffic is concurrent with additional visits or visitors.

Overall traffic volume is one Web analytics metric that is best received in "real time" (see Chapter 3 for more on real-time data delivery). Having this information as close to the time the data is actually generated allows for you to respond rapidly to changes, either beneficial or detrimental.

Usage

You should pay close attention to overall traffic volumes simply because this metric is the single best indicator that something has changed in your relationship with your online visitors. Pronounced peaks and valleys will appear in your traffic volume reporting more quickly than higher-level data such as leads, purchases or complaints to your customer service phone center.

Interpretation

In general you are looking for either spikes or dips in traffic that exceed the average for your timeframe or simply "look different." If you get into the habit of checking this metric two or three times each day you will easily pick out changes in normal patterns that will alert you that additional research is necessary. Overall traffic volume is not an interesting metric in and of itself; the value this metric provides is to serve as a guide, letting you know when you should look more closely at information about changes in the relationship between your Web site and the visitors who are currently seeing your marketing message.

Example

BackcountryStore.com watches its traffic volumes closely to ensure it is able to capture emerging trends and activity exhibited by its customers. One of the things

BackcountryStore.com watches most closely for is the traffic pattern exhibited in Figure 23.

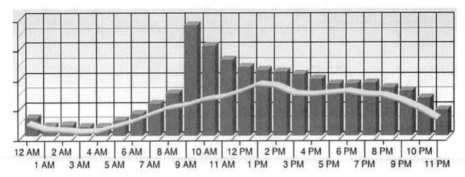

12 AM 1 AM 2 AM 3 AM 4 AM 5 AM 6 AM 7 AM 8 AM 9 AM 10 AM 11 AM 12 PM 1 PM 2 PM 3 PM 4 PM 5 PM 6 PM 7 PM 8 PM 9 PM 10 PM 11 PM

Figure 23: Traffic pattern measured for a single day on BackcountryStore.com's Web site.

The yellow line on the graph in Figure 23 indicates the average traffic volume, measured in page views, for the day in question. The large spike in traffic occurring at 9:00 A.M. was strongly correlated to an outbound email campaign advertising large holiday discounts on gear sold at BackcountryStore.com. Based on nothing more than this pattern, the marketing group at BackcountryStore.com can be assured that their campaign is working. Still, they would want to drill-down and determine A) how much of this spike can be attributed directly to the email campaign and B) what percentage of email recipients responded.

Related Metrics

The metrics most commonly tied to the interpretation of changes in overall traffic volume are the referring source metrics discussed in Chapter 12: referring domains and URLs, search engines and search keywords and phrases. Campaign analytics are also very closely tied to changes in overall traffic volumes.

Number of Visits

Visits are closely related to overall traffic volume as a direct measure of the number of people you are able to successfully reach online. Visits are important to examine in this context since page views do not convey all of the necessary information about the traffic coming to your Web site. Page views are about the number of "clicks" a person makes, whereas visits are about the people themselves.

How to Calculate

Similar to overall traffic volume measured by page views, visits are typically reported directly by your Web analytics package. Ideally your application also provides averages and forecasts to help visualize the effects of changes in visit and visitor patterns. An important thing to remember is the definition of visit from Chapter 4: a visit is composed of measured page views or requests followed by at least 30 minutes of inactivity.

Dependence

Like overall traffic volume, visits are dependent on the number of visitors coming to the Web site. Often times when you observe a large spike in page views it is worthwhile to immediately check visits to see whether the spike can be attributed to a similar spike in the number of visits to the Web site.

Usage

While it is good to use visits as a "level set" for overall traffic volumes, visits are also a key indicator for how effectively you are able to reach and begin to acquire visitors. There are two common and useful comparisons you can make with the visits metric:

- Total volume of visits compared to previous similar timeframes
- Total volume of visits compared to online marketing activity

To get a clear picture of how traffic measured in visits is changing you should be sure to compare current visits to visits from recent timeframes. For example, compare the current week's Monday to last week's Monday, the current full week to the last full week or the current weekend to the last two or three weekends. The measurement should be a percentage increase or decrease from period to period. Comparing current volume of visits to the volume from last year can be informative from a gross reporting perspective (saying "We have successfully grown traffic year over year by 25 percent, measured by total visits to the Web site"), but this information is typically less actionable in the continuous improvement model since your Web site has, hopefully, changed over this period of time.

When comparing visits to online marketing activity you simply want to be able to annotate any chart or graph describing the number of visits to the Web site with information about which portions of your current marketing program are likely driving visitors to your site. It is important to keep in mind that not everyone will take the time to read a book like *Web Analytics Demystified* and understand what these numbers mean and what they can tell you. Annotation and the direct mapping of this data back to information that is common to your business (marketing campaigns, partnerships, relevant keywords being searched for at Google, and so on) will help others connect with this data in meaningful ways.

Interpretation

Similar to overall traffic volume you should be looking for changes in visit patterns that are indicative of a change in the relationship between the people you are trying to reach and your Web site. While slightly more useful than page views by virtue of being about people, not just clicks, the real value of visits is found in comparative analysis.

Example

Holiday traffic is perhaps the single most important source of income to online retailers, including BackcountryStore.com. Growth in the number of visits is a key indicator of the likelihood of revenue growth, as some known percentage of these visits will convert into purchases. BackcountryStore.com's visiting traffic pattern leading into Christmas 2003 shows nothing but excellent news (Figure 24).

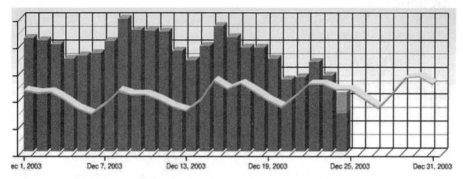

ec 1, 2003   Dec 7, 2003   Dec 13, 2003   Dec 19, 2003   Dec 25, 2003   Dec 31, 2003

Figure 24: Graph of visits to BackcountryStore.com in December 2003. The yellow line represents the period average, which BackcountryStore.com clearly exceeded right up until the last few days before the holiday.

While BackcountryStore.com pays close attention to the raw numbers of visits to their Web site, of greater interest is the year-over-year growth (not shown). Having this information helps BackcountryStore.com understand not only how it is exceeding recent traffic patterns but also how their business is truly growing over time.

Related Metrics

Similar to overall traffic volume as measured by page views, the metrics that are most commonly tied to interpretation of changes in number of visits are the referring sources metrics discussed in the chapters on acquisition and campaign analytics.

Number of New Visitors

The number of new visitors you are able to attract to your Web site is a direct measure of the efficacy of your reach. New visitor metrics reported by Web analytics packages generally attempt to quantify the number of "new ever" visitors, that is, those visitors who have never been to your Web site previously. Like page views and visits, new visitors is a measurement that spans both reach and acquisition.

How to Calculate

New visitors is a metric that most reporting packages provide with no additional setup. Check your solution, but this metric should provide information about the number of visitors who have never been to your Web site previously and who have visited in the timeframe under analysis.

Dependence

The primary dependence of any new visitors report is on the method for determining the "newness" and uniqueness of a visitor. Cookies are the preferred method since they provide a long-term storage mechanism for keeping track of this information. But even with cookies there is always the issue of whether a visitor is "new" on one computer/browser but has visited previously on another computer/browser (see Chapter 3 for more on cookies used by Web analytics applications). The only sure way to determine whether a visitor is truly new is to require visitors to log in—an impractical request for most online businesses.

Usage

The new visitor metric is typically used in conjunction with a count of returning visitors, or all visitors, to calculate ratios useful in determining the quality of visitor acquisition. As a stand-alone metric it is good to watch new visitor acquisition patterns to answer questions like:

- Do you reach new people more effectively on weekends, early in the week or later in the week?
- Are new visitors more likely to visit during the daytime or in the evening?
- Do new visitors react to new marketing materials immediately or is there lag time between media drops and new visitor response?

Correlating new visitor acquisition to campaign activity can provide valuable data for optimizing future campaigns. Consider two media campaigns, one launched on a Saturday morning and the other on a Monday afternoon. Watching the growth of new visitor acquisition after each drop can help you understand which time is more likely to attract the greatest percentage of new visitors relative to overall visitor traffic.

Interpretation

For any given time period, the number of reported new visitors is simply that, the number of visitors who have visited the Web site for the first time ever.

Example

One thing that BackcountryStore.com pays close attention to is its rate of growth or shrinkage in the volume and percentage of new visitors it attracts to its Web site. As you can see in Figure 25, BackcountryStore.com experienced a steady growth in the number of new visitors coming to the Web site throughout the fourth quarter of 2003.

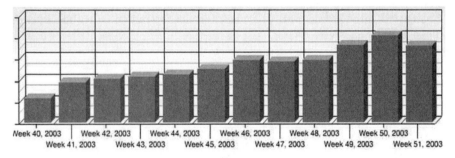

Figure 25: Steady, continuous growth in the raw number of new visitors to the BackcountryStore.com Web site in Q4, 2003. While this growth is clearly good news, a better analysis would be to compare this growth to the total number of visitors to the Web site to determine whether the percentage of new visitors is also growing.

Related Metrics

Perhaps more important than the raw number of new visitors is the relationship between new and returning visitors and that between new visitors and all visitors, discussed below. Additionally, the number of new visitors acquired is tied to referring sources metrics discussed in the chapters on acquisition and campaign analytics.

Ratio of New Visitors to Returning Visitors

The ratio of new to returning visitors is a key performance indicator for reach and acquisition, one that can help you easily determine your Web site's current "acquisition mode." Essentially a simple calculation, the ratio tells you how many new visitors you reach and acquire compared to the number of visitors you retain for any given timeframe. This metric is an excellent key performance indicator.

How to Calculate

Divide the number of new visitors by the number of returning visitors reported for the timeframe under analysis:

```
NEW VISTORS / RETURNING VISITORS = "ACQUISITION MODE"
```

It is very important to use returning visitors that are directly comparable to your new visitor metric, most likely day, or daily returning, visitors. Since new visitors are most typically reported on a daily basis, if you are to use a non-day metric for returning visitors you will skew the measurement of acquisition mode.

Consider 100 new visitors summed over a single week, 50 daily returning visitors summed over the same week and 30 weekly returning visitors for the week. The calculation for each would be:

- 100 new visitors / 50 daily returning visitors = 2.00
- 100 new visitors / 30 weekly returning visitors = 3.33

From an interpretation standpoint these two measurements of "acquisition mode" are 66 percent different, certainly a large enough variance to result in potentially different actions taken.

Dependence

The ratio of new to returning visitors depends on an accurate measurement of the individual numbers. The use of cookies is preferred for accurately measuring of new and returning visitors, but you are encouraged to read the section in Chapter 3 on cookie usage in analytics programs.

It is important to note that if you have recently moved to a new application or strategy for measuring new visitors that this metric will be meaningless due to the fact that nearly all of your visitors will be counted as "new visitors." If this is the case you should consider measuring, but not acting on, this measurement for some period of time, allowing visitors to be counted as new for the first time and time for their retention patterns to develop.

Usage

This ratio is a key performance indicator for any Web site, one that should be an integrated part of your regular reporting program. You should monitor this ratio on a daily or weekly basis, watching for pronounced changes, which can be leading indicators of a significant change in the relationship between your marketing programs, the Web site and the audience you are trying to reach. This KPI has the ability to inform on the efficacy of both acquisition and retention marketing programs.

Interpretation

Consider three examples:

- Company "A" reports 100,000 new visitors and 30,000 daily returning visitors summed for the month. The acquisition mode calculation for company "A" is 3.33. This means that for each visitor that returns to this company's Web site, 3.33 new visitors are successfully reached and acquired.
- Company "B" reports 50,000 new visitors and 80,000 daily returning visitors summed for the month. The acquisition mode calculation for company "B" is 0.63. This means that for every two new visitors that comes to this company's Web site, three visitors return in the same timeframe.
- Company "C" reports 180,000 new visitors and 176,000 daily returning visitors summed for the month. The acquisition mode calculation for company "C" is 1.02. Company "C" gets about one new visitor for every one returning visitor in the timeframe.

From the above data we can determine that company "A" is in new visitor growth and acquisition mode, company "B" is in active retention mode and company "C" has found a healthy balance of growth and retention. Depending on your acquisition model there are optimal targets for this calculation:

- If your business is in a strong growth mode, perhaps because you are new or you are releasing a new product or product line, this ratio should be between 2.00 and 5.00. Less than 2.00 and you would not describe your new visitor reach and acquisition as "strong." More than 5.00 and you are likely not doing enough to retain visitors.
- If your business depends on visitors returning, either because you have a complex sales process or you are working to develop an online community of loyal visitors, this ratio should be between 0.25 and 2.00. Less than 0.25 and you are simply not attracting many new visitors. More than 2.00 and you are beginning to drift into positive acquisition mode.
- If you are doing little marketing but have a well-designed Web site that offers compelling information or products, likely your ratio is somewhere between 0.75 and 1.25. This is an indicator of a healthy Web site but one that is not actively trying to acquire either new or returning visitors.

Related Metrics

New visitors reached and returning visitors retained are tied to referring sources metrics discussed in the chapters on acquisition and campaign analytics, as well as the retention metrics discussed in Chapter 14.

Percentage of New Visitors

The percentage of new visitors to total visitors is perhaps the best measure of how effectively you are able to reach people on the Web. The ratio is a straight percentage telling you how many people, out of your total audience, were new prospects who had somehow been attracted by your marketing program. This metric is an excellent candidate for usage as a key performance indicator.

How to Calculate

Divide the number of new visitors reported by your analytics package by the number of visitors that visited in the same timeframe.

```
NEW VISITORS / UNIQUE VISITORS = PERCENT NEW VISITORS
```

One subtlety is that many analytics packages will report different types of visitors—daily, weekly, monthly and occasionally for odd timeframes. You want to be careful you understand what "kind" of visitors you are using for your comparison.

Dependence

This number is dependent on how your particular analytics package measures new and unique visitors. Ideally someone can only be a new visitor to your Web site one time ever (see "number of new visitors" discussion). Visitors, on the other hand, can be measured a number of different ways (see Chapter 4). The most important thing is that you are using the same timeframe to get both numbers, as failure to do so will skew the resulting percentage. In general it is best to use the same type of unique visitors for the reporting timeframe, that is, if you are looking at new visitors for the week use weekly unique visitors.

Usage

The percentage of new visitors is an excellent key performance indicator for your marketing programs. It is a single number that can be tracked on a daily basis that allows you to quickly determine the effect of active marketing programs. If the percentage of new visitors is increasing day-over-day you know that your marketing programs are having a positive effect—you have successfully reached more new prospects today than you did yesterday. The converse is also true.

Interpretation

The number generated is the percentage of all visitors to your Web site in the timeframe under examination who were completely new to your site. A value of "30 percent" means that 30 percent of your visiting traffic was made up of new people successfully reached and brought to your Web site for the first time ever.

Example

BackcountryStore.com keeps track of the percentage of new visitors that are coming to its Web site to achieve and preserve an optimal mix based on past performance. It knows that its customers are unlikely to make more than a handful of purchases throughout the year so BackcountryStore.com depends heavily on attracting new visitors in hopes of converting them to loyal, lifetime customers.

Over time, BackcountryStore.com has learned that about 75 to 85 percent is the best mix of new to returning visitors coming to its Web site, and, using automated reporting provided by their Web analytics vendor, it monitors the percent of new visitors coming to the Web site (Figure 26).

Week of:	10/12	10/19	10/26	11/02	11/09	11/16	11/23	11/30	12/07	12/14
Percentage New Visitors:	81.0%	83.2%	81.8%	82.3%	82.3%	81.3%	81.0%	83.1%	82.6%	80.9%

Figure 26: Percent new visitors monitored on BackcountryStore.com via regular KPI reporting. BackcountryStore.com has optimized its marketing mix to achieve a roughly 75 to 85 percent mix of new to returning visitors.

Related Metrics

New visitors are tied to the ratio of new visitors to returning visitors ("acquisition mode"), as well as the referring sources metrics discussed in the chapters on acquisition and campaign analytics, as well as the retention metrics discussed in Chapter 14.

Entry Pages and Contents

Entry pages and contents are the way that many Web analytics applications refer to the first pages and first content groups that a visitor sees when they visit your Web site. If you consider the definition of a "visit" (Chapter 4), you will see that visit implies a first and last page in every visit, although they may be the same page. Paying close attention to entry pages and entry content is an excellent way to increase your chances of acquiring and converting the visitors you are able to reach.

How to Calculate

Entry pages and contents are metrics that are typically reported by your Web analytics application. Often grouped under "page" and "content" metrics, most vendors report the number of visits that begin at each page or content group listed.

Dependence

Entry pages and contents are dependent on how your application defines a visit or "session." If your application is not collecting information about pages viewed on a "per visit" basis you will likely be unable to make use of these metrics.

Usage

Entry pages and contents are critical to ensuring that you maintain a good chance to connect with each visitor you are able to reach. An important factor in reaching and acquiring visitors to your Web site is expectation setting—making sure that the message a prospect sees when they view your banner, read your email, find your search results, and so on, is consistent with the message a visitor sees when they land on your Web site. If a visitor thinks they are getting "A" when they click on your link or type in your URL but don't see any reference to "A" when they arrive on your site, the chances that they will click the back button increases significantly.

Monitor your top entry pages and content areas closely to ensure that the message on these pages is consistent with your overall marketing program. If you observe that a page or content area is appearing unexpectedly high on this list take a closer look at it to ensure that the message is consistent.

Interpretation

If your Web analytics package reports that "entry page A had 10,000 visits" this tells you that 10,000 visits to your Web site started at page "A." Your particular analytics package may also report that "5,000 visitors entered your Web site at page B," which is slightly different but still a measure of the relative popularity of page "B" as an entry point into your Web site.

Example

BackcountryStore.com keeps track of the most popular entry pages to its Web site in order to make sure that the home page features the products that its visitors are most interested in (Figure 27). By monitoring the percentage of entries into the Web site by page and product category, BackcountryStore.com is able to ensure that the new visitors, who make up the largest part of their visiting audience, are able to find the most popular items quickly.

	Name	%
1.	/Introduce BackcountryStore/BackcountryStore Home	19.70
2.	/Sell Products/The North Face/The North Face	7.03
3.	/Sell Products/Ski/Alpine Touring/Winter Packs/Winter Packs	3.49
4.	/Sell Products/Ski/Ski	2.75
5.	/Facilitate Search/Search for ski boots	2.42
6.	»/Sell Products/Womens Clothing/Womens Winter Clothing/Womens Fleece Jacket...	1.85
7.	/Sell Products/Snowboard/Snowboard	1.84
8.	/Sell Products/Camp Hike/Sleeping Bags/Sleeping Bags	1.65
9.	/Sell Products/Mens Clothing/Mens Clothing	1.45
10.	/Sell Products/Burton/Burton	1.41

Figure 27: Top ten entry pages by percentage of entry page views.

Related Metrics

Entry pages and contents are closely related to other marketing reach and acquisition metrics described in the chapters on acquisition and campaign analytics. Also, entry pages and content are closely reported to the acquisition metrics of "immediate abandonment" reported in Chapter 12.

Visitor Geographic Information

Keeping an eye on visitor geographic information is a simple recognition that the Internet is global, even if your marketing programs are local. Monitoring where your incoming traffic is coming from geographically will increase your chances of taking advantage of unexpected traffic from outside your target market.

How to Calculate

Visitor geographic distribution is often included in Web analytics packages, typically organized with "visitor" or "demographic" metrics. Different analytics packages report this information to different levels of granularity—some only reporting to the level of continent, others going down to the level of state, city and even zip code.

Dependence

Visitor geographic information is dependent on the method used to assign an anonymous visitor to a geographic region. Some Web analytics packages, notably those that depend on Web-server log files, have some difficulty with this since visitor IP address is often not the best data source for this assignment. Still, some vendors have partnered with content delivery networks like Akamai and Speedera to refine IP addresses to physical locations with a high degree of accuracy (see http://www.akamai.com/en/html/services/edge_how_ it_works.html for an example of the kinds of data that are available in a model like this).

Usage

It is recommended that you monitor the geographic distribution of your visitors occasionally to watch for spikes in traffic from locations you do not expect. The classic example of this is the online business that was doing no marketing or promotion overseas but who observed a significant traffic presence coming from Japan. Knowing this allowed the company to experiment with landing pages and marketing campaigns to better speak to this specific audience. The end result was a significant increase in overall online revenue from Japanese visitors.

Interpretation

Again, most Web analytics packages report geographic information on either a visitor or visit basis. If your Web analytics package reports that you had "100,000 visitors from Canada" in the last month or "50,000 visits were from visitors in China" you can determine if you should attempt to reach visitors you currently consider to be "out of market."

Example

As BackcountryStore.com expands into the offline world of catalog sales it has an increased interest in knowing more about its visitors' specific locations. Knowing more about where people are geographically when they find BackcountryStore.com online can help better target catalog mailings, especially considering the cost of lists of names. BackcountryStore.com's analytics provider is able to provide visitor geographic information down to the level of the city, allowing BackcountryStore.com's catalog group the ability to watch for cities and states that may stand out as being more active online.

	Name	%
1. ⊙	New York, New York -- United States	4.17
2. ⊙	Atlanta, Georgia -- United States	2.56
3. ⊙	Seattle, Washington -- United States	2.38
4. ⊙	Cherry Hill, New Jersey -- United States	2.29
5. ⊙	Chicago, Illinois -- United States	2.10
6. ⊙	Los Angeles, California -- United States	2.00
7. ⊙	San Francisco, California -- United States	1.64
8. ⊙	Denver, Colorado -- United States	1.63
9. ⊙	Washington, District of Columbia -- United States	1.37
10. ⊙	Boston, Massachusetts -- United States	1.26
11. ⊙	Saint Louis, Missouri -- United States	1.18
12. ⊙	Philadelphia, Pennsylvania -- United States	1.06
13. ⊙	Toronto, Ontario -- Canada	1.04
14. ⊙	London, England -- Great Britain	1.04

Figure 28: Visitor cities by percent of visitors visiting BackcountryStore.com.

As you can see in Figure 28, with the exception of New York, New York, visiting traffic is pretty well distributed throughout North America. It is interesting to note the traffic coming from Canada (line 13) and Great Britain (line 14), both areas that BackcountryStore.com currently considers "out of market" for shipping.

Error Pages

Often overlooked in a Web analytics program, since it is perceived as being more IT's responsibility than marketing's, is monitoring error pages—typically "file not found (404)" errors. Nothing is more frustrating for a new visitor than getting an error or running into a dead end. Even if you have created a nice looking "we're sorry but that documents has moved …" page you are still making a visitor wait for a page to load that was not what they were looking for or requesting. Error pages make a valuable addition to your key performance indicator program for reach and acquisition.

How to Calculate

Your Web analytics package should either generate error page information for you automatically (common in Web-server log-file-based applications) or provide an optional script to allow you to track these pages. Web-server log-file-based solutions will typically report on a variety of errors (file not found, server errors, and so on) since this information is freely available from the log file. Client-side data collection solutions are typically more limited in their ability to report, often depending on a custom error page being delivered by your Web server.

Dependence

Tracking error pages is wholly dependent on your Web analytics applications ability to record and present this information.

Usage

Error page reporting should be monitored on a weekly, if not daily, basis. Considering the amount of time, effort and money that most online businesses spend on marketing and marketing optimization, and since nothing good comes of a visitor seeing an error page, it only makes sense to work diligently on reducing the number of times visitors get errors during a visit.

Follow your error report closely and do two things to any page that is being requested "in error" as quickly as possible. First, implement a redirect of some kind from the error page to the correct page or at least a closely related page. Second, if your analytics package also reports on the pages that contained links to the broken page, correct the linkage on those pages if they are on your site or, if the links are on another Web site, write to the owners of the site and ask them to correct the broken links.

Interpretation

Most error page reports indicate the name or URL of the page that the visitor was ultimately looking for and the number of times visitors saw the error page. You should be watching closely and looking for error pages that are a receiving a significant amount of traffic as measured by total number of page views or as a large percentage of all error pages.

Interested Visitor Share

Adapted from Bryan Eisenberg and Jim Novo's *Guide to Web Analytics* description of "committed visitor share," this metric can help the online business understand what percent of visitors spend a moderate period of time interacting with the Web site. Much like average time spent on site, interested visitor share can be a powerful performance indictor for reach, helping you to identify changes in the composition of the audience you are reaching.

How to Calculate

The interested visitor share calculation is simply the number of visits that lasted longer than "n" minutes divided by the total number of visits:

```
VISITS OF MORE THAN "N" MINUTES / TOTAL VISITS = INTERESTED
VISITOR SHARE
```

Eisenberg and Novo do not recommend a value for "n" that will specifically indicate that a visitor is in fact "interested" in your Web site. Rather their description of "committed visitor index" discusses visitors who spend more than 19 minutes interacting with the Web site. One can reasonably set this number, however, by examining the average time spent on site, commonly available in most Web analytics packages. It would be reasonable to set "n" to the average number of minutes visitors spend on your Web site, thus providing an easy KPI for the percent of visitors who spend more than an average amount of time browsing.

Dependence

To calculate the interested visitor share all you need be able to do is determine the total number of visits exceeding "n" minutes for any period of time. If your Web analytics application has a "time spent on site" metric or report this is the most likely source for the data required to calculate interested visitor share.

Usage

The interested visitor share can be used to understand changes in the audience you are currently reaching and bringing to the Web site. If your goal is to bring visitors to the site that will spend five or more minutes interacting with the site then it would be useful to set "n" to "5 minutes" and calculate the total share of visitors who are spending more than five minutes, showing greater a than average interest in your message and content.

Interpretation

The interested visitor share is a percentage of all visitors who spend more than "n" number of minutes on your Web site. The actual number of minutes will depend on your specific business model and Web site goals. An educational, news or entertainment Web site would want to have a much higher interested visitor share than would a customer support site. In the former case, a visitor spending more time is a good thing as they are likely to connect more closely with the content and generate additional advertising views in the process. In the latter case, someone spending more time is potentially a bad thing, serving as an indicator that they are struggling to find the information they need to troubleshoot whatever problem they may be having at the time.

Example

BackcountryStore.com keeps track of its interested and committed visitor share and compares these numbers to its overall conversion rate (Figure 29). BackcountryStore.com is not necessarily interested in visitors spending long periods of time browsing their Web site—its hope is that visitors are able to find what they are looking for and make purchases quickly and easily—but it recognizes that there is some correlation between the site's conversion rate and visitors being "interested" and "committed."

Week of:	10/12	10/19	10/26	11/02	11/09	11/16	11/23	11/30	12/07	12/14
Interested Visitor Share:	19.9%	19.8%	20.6%	20.4%	21.1%	21.4%	22.3%	22.5%	22.2%	22.1%
Committed Visitor Share:	11.6%	11.6%	12.3%	12.0%	12.5%	12.9%	13.5%	13.7%	13.5%	13.5%

Figure 29: Interested and committed visitor share measured for BackcountryStore.com.

Related Metrics

Interested visitor share is related to all time spent on site metrics, including average time spent on site and percent of visits less than 90 seconds presented in Chapter 12.

Campaign Reach Metrics

Throughout *Web Analytics Demystified* we will revisit the metrics used to measure the effectiveness of campaigns designed to drive traffic to one's Web site. While the majority of the value derived from the campaign analysis tools described in Chapter 8 is associated with measuring acquisition and conversion, the following two metrics used to measure the effective reach of a campaign are important to creating a holistic view of how your campaigns support your online business.

Impressions Served

The measurement of campaigns crosses over all stages in the customer life cycle. Robust and well-implemented campaign analysis tools will help you to understand the reach and frequency for each ad, the response rate for the campaign as a measure of acquisition, the conversion rate—even metrics of retention and loyalty. To calculate reach and frequency, the primary metric used is the number of impressions served.

How to Calculate

Measuring and calculating impressions served is highly dependent on both your Web analytics package and the type of impression you are attempting to measure. In many instances the measurement of impressions served must be made by the vendor serving the impressions, as in the case of running your ad on a banner network or purchasing search engine keywords for placement via Google or Overture. In other instances Web-server log analysis applications are able to report the number of impressions served (if images are requested from the local Web server) simply by determining the number of requests for campaign images. In still other instances impressions can be tracked from within HTML email campaigns by sending a simple image request back to a Web server.

In general it is best to consult your Web analytics software or service provider for the details about how to get this information if you are not already able to get it from the vendor serving the ads.

Dependence

Measuring impressions served for a particular campaign is dependent on your ability to do so within or outside of your Web analytics application. In general it is far more common to get this information from an outside vendor, such as a banner network, search engine or email campaign management solution, than it is to be able to measure using your own Web analytics application. With this in mind it is important to understand how the outside vendor makes the impression measurement—is it based on page views or some visitor measurement? Is it set up to record immediate subsequent impressions (such as a reload) or ignore them?

Making sure that you can reconcile and understand how these measurements are made will allow for more meaningful integration of this data into your overall Web analytics program.

Usage

Impressions served are an important metric for calculating the reach and overall success of any campaign. Without knowing how many people saw the message it is impossible to know how compelling the message was or calculate the overall response rate for the campaign. Again it is important to reconcile any differences in how impressions served are measured with the method for measuring responses to be sure you are making an "apples to apples" comparison.

Interpretation

Impressions served are critical to determining the quality of any online opportunity to present your marketing message. You want to compare the number of impressions served with the number of impressions you purchased or were promised to ensure you are getting what you are paying for. You want to compare this number with the number of visitors who viewed the impression to calculate reach and frequency, that is, if you serve 100,000 impressions to 50,000 visitors to a Web site over a month your reach is 50,000 and your average frequency is 2.00 impressions per visitor.

In the end the most important reason to measure impressions served is to provide the denominator for the calculation of response rate for a campaign; you need to know how many people saw an ad to determine the rate at which people actually responded.

Open Rates

Open rate is a campaign analysis metric specific to email indicating the percentage of all emails sent that were actually viewed. The open rate is important, especially when you are purchasing a list of names and email addresses, as your message only has a chance to reach people when they actually see and read the message.

How to Calculate

Open rate is calculated by dividing the number of email addresses the message was sent to by the number of unique visitors who opened the mailing. Ideally:

```
UNIQUE READERS / TOTAL EMAIL ADDRESSES = OPEN RATE
```

Since it can be very difficult to measure the number of unique readers it is reasonable to use the measure of impressions served and assume a 1:1 ratio of impressions to unique readers. This is potentially dangerous if you consider a reader who is so interested in your message that he or she opens the email and reads the message several times but with large numbers this effect is minimized and it's better to have a "rough" open rate than no information about the number of readers at all. So:

```
AUDIENCE IMPRESSIONS / TOTAL EMAIL ADDRESSES = "ROUGH" OPEN
RATE
```

Dependence

Since it is more likely you will be generating a "rough" open rate you should also keep in mind that this calculation depends on the likelihood the email addresses you use are viable, that is that your emails will actually be delivered to people. Ideally you are able to keep track of both bounced emails (for whom no recipient could be located) and your opt-out rate. If you send a message to 100,000 email addresses and get 18,000 bounce backs and 2,000 opt-out requests your revised total email addresses should be 80,000 (100,000 - 18,000 bounces - 2,000 opt-outs = 80,000 total email addresses). Doing so will increase the accuracy of the calculation.

Measuring open rates is dependent on your ability to accurately measure the number of emails actually opened, often using some type of impression measurement tool. Both Web-server log file and page-tag-based applications are able to support this, typically by embedding an invisible image into the email. It should be noted that this technique *only* works for HTML emails, not text-based emails. But many businesses have expressed their comfort in generating an open rate for HTML email and then using the same percentage when analyzing text-only email.

Usage

Calculating the open rate for any email message you send to people will let you determine three things:

- Quality of email list
- Receptiveness of the recipients to the message subject
- Trustworthiness or "strength of brand" for your company

All a prospect sees when they get an email, unless they have some kind of preview pane, is a subject line and an idea of who was sending the email in the "From" line. If your subject line is not well written or the recipient has no idea who the sender is, especially in this age of spam and email-delivered viruses, chances are your email will be deleted, unopened. If your brand is a known quantity, you may have a slightly higher chance of having your message viewed. Regardless, open rate provides a good opportunity to test the relative quality of subject lines.

Given a large enough number of addresses it is relatively simple to test subject lines by simply dividing your audience up into test groups. A recommended method for testing is to separate out enough of your audience to test two or three different subject lines in an effort to optimize your open rate and still have enough audience left over for a mass-mailing.

Consider a total audience of 100,000 email addresses:

- Separate out 18,000 for testing, leaving 82,000 email addresses.
- Split the 18,000 into three groups of 6,000 "test subjects."
- Send each of the three groups the same email, from the same person or email alias, with three different subject lines.
- Measure the open rates for each of the three audiences. Take this a step further and measure response and conversion rates for each (Chapters 12 and 13).

Following this simple testing strategy will allow you to determine which subject line your total audience is most likely to be most receptive to. In a perfect world one of the subject lines will stand out as "most likely to be opened" and will have a response and conversion rate that is equally high as the other test messages. This subject line would be the best candidate to use for the remaining 82,000 recipients and will, hopefully, deliver the largest number of responses and conversions.

Interpretation

Open rate is simply the percentage of emails received that were actually opened for viewing; higher percentages indicate more actual messages viewed. This number can be inflated, dramatically in some instances, by the use of a preview pane in some email browsing applications. Unfortunately the author knows of no way to measure the percentage of messages browsed in a preview pane versus the number opened intentionally.

About Email Marketing

Open rates are a metric specific to a very important category of measurement, that of the efficacy of your email marketing. Jim Sterne, a recognized authority on email marketing and the author of *Advanced Email Marketing* has this to say about email marketing: "Email is an effective message-testing tool. While you have likely used email to drive Web traffic and sales, you may not have used it as a tool for testing your brand message." Jim makes an excellent point, that email is both an effective tool for communication but also a very valuable component in the continuous improvement process on one's Web site.

In his book, Jim discusses a handful of fundamental email marketing metrics that are not explicitly dealt with in *Web Analytics Demystified*. Briefly, these metrics are:

- **Total Sends** – the number of email addresses you originally sent your message to, before any bounces or failed notifications have returned.
- **Successful Sends** – the percentage of total sends that are not returned for some reason.
- **Hard Bounces** – the number of undelivered mails that are due to an address no longer being valid.
- **Soft Bounces** – the number of undelivered mails that are only temporarily undelivered due to software or server error. The author of *Web Analytics Demystified* also considers "out-of-office" messages soft bounces since some people will ultimately read your message but alas, many will not.
- **Messages "Missing-in-Action"** – the very difficult to track number of messages that get caught in anti-spam software, etc.
- **Tracked Opens** – the number of HTML emails opened tracked using an impression measurement tool, such as the one described in this chapter.
- **Estimated Opens** – the estimated number of total emails opened for both HTML and text messages.
- **Tracked Clickthroughs** – even though the author does not like the term "click-through" (see Chapter 4), Mr. Sterne cites this metric as the number of successful "clicks" on a link in an email. The author prefers to measure the number of responses and respondents (described in Chapter 12).
- **Forwards and Referrals** – difficult to accurately measure but invaluable in understanding how your message was ultimately received by your target audience.

Rather than spend too much time drilling-down into the subtleties of email marketing, the author instead gleefully refers the reader to Mr. Sterne's book. If you're doing any kind of email marketing you definitely should get a copy of this book from Lyris Technologies (www.lyris.com) and make sure that you A) read it and B) understand it.

Key Performance Indicators Recommended for Measuring Reach

Part of the demystification process is helping you to understand the metrics listed in this chapter and make good use of them on a regular basis. To this end, several of the metrics have been identified as "good candidates for regular key performance indicators." Ideally any reader of *Web Analytics Demystified* will, upon finishing the book, be able to construct a KPI report for their online business and make these metrics available to others within their organization on a regular basis.

To summarize, the key performance indicators the author recommends for reach, keeping in mind that these are metrics that are typically useful for *all* business models, include:

- Overall traffic volumes, to ensure that you are tracking large spikes or dips in the number of page views being requested.
- Ratio of new to returning visitors as an indicator of changes in the overall makeup of your audience.
- Percentage of new visitors, to observe the effect of changes to your marketing reach and acquisition efforts.
- Average pages viewed per visitor, to check whether dramatic changes in your overall traffic volume are due to a similar change in the number of visits to the site. Similarly, some businesses will want to monitor interested visitor share.
- Top five or ten error pages and the number of times each is seen by visitors to quickly resolve problems in the visitor experience.
- All campaign metrics presented in this chapter.

As you should see, the KPIs recommended are, for the most part, ratios, percentages or averages. These types of numbers are typically more useful as they are able to convey a greater amount of information via a single number, one which can be easily compared to previous time periods. Refer to Chapter 15 for additional information on these KPIs and how they should roll up into a regular, automated reporting program.

Metrics You Should Be Asking for Before You Spend Advertising Dollars

Before you spend any money on advertising with any other online business you should ask a handful of very specific questions about the type of audience they reach and how they measure reach and frequency. These questions apply to any Web site you are considering advertising on to drive traffic to your site, regardless of whether you are going to run banner ads, sponsor content or enter into a full-blown business partnership. There are slightly different measurements of reach for keyword buying opportunities and email campaigns (discussed below).

Important questions to ask include:

- How many page views does your Web site serve in an average day?
- How many page views did your Web site serve last month?

- How many unique visitors did you serve those pages to?

The answers to these questions will help you get a better handle on whether the site is likely to provide a good opportunity to reach people with enough frequency that your ad will likely be seen and remembered. If you are looking to buy a million impressions served over the month, but the Web site in question only saw a million page views last month, then you will be super-saturating the site and annoying more people than you attract. Alternatively if you are looking to buy 10,000 impressions and the site is serving ten billion page views your advertising will probably be viewed infrequently and either missed or just not remembered, unless you are targeting a very specific page or content area.

The ratio of page views to unique visitors, both the daily average and monthly measurement, will also help you determine whether the Web site has the right type of audience for you. If the site reports one million page views from 900,000 unique visitors you can determine that each visitor is viewing a little more than one page, on average. In this case, depending on the quantity of impressions you purchase, you will either be seen only once or not at all. Conversely, one million page views and 100,000 unique visitors yield an average of 10 pages per visit. Conventional wisdom dictates that the higher this number the more interested the site visitor is in the content provided; and the more interested the visitor the more likely they are to at least *see* your ad, if not respond.

You also want to be sure to ask how they measure their Web site's traffic. Consider what you learned in chapters 2 and 3 regarding differences in data sources informing Web metrics, such as the ratio of page views to visitors. Accuracy is very much an issue if the information is based on Web-server log files, unless the Web site operators are diligent in their attempts to determine the uniqueness of visitors and excluding non-human viewers when recording page views. It is better to have these numbers based on a client-side data source or to get audited numbers from a source like I/PRO.

If you do not trust the validity of the sources of data provided by the advertising site you should be extra careful to measure the response and conversion of traffic from that advertising venue. This is not to say that you should choose not to advertise with any Web site that does not have highest-quality metrics reporting, just that you should establish a vigorous program for determining success on your end.

Another critical question to ask is, "What is the demographic and technographic makeup of your audience and how do you measure that information?" More important than the number of impressions that a Web site will be able to serve is the type of audience they are able to reach and the quality of fit its audience has with the audience you have identified as being predisposed to respond to your message. Age, race, gender and socioeconomic factors are just as important online as they are offline when determining how advertising dollars should be spent. Unfortunately, accurately measuring these factors is extremely difficult and is often achieved using panel-based measurement services such as Nielsen/NetRatings.

Many Web sites are now taking advantage of visitor segmentation tools by capturing demographic information out of their registration process to further examine numbers and activity around key demographic segments. Done well, and providing the Web site is able to segment a statistically relevant population, this type of information can be very valuable in terms of understanding quality of fit for advertising buyers. Additional information regarding this segmentation strategy is provided in Chapter 14.

CHAPTER **12**
MEASURING
ACQUISITION

"The closer the match between the capabilities of the Web site and the needs of the customers, the greater the likelihood of success in the [acquisition] stage [of the customer life cycle]."
Hurol Inan in *Measuring the Success of your Web site*

Compared to measuring reach, measuring acquisition is relatively easy; there are several well-defined metrics that report on the number of people who have expressed at least some interest in your Web site. The most important differentiator is that, whereas many measures of reach depend on information from other sources, measurements of acquisition can be made from one's own Web analytics data.

For the most part the focus on acquisition measurement is, "How many visitors are we acquiring" and, "Where are we acquiring these visitors from?" The answers to these questions become very important when we move on to examine conversion and retention. Knowing one's conversion rate without knowing where the most likely converters come from is a good start but it's not enough to truly be effective on the Internet.

Note that all of the metrics presented in Chapter 11 on reach make good acquisition metrics in many instances.

General Metrics to Help Measure Acquisition

The following are metrics recommended to help better understand how successfully your Web site and online marketing programs are at helping you acquire visitors.

Percent New Visitors

The percentage of new visitors, also presented in the Chapter 11, as a reach metric is perhaps a better measurement of acquisition. Usually reported by Web analytics packages as the number of "new ever" visitors, those visitors who have never been to your Web site previously, new visitors are an audience segment that you want to focus much of your efforts on from an acquisition/conversion standpoint.

The percentage of new visitors in relation to all visitors is an excellent acquisition performance indicator. Please see the description of percent new visitors in Chapter 11 for details about percent new visitors.

Average Number of Visits per Visitor

The measurement of the average number of visits per visitor is used to help you understand the overall level of interest exhibited by active visitors. The more active or interested a visitor, the greater the likelihood they will return to your Web site and visit repeatedly. Keep in mind that for some business models increased activity is not necessarily a good thing. The average number of visits per visitor is an excellent acquisition performance indictor.

How to Calculate

The average number of visits per visitor is simply calculated by taking the total number of visits in the timeframe and dividing by the number of unique visitors in the same timeframe:

```
VISITS / VISITORS = AVERAGE VISITS PER VISITOR
```

This calculation should always give you a number greater than 1.00.

If you have access to the visitor segmentation tools discussed in Chapter 7 you may want to consider generating this calculation for different segments of visitors—new visitors, returning visitors, existing customers, and so on. Doing so will let you better understand what factors may be behind any changes observed. An increasing number of visits per visitor may be good for new visitors but bad for existing customers on the same Web site.

Dependence

The major dependence in this calculation is on the "visitors" measurement. As discussed in Chapter 7 there are several "types" of visitor:

"A daily unique visitor should be counted the first, and only the first, time a unique visitor visits a Web site on any given day. A weekly unique visitor should be counted the first, and only the first, time a unique visitor visits a Web site in a given week. A monthly unique visitor should be counted the first, and only the first, time a unique visitor visits a Web site in a given month."

With this in mind you should always attempt to use the most relevant definition of visitor for the timeframe in question. If you are trying to determine the average number of visits per visitor for a week, use weekly unique visitors. If you are trying to determine the average number of visits per visitor for a month, use monthly unique visitors, and so on.

Usage

The average number of visits per visitor should be used in conjunction with marketing activities to understand how interested different audiences are in the content, products or information you provide. Additionally, you should be careful to examine this metric in the context of your business model—it is not necessarily good news when this ratio increases on all sites. Having a higher average number of visits per visitor is preferred for most online stores where more visits potentially indicates a greater likelihood that the average visitor will make a purchase. A customer support site with a high average of visits per visitor may indicate an expression of frustration with a product or service.

Interpretation

The number provided by this calculation will simply be a number greater than 1.00, which indicates the average of all visits per all visitors, measured in the timeframe. A ratio of "3.5" tells you that the average visitor came to the Web site 3.5 times in the timeframe under examination. Another way to think about the average number of visits per visitor is as the average frequency of visit for the timeframe.

Example

The folks at BackcountryStore.com know that most of their customers are new visitors and that visitors return infrequently to purchase new gear. They keep track of the average number of visits per visitor to watch for any changes in this trend but they know that, unless they offer some dramatically different service, these numbers are unlikely to change (Figure 30).

Week of:	10/12	10/19	10/26	11/02	11/09	11/16	11/23	11/30	12/07	12/14
Visits per Visitor:	1.17	1.17	1.18	1.18	1.18	1.19	1.19	1.20	1.20	1.20

Figure 30: Weekly reporting on the average number of visits per visitor for BackcountryStore.com, calculated using "weekly" unique visitors.

Average Number of Page Views per Visit

The average number of page views per visit is also an excellent measurement of acquisition, as well as the likelihood for overall conversion in some situations. A measure of the likely depth of visit, measured by the number of pages the average person is likely to see in a given visit, this measurement is another good proxy for the level of interest in your content, products or offers. If one measure of success is getting visitors to look at a large number of pages, the larger this number the greater number of pages viewed in an "average" visit. The average number of page views per visit is an excellent acquisition performance indicator.

How to Calculate

To calculate the average page views per visit simply divide page views into visits:

```
PAGE VIEWS / VISITS = AVERAGE PAGE VIEWS PER VISIT
```

This calculation should always give you a number greater than 1.00.

Much like average visits per visitor, if you have access to the visitor segmentation tools discussed in Chapter 7 you may want to consider generating this calculation for different segments of visitors—new visitors, returning visitors, existing customers, and so on. Doing so will let you better understand what factors may be behind any changes observed. Much like visits per visitor, an increasing number of page views per visit may be good for new visitors but bad for existing customers on the same Web site.

Dependence

This calculation depends only on having accurate, consistent measurements for page views and visits.

Usage

Average page views per visit is used much like visits per visitor—to help you understand the changing nature of the visitors you are able to attract to your Web site. Similarly you want to be sure to consider your business model and what you are trying to get visitors to do online when you examine this average.

Much like the interested visitor share described in Chapter 11 there are optimal values for average page views per visit depending on your particular business goals. Obviously if your business model depends on visitors viewing a larger number of pages because those pages are tied to advertising views you hope this number will be as large as possible. Conversely if your visitors are looking for specific information on your Web site, perhaps to learn more about your business, larger numbers do not necessarily mean good news.

One valuable activity is to map out different scenarios that you'd like visitors to accomplish on your Web site and count the number of page views each would take. Depending on the scenarios, and the number of scenarios you can reasonably expect a visitor to complete in a single visit, you will begin to gain an understanding of what the optimal number of page views per visit is for your Web site. This number can then be used for a performance target and incorporated into your KPI program.

Interpretation

Like visits per visitor this number should always be a number greater than 1.00 and reflects the number of pages the average visitor saw in a visit. So a ratio of "10.8" tells you that during an average visit, visitors are seeing slightly less than 11 pages.

Example

Much like monitoring the average number of visits to visitors, BackcountryStore.com keeps track of the ratio of page views per visit to monitor for any dramatic changes in the number of pages the "average" visitor is viewing in a visit (Figure 31).

Week of:	10/12	10/19	10/26	11/02	11/09	11/16	11/23	11/30	12/07	12/14
Page Views per Visit:	16.31	16.11	16.43	16.16	16.58	16.67	17.36	17.20	16.65	16.47
Visits per Visitor:	1.17	1.17	1.18	1.18	1.18	1.19	1.19	1.20	1.20	1.20

Figure 31: Page views per visit, part of BackcountryStore.com's regular site performance reporting.

The major influence on page views per visit, at least on the BackcountryStore.com Web site, appears to be sale activity. When sales are announced via marketing channels such as banner ads and the retention email program, BackcountryStore.com is able to see more page views per visit. In the example provided in Figure 31 there was a large, advertised sale that ran from the week of November 23 to the week of December 7. During this timeframe you can see that the average number of page views per visit was up between 6 and 8 percent over non-sale periods.

Average Pages Viewed per Visitor

The average number of pages viewed per visitor is an excellent indicator of the quality of fit to the audience you are trying to acquire. The better targeted your marketing program, the greater the number of pages the responding visitors will likely browse. This metric is referred to as "attraction" since you can loosely state that if you find the right people they will be more attracted to your Web site and your content.

Not all business models are necessarily trying to get visitors to view many pages of content. This metric does serve most business models well, however, and it should be used as a key performance indicator for reach and acquisition.

How to Calculate

Divide the number of page views for a time period by the number of visitors:

```
PAGE VIEWS / VISITORS = AVERAGE PAGES VIEWED PER VISITOR
```

Dependence

This number is *highly* dependent on the reporting period, especially in the denominator. Hopefully your Web analytics application is able to measure at least daily and monthly unique visitors. Page views are a daily statistic, so if you are looking at a month's page views you are looking at the sum of page views for each day in the month. You can calculate both a daily and a monthly average page views per visitor measurement for your Web site, but these numbers will be different.

Usage

The daily average page views per visitor measurement can be used to determine, on a short-term basis, how effectively a Web site is able to draw visitors past the home (or landing) page. The monthly calculation is a better measurement of the true average depth of visit for the Web site on a per-visitor basis. Use the monthly calculation to help you determine whether your Web site's average visitor will have the opportunity to view your message with enough frequency.

Practically speaking, unless you dramatically change the content or information architecture of your Web site this number does not change much month-to-month. You should incorporate this metric into your regular monthly reporting and compare the current month to the previous month, watching for a percent change of more than 10 percent. The one activity that has the potential to change your site's value for average page views per visitor is a dramatic change in the audience you are trying to reach and acquire. Imagine that you have been advertising to a highly qualified audience and these respondents are looking at five pages on average when they come to your Web site. Imagine now that you begin to advertise to a much larger but less-qualified audience. As these visitors come to your Web site, assuming they are truly less qualified, you may see your average page views per visitor metric *decrease*. Because of this it is worthwhile to keep an eye on this metric in your regular reporting program and, if the number decreases, always ask yourself, "Did anything change in our marketing program recently?"

Interpretation

The ratio for this metric will always be greater than one, and the value represents the average number of pages that a visitor will view in the timeframe. Higher numbers, at least in terms of advertising reach and frequency, are better. A value of "1" indicates that the average visitor only sees one page. A value of "10" indicates that the average visitor sees 10 pages. There is no "optimal range" for average pages viewed per visitor; every Web site will have a different value. The range for your particular Web site is a function of your information architecture, your content and the audience you attract.

Related Metrics

Average pages viewed per visitor can also be calculated for content groups (discussed below). Some Web analytics applications provide a "depth of visit" metric that reports on the measured number of visitors viewing "one page," "two pages," "three pages," and so on. This metric can be used as a supplement to average pages viewed per visitor, if it is available, to determine whether there is a "sweet spot" of pages viewed. Average pages viewed per visitor can also be compared to time spent on site to see how page views relate to time spent on a global scale.

Page "Stick" and "Slip"

One of the most important measurements in reach and acquisition is the ability of the landing page to keep visitors' attention and draw them deeper into the Web site. While some authors use this term differently, the author of *Web Analytics Demystified* uses the term "stickiness" to describe a page's ability to keep a visitor engaged. The "stickiness" of any landing or entry page is critical to acquisition efforts as a direct measure of the ratio of visitors who start their visit on any given page to the number of visitors who *only* see that page. Put another way, the opposite of "stick," sometimes referred to as "slip," is the number of visitors who see your home page/entry page but immediately back up or leave the Web site. For most marketing and Web site entry pages, page "stickiness" is a critical acquisition performance indicator.

How to Calculate

For any given page under investigation:

```
SINGLE ACCESS PAGE VIEWS OF A PAGE / ENTRY PAGE VIEWS OF THE
SAME PAGE = PAGE "SLIP"

1 -(SINGLE ACCESS PAGE VIEWS OF A PAGE / ENTRY PAGE VIEWS OF
THE SAME PAGE) = PAGE "STICK"
```

The ratio of single access page views— the number of times the page was the only page viewed in a visit divided by the number of times the page was the first page in a visit—provides us a measure of the percentage of times a visitor sees the particular page and no other; we refer to this as page "slip." Subtracting this from one provides us a more optimistic key performance indicator, the percentage of visitors who start a visit at this page and get at least one page further; we refer to this as a page's ability to create "stick."

Dependence

Page "stick" and "slip" are dependent on being able to get a single access and entry page measurement for individual pages but most known analytics packages provide both of these metrics on a page-by-page basis, at least for the most popular pages on a site.

Usage

From an acquisition standpoint this metric is one of the most important performance indicators for the home page or any page designed to be an entry point into the site. As with all KPIs you are watching for both lower numbers than expected— a low percentage of visitors "sticking" on the page—as well as for large swings up or down. If, aside from your home page, you are unsure which pages should be tracked using this metric you should examine your "entry page" report for the top three to five most popular points of entry to your Web site and then monitor those pages.

You should always make this measurement for campaign landing pages since there is a gap between measuring open rates, response rates and conversion rates. Remember that open rates or impressions tell you only how many people viewed a message and that response rate tells you how many people clicked to your Web site. Conversion rate, which you will learn more about in Chapter 13, tells you how many respondents completed a specific action or actions. Making a page "stickiness" measurement for the campaign landing pages, you can begin to estimate the percentage of visitors who are going to be available to convert— if you have 1,000 respondents and a page "stickiness" of 20 percent you only have 200 potential converts, not 1,000.

Interpretation

If the page "stickiness" metric for your home page is "45 percent" (0.45) this tells you that only 45 percent of the visits to your home page during the timeframe under analysis went any further than the home page. Since most pages are designed to drive traffic to additional pages, the ideal situation is where the "stickiness" metric is relatively high (in the 70 to 80 percent range). Unfortunately this is rarely the case; some very common reasons that "stickiness" is low for entry pages include:

- Long load times for entry pages, especially critical for modem users
- Poor fit between the message that prompted the visitor to visit the page and the message presented on the page itself
- Poor page design in general
- Poor reach for marketing campaigns driving high volumes of traffic

Fortunately all of these issues are easily corrected. Any time you see lower than expected "stickiness," certainly for any entry page where at least 50 percent of all visitors immediately bail out, you should perform additional analysis to determine the cause and implement corrective action.

Occasionally there are pages that are designed to have low "stickiness" but most often these are portal-type pages designed to drive traffic directly to different Web sites that are outside of the realm of the analysis, different domains for log-file analysis or differently coded pages for tagged pages. In these situations you can perform a similar analysis if you have some type of "exit link" measurement available to you to determine whether visitors who are leaving that page are, in fact, clicking the appropriate links.

Example

The folks at BackcountryStore.com pay close attention to the stickiness of key entry pages on their Web site, especially those that they drive visitors directly to via marketing activities. To this end, in their regular KPI reporting they have built-in alerts to let them know when pages have slipped below acceptable thresholds (Figure 32).

Page Name	Stickiness
/Introduce BackcountryStore/BackcountryStore Home	82.4%
/Sell Products/The North Face/The North Face	90.6%
/Sell Products/Ski/Alpine Touring/Winter Packs/Winter Packs	11.7%
/Sell Products/Ski/Ski	83.9%
/Facilitate Search/Search for ski boots	65.2%
/Sell Products/Snowboard/Snowboard	81.6%
/Sell Products/Womens Clothing/Womens Winter Clothing/Womens Fleece	43.1%
/Sell Products/Camp Hike/Sleeping Bags/Sleeping Bags	81.2%
/Sell Products/Mens Clothing/Mens Clothing	66.9%
/Sell Products/Burton/Burton	84.4%

Figure 32: Page "stickiness" reporting for BackcountryStore.com, part of their regular, automated KPI report. Note that "Winter Packs" falls well short of a 60 percent threshold for the percent of visitors who click at least one-page further, highlighted in bold. Also note that "Women's Fleece Jackets" are of some concern with only 43.1 percent of visitors going any further.

BackcountryStore.com has set one threshold at 60 percent and another at 40 percent to indicate pages that need attention and pages that need *serious* attention. If a page is designed to move visitors more deeply into the Web site, it should be able to do so at least 60 percent of the time. The 40 percent threshold is an emergency warning, indicating that perhaps something has gone wrong with the page being monitored, as every page on the Web site reasonably leads somewhere else that should be of interest to visitors.

Having regular reporting such as that shown in Figure 28 helps BackcountryStore.com respond proactively, rather than reactively, towards its Web site. Being proactive lets the company ensure that the customer experience is always a positive one, keeping conversion rates higher than they would be if customers were constantly experiencing errors and ending up at dead-ends.

Related metrics

The most closely related metrics are single access page views and entry page views, the critical components of this metric. Also related are the reach and acquisition metrics for campaign analysis as well as referring source metrics, both of which are driving traffic to entry pages. Eisenberg and Novo in their *Guide to Web Analytics* refer to this metric as the "site penetration index" when it is calculated for the home page.

Cost per Visitor

Eisenberg and Novo state that "(cost per visitor) is a very useful way to measure what your traffic is costing you. (A) simple calculation to get an important number that can't be overlooked." Essentially cost per visitor can be used to determine how effective your overall marketing program is at driving traffic to your Web site, a measurement of reach and acquisition. The ultimate goal of online businesses, especially those selling directly via the Internet, is to lower cost per visitor while increasing sales per visitor (see Chapter 13 for more).

Given the ability to accurately and easily determine the "cost" part of this equation, cost per visitor can be an important acquisition performance indicator.

How to Calculate

Cost per visitor is based on being able to measure your costs for any marketing program designed to drive traffic to your Web site.

```
MARKETING EXPENSES / VISITORS = COST PER VISITOR
```

Dependence

As you can see, this calculation is dependent on being able to easily determine your marketing expenses for the same period of time you make the visitors measurement. Some businesses are able to grab this number with ease; others are unable to assign a fixed dollar value to marketing expenses. The problem with this number is that A) if you are spending any appreciable amount of money it can be difficult to know how much was actually spent in any short period of time, such as a day, and B) often it can take more time than is reasonable to determine this number and so the act of building this ratio effectively sidetracks the Web analytics process.

There appears to be a direct correlation between the size of a business and the difficulty in determining the marketing spend for a given day, week or month. Keep this in mind when determining whether to use this number or not; if it will take you much more than 15 or 20 minutes to get an answer to "how much did we spend on marketing last [timeframe]?" and you cannot automate the process, consider passing on cost per visitor and focusing on metrics more easily calculated.

Usage

Dependence aside, knowing your cost per visitor and watching it increase and decrease over time can help you understand the effect that decreasing marketing spend can have on acquiring visitors. Ideally, at some point, you can decrease your monthly spend on marketing without also decreasing the number of visitors coming to your Web site. You would know that you are at this point because your cost per visitor will begin to decrease while your average order size, purchase conversion rate and sales per visitor will stay roughly the same.

Interpretation

Cost per visitor is a dollar amount, such as, "$0.50 cost per visitor." Obviously lower amounts are better. Hopefully you would never end up in a situation where your cost per visitor is the same as, or higher than, your sales per visitor; this situation would mean that you lose money with every visitor who comes to your Web site.

Related metrics

Cost per visitor is closely related to sales per visitor, average order value and site-wide (purchase) conversion rates, all described in Chapter 13, Measuring Conversion.

Ratio of New Visitors to All Visitors

See "number of new visitors," above, for discussion of this ratio.

Heavy User Share

Taken from Bryan Eisenberg's *Guide to Web Analytics*, heavy user share is the number of visitors who view more than "n" pages in a visit divided by the total number of visits. As long as your Web analytics application is able to provide you the distribution of number of pages per visit, "n" in this case, you should be able to calculate this ratio.

Heavy user share can be a valuable performance indicator for online businesses focused on having visitors stay engaged for longer visits.

How to Calculate

Simply, for any "n" pages per visit:

```
NUMBER OF VISITS OF "N" OR MORE PAGES / TOTAL VISITS = HEAVY
USER SHARE
```

In *The Guide to Web Analytics* Mr. Eisenberg recommends setting "n" to 11 pages to account for visits of 10 or more page views.

Dependence

The only dependence is your application's ability to report on the number of pages viewed per visit.

Usage

Eisenberg states that heavy user share is useful in determining the percentage of users who are highly attracted to content on your Web site and, as a metric, to help you understand the quality of fit for the audience you are currently reaching. The assumption is that a more qualified audience will view more pages in a given visit, thus increasing the likelihood they will be counted as a "heavy user."

Depending on how you define "n" you can tweak this ratio to serve your particular businesses needs. If you determine that the average number of page views per visit (see average page views per visit) is five pages per visit then you could set "n" to seven or eight to measure the percentage of visits that are 50 percent greater than your average number of page views per visit. Conversely you could halve the average number of page views per visit and calculate a "light user share," depending on your specific business needs.

Interpretation

Depending on your Web site's goals you may or may not want to have a high heavy user share. If you present content it is likely that you would prefer to have a higher heavy user share, which indicates that you are attracting visitors who are interested in your content. Conversely if you are making this measurement for a support site you may want visitors to be able to find the information they need in as few clicks as possible, leading to a lower heavy user share.

Your particular business model will dictate whether heavy user share can be used as a performance indicator to help you determine if current and emerging marketing campaigns are having the desired effect in terms of audience reach and acquisition.

Top Pages and Content Requested By New Visitors

One of the most important data points for acquisition is the pages and content that new visitors are viewing on your Web site. This is the information that you provide that they find "most compelling" and thus the area on which you may want to focus your acquisition efforts. Keep in mind that the "new" or "first time" visitor experience may differ from that of a returning visitor or someone who was purchased or otherwise made a commitment to you in the past. Tracking what early-stage prospects are doing on your site can help you to significantly improve the quality of outbound marketing you do to attract other new visitors in the future.

How to Calculate

Since all known analytics applications report on some kind of "page analysis," and most provide similar analysis for hierarchical content, the important component for this metric is being able to tie page and content views to "new" visitor status. In many applications this is accomplished using the visitor segmentation tools described in Chapter 7, using the following rough strategy:

1. Create a system to cookie visitors based on the number of visits they make to your site (see below).
2. When any visitor comes to your site, first test to see if this cookie exists. If it does not, assume they are a "first time" visitor and segment as such.

One advantage of creating a system to cookie visitors on a "per visit" basis is that you can then likely generate a number of useful reports based on the number of lifetime visits your visitors are making.

Dependence

This metric is wholly, but only, dependent on your analytics application's ability to differentiate new from returning visitors and report on the pages and content new visitors are most interested in. Ideally your application provides page views, content views, campaign responses and referring source (domains, search engines and search terms) for new and returning visitor segments.

Usage

The most typical use for this information is to determine what content and information presented on your Web site is most compelling to newly acquired visitors. This same logic will apply to returning visitors and visitors in other customer life cycle categories (converted, retained), but by mining this type of information you can determine what products, offers and/or information you provide are most likely to A) help you move these visitors along the customer life cycle and B) acquire more visitors in the future.

Interpretation

Having this information available can highlight particular pages and content that are visited more frequently by new visitors as opposed to returning visitors. By knowing what percentage of time key information is viewed based on percentage of page views for new visitors and comparing that to the total number of page views for the content area for all visitors you can begin to interpret the goals of newly acquired visitors in an effort to increase new visitor conversion.

Related metrics

Closely related to information preferences for new visitors are both visitor segmentation and page/content view metrics. Please refer to the section below on setting up a visit cookie system for specifics on how this metric can be made if your analytics application does not provide it automatically.

An Important Note about Setting up a "Visit" Cookie System

One aspect of tracking acquisition and retention is the ability to differentiate new from returning visitors and to be able to see what pages, content, processes, and so on, these different classes of visitors engage in. Ideally your analytics package will provide this information to you without any additional setup. If it does not, but does provide some ability to segment visitors within the reporting interface, you may want to consider setting up a visit tracking system of your own using cookies.

All that is required to do this is the ability to set and read cookies from a visitor's browser and the ability to determine the number of minutes since the last page "click." The basic logic involved is:

1. Check and see if the cookie exists already:
2. If it does, grab the number of visits and the date/time of the last click.
3. If it does not, write the current date/time and the number "1" for number of visits to the cookie. This visitor would be classified as a "first visit" visitor.

4. If in step 1 there was a cookie, compare the current date/time with the date/time of the last click:
5. If the number of minutes since the last click was greater than 30 minutes increase the number of visits by "1" and write that number and the current date/time to the cookie.
6. If the number of minutes since the last click was less than 30 minutes simply write the current date/time to the cookie (but do not increase the number of visits).

```
//      Set cutoff amounts
var durationCutoff = 23;  // Set the duration high/low to 23 minutes
var visitCutoff = 3;  // Set the visit high/low to 3 visits
var sessionCutoff = 30;  // Set the session timeout in minutes to 30 m

function _read_cookie( begin ) {
   var end=document.cookie.indexOf(";,"begin);
   return unescape(document.cookie.substring
(begin,end<0?document.cookie.length:end));
}
function _write_cookie(name,value,expires,path,domain,secure) {
   document.cookie= name+"="+escape(value) +
      ((expires == null) ? "" : ("; expires=" +
expires.toGMTString())) +
      ((path == null) ? "" : ("; path=" + path)) +
      ((domain == null) ? "" : ("; domain=" + domain)) +
      ((secure == true) ? "; secure" : "");
}
function GetCookie( name ){
   var arg = name + "=";
   var alen = arg.length;
   var clen = document.cookie.length;
   var i = 0;
   while( i<clen ) {
      var j = i + alen;
      if(document.cookie.substring(i, j) == arg)
         return _read_cookie(j);
      i = document.cookie.indexOf(" ," i) + 1;
      if (i == 0) break;
   }
   return null;
}
function SetCookie(name,value,expires_in_minutes,path,domain,secure) {
   var expdate = new Date ();
   expdate.setTime(expdate.getTime() + (expires_in_minutes * 60 *
1000));
   _write_cookie(name,value,expdate,path,domain,secure);
}

//      Load the cookies with previous values if present
var oldTime = GetCookie('visit_time');
var oldVisitCount = GetCookie(' visit_count');
var oldMonth = GetCookie(' visit_month');
var oldSessionStartTime = GetCookie(' visit_ss_time');
var timeDiff = 0;
var thisCount = 1;
var thisDate = new Date();
var thisTime = thisDate.getTime();
var thisMonth = thisDate.getMonth();
var thisSessionTime = oldSessionStartTime; // Don't update this unless
it's a NEW VISIT

// Test to see if this is a first monthly visit
if (oldMonth == thisMonth) {
```

```
        // Set thisCount to the value in the cookie
        var thisCount = oldVisitCount;

        // No, they've been this month so set their QUAD level
        var difference = thisTime - oldTime;
        var minutes = Math.round(difference / (1000 * 60));
        var session_difference = thisTime - oldSessionStartTime;
        var session_minutes = Math.round(session_difference / (1000 *
60));

        timeDiff = minutes;
        session_timeDiff = session_minutes;  // Use this to test for
SESSION duration

if (timeDiff > sessionCutoff) {  // If there has been "sessionCutoff"
mins of inactivity BETWEEN CLICKS, increase visit count and reset the
session time
        thisCount = (oldVisitCount/1) + 1;
        thisSessionTime = thisTime;

} else {

// Yes, first visit this month so reset
thisCount = 1;
thisSessionTime = thisTime;
session_timeDiff = 0;

};

// Update cookies
var expires_in_days = 30 * 24 * 60 * 1000;
SetCookie('track_time',thisTime,expires_in_days);
SetCookie('track_ss_time',thisSessionTime,expires_in_days);
SetCookie('track_count',thisCount,expires_in_days);
SetCookie('track_month',thisMonth,expires_in_days);
```

Figure 33: Sample code for setting up a cookie-based "visit" tracking system, written in JavaScript by the author in as inelegant a fashion as humanly possible.

With each test run—and you should run this test on every page, if possible—this logic will update the time of "last click" in all cases and in some cases (if this is a new visit, for example) will update the total number of visits. One variation on this is to determine whether the visit is in a new month (that is, the last visit was in a previous calendar month), in which case you can count monthly visits.

From this logic you can easily derive whether the visitor is a "new" or "returning" visitor and also begin to classify the visitor into visit categories, "2 to 5 previous visits," "6 to 10 previous visits," and so on. Using this in tandem with whatever system for visitor segmentation your analytics application provides can be a very powerful strategy for understanding visitor acquisition and retention.

Content "Focus"

The concept of content "focus" was first presented by Sterne and Cutler in *E-Metrics: Business Metrics for the New Economy,* and relates the average number of pages visited in a content area to the total number of pages in the section.

How to Calculate

In order to calculate content focus you first need to calculate the average number of pages viewed per visitor for the content group of interest. Similar to the average number of page views per visit, this ratio is specific to a single content grouping on your Web site.

```
CONTENT PAGE VIEWS / CONTENT UNIQUE VISITORS = AVERAGE NUMBER
OF PAGES VIEWED PER VISITOR BY CONTENT
```

Once you have made this calculation, content focus can be found by dividing this value by the total number of pages contained in the content group.

```
AVERAGE NUMBER OF PAGES VIEWED PER VISITOR BY CONTENT/ TOTAL
NUMBER OF CONTENT PAGES = CONTENT FOCUS
```

Dependence

This metric is dependent on being able to determine the number of page views and visitors for an individual content group, numbers that are not necessarily available in all Web analytics packages. You should consult your vendor to determine if these numbers are available.

Obviously this metric is also dependent on knowing how many total pages are contained in a content grouping, which is often difficult to determine—especially for content-rich sites or online businesses that sell many different products,

Usage

According to Sterne and Cutler, this calculation will help you determine whether the average visitor has a *wide* or *narrow* focus regarding the content in question. While the desire to have a wide or narrow focus will likely change by content presented, making this calculation for key areas of your Web site will allow you to understand when your audience makeup changes significantly, thereby allowing you to react to those changes.

Interpretation

According to Sterne and Cutler smaller values indicate a *narrow focus* while larger values indicate a *wider focus* on the content in question. These authors cite the example of narrow focus being good in customer service and support areas of a Web site, where it is important that visitors are able to quickly find information and move on, whereas a wider focus is preferable in an online auction or product catalog, where one hopes that visitors browse a number of products, increasing their likelihood of conversion.

Sterne and Cutler also relate content focus to the "stickiness" of the Web site but it is worth noting that their definition of "stickiness" and that used in *Web Analytics Demystified* are different.

Percent of Visits Under 90 Seconds

For most Web sites it takes visitors at least 90 seconds to become engaged in reading content or finding information. Certainly there are exceptions—news and sports Web sites with regularly changing headlines on the home page are a good example—but for the most part any visit lasting less than 90 seconds can be considered a visit that was probably not long enough for a visitor to become connected with the site.

The percent of visits under 90 seconds is an important acquisition performance indicator.

How to Calculate

The calculation is simply the number of visits lasting 90 seconds or less on the Web site divided by the total number of visits in the timeframe.

```
VISITS UNDER 90 SECONDS / ALL VISITS = PERCENT OF VISITS UNDER
90 SECONDS
```

Dependence

The only real dependence is your analytics package's ability to report on the distribution of visits in half-minute increments or groupings that include 90 seconds and under. If only minute increments are available it is acceptable to calculate percent of visits lasting less than a minute.

Usage

Percent of visits under 90 seconds is an important acquisition performance indicator helping you to observe gross changes in the type of audience you are bringing to your Web site. If you are consistently seeing this number reported in the 25 to 30 percent range and then suddenly it spikes to 50 percent you know that either you have just attracted a large number of visitors who are not interested in what you have to offer or for some reason you are no longer attracting the visitors who had been interested in your site (the percentage will change due to changes in either the numerator or the denominator).

Any time you see dramatic changes in this metric you want to immediately ask yourself what may have changed in your marketing program and the type of visitors you are trying to reach. If you start a marketing campaign that is bringing you thousands of respondents, but your percent of visits under 90 seconds spikes dramatically, you can reasonably assume that most of the respondents are not as interested as they thought they might be. Conversely if your campaign is bringing you large volumes of visitors and your percent of visits under 90 seconds stays relatively stable or decreases you know you have identified a good advertising opportunity.

Interpretation

The percent of visits under 90 seconds is simply a percentage describing the total volume of traffic spending little or no time interacting with your Web site.

Example

BackcountryStore.com pays close attention to how visitors interact with its Web site. As shown in Figure 29, the marketing group pays close attention to the "interested" and "committed" visitors who visit the site. Because they are realists, they also pay attention to the number of visits that are under 90 seconds in length (Figure 34).

Week of:	10/12	10/19	10/26	11/02	11/09	11/16	11/23	11/30	12/07	12/14
% Visits under 90 seconds:	23.0%	22.7%	22.2%	22.2%	22.2%	21.7%	22.0%	21.8%	22.0%	21.9%
Interested Visitor Share:	19.9%	19.8%	20.6%	20.4%	21.1%	21.4%	22.3%	22.5%	22.2%	22.1%
Committed Visitor Share:	11.6%	11.6%	12.3%	12.0%	12.5%	12.9%	13.5%	13.7%	13.5%	13.5%

Figure 34: Percent of visits under 90 seconds included with "interested" and "committed" visitor shares in BackcountryStore.com's regular and automated KPI reporting.

While BackcountryStore.com knows that it will never have "0.0 percent visits under 90 seconds" it works to ensure that its Web site loads quickly and presents compelling products and information on key entry pages. The fact that its visits under 90 seconds runs roughly parallel to its interested visitor share means that for every visitor it loses to disinterest it retains one who may be interested enough to make a purchase.

Average Time Spent on Site

Average time spent on site is less a metric that needs to be calculated and more a metric that needs to be watched as part of a regular reporting program. Considered here under the umbrella of "acquisition" this measurement truly spans all phases of the customer life cycle. In fact, a strong use of the visitor segmentation tools described in Chapter 7 would be to segment visitors based on their phase in the customer life cycle and observe how the average time spent on the site changes as the visitor's progress.

How to Calculate

The rough calculation is the total time spent surfing all pages in a visit divided by the number of visitors in the same timeframe. In nearly all instances the average time spent on site is calculated and presented by the analytics application. Any application that does not provide this metric should be considered suspect and replaced.

Dependence

The only major dependence average time spent is known to have is how the calculation treats the final page in the visit (the exit page in some applications). Because there is no subsequent "click" it is impossible for the analytics application to assign an amount of time spent on the final page in a visit. It is best if the application excludes the final page view in a visit from the calculation, if possible.

Consult your application vendor to determine how they treat the final page in a visit when it comes to both average time spent on site and also time spent on pages.

Usage

Average time spent on site is used to watch for gross changes in the total audience visiting the Web site. Not limited to visitor acquisition programs, this value can be heavily influenced by the type of visitors you reach and acquire via marketing programs. If, much like percent of visits lasting under 90 seconds, new inbound marketing activity can be correlated to a decrease in the average time spent on site, the quality of the audience being acquired should be more closely examined for true quality of fit.

Interpretation

Simply a report of the average number of hours, minutes and seconds all visitors spend interacting with your Web site.

Campaign Response Metrics

One of the most important aspects of measuring reach, acquisition and conversion on any Web site is the measurement of marketing activities designed to bring visitors to the Web site. Regardless of whether your online strategy uses banner ads, opt-in email, non-opt-in email (nice word for "spam"), direct mail, pop-up ads, keyword buying, print advertising, television, billboards or roving gangs of thugs wearing t-shirts bearing your logo and URL, you should be measuring the effect this campaigning has on your online business. Not to do so is irresponsible, period.

To this end, hopefully the Web analytics package you have chosen supports the type of robust campaign analysis tools described in Chapter 8. Key to measuring the effect online marketing has on customer acquisition is the ability to somehow "tag" media and links in such a way that you are able to differentiate campaign responders from other traffic.

Note that ultimately the concept of "other traffic" is fallacious, since everyone had to learn about your Web site via some marketing effort. But it can be difficult to measure returning visitors with anything other than "lifetime returning visitor" metrics (which will be described in Chapter 14).

Responses and Respondents

The second most important metric when measuring the effectiveness of any marketing campaign is the response rate for that campaign. When online businesses first start to attempt to quantify the effect of marketing, response rate is one of the first metrics examined and tracked. While this is tremendously important, it is perhaps more important to understand what these respondents are doing on the Web site (see campaign discussion in Chapter 13).

How to Calculate

Any Web analytics application that supports campaign analysis of some kind should be able to provide the number of responses and respondents to a given campaign. Remember from the discussion in Chapter 8, respondents are real people who perform some activity you have designed to bring them to your Web site (click a link, type a URL, and so on). When these people perform this activity it is said to be a "campaign response" and the percentage of campaign responses divided by the total impressions is the response rate.

```
RESPONSES / TOTAL IMPRESSIONS = RESPONSE RATE
```

You should calculate the response rate for any active campaign on a daily basis.

Dependence

The response rate calculation depends on you being able to accurately track or know the number of impressions served and the number of responses for a given campaign. If you are unable to measure the number of impressions served for a campaign but you have a rough idea of how many impressions were delivered (you sent an email to 100,000 addresses but have no idea what the open rate was) you can calculate response rate based on this estimate but keep the fact that you are working from an estimate in mind when you are tempted to use the resulting data.

Usage

Response rate is critical to the continuous improvement process when it comes to acquisition and conversion. Presumably you have some experience with online marketing and have discovered independently that not all campaigns are created equally. If open rate is an indicator of how compelling your subject line is for an email, response rate is a measure of how compelling the overall message is once it has been viewed. Response rate is critical in helping you diagnose issues of message and packaging, as well as the quality of reach through a given delivery mechanism.

While response rate is not the most important metric of campaign success it is an important indicator of whether a campaign will be successful. The more respondents you are able to acquire the greater the likelihood you will find qualified respondents who will potentially convert.

Interpretation

Response rate is simply a percentage that tells you, "What percentage of all impressions served for this campaign turned into visits to my Web site?" Higher percentages can tell you either that the message was well-received by the audience you were attempting to reach (a strong fit between audience and message) or that the message was so compelling that people were responding regardless of the quality of fit between audience and message. Lower percentages are, of course, an indicator that there is some disconnect between the message and the audience.

Example

The author of *Web Analytics Demystified* was engaged in a handful of marketing campaigns to drive traffic to the companion Web site for this book throughout the last half of 2003. These campaigns included email, keyword buying through Google.com and a handful of vanity URL landing pages (Figure 35).

	ID	Description	New Respondents	Repeat Responses	Responses
1.	KNL-Google	KNL-Google	174	62	236
2.	OTL-Open Preview	OTL-Open Preview	64	41	105
3.	EML-Updaters	EML-Updaters	29	10	39
4.	OTL-Stanford	OTL-Stanford	5	6	11
5.	EML-Sterne Measures	EML-Sterne Measures	2	1	3

Figure 35: Sample data from the author's Web site showing active campaigns and number of responses, broken down by new respondents and repeat responses.

Depending on the campaign type, the author calculated response rates differently. For the "KNL-Google" campaign, impression data came from the Google AdWords™ application interface (Figure 36). For email programs, response rate was generated based on the total number of emails sent. For vanity URL landing pages, rates were generated using page views.

Keyword	Status	Max. CPC	Clicks	Impr.	CTR	Avg. CPC ▾
Total — search			178	33,891	0.5%	$0.06
Total — content targeting			15	16,538	0.0%	$0.06
web analytics	Strong	$0.10	12	711	1.6%	$0.08
web analysis	Strong	$0.10	56	7,086	0.7%	$0.06
traffic analysis	Moderate	$0.10	6	1,976	0.3%	$0.06
log analyzer	Moderate	$0.10	10	1,680	0.5%	$0.06
traffic statistics	Strong	$0.10	13	1,394	0.9%	$0.06
web logs	Moderate	$0.10	26	3,912	0.6%	$0.06

Figure 36: Response rates (called "click-through-rate" in Google-ese) for a handful of keywords that the author purchased in the last half of 2003 (data provided by Google AdWords).

Of each of the different kinds of campaigns that the author was running at the time, direct email campaigning had the best response rates, averaging more than 20 percent. This was followed by vanity URLs, averaging around 7 to 9 percent and then keyword buying, averaging around 0.5 percent. In the context of the author's marketing program for driving people to download a preview copy of *Web Analytics Demystified* this made perfect sense. The people whom the author had previously had the most contact (through email) had the highest conversion rate, followed by people with whom he'd had peripheral contact (vanity URLs were being fed by others in the Web analytics space such as Jim Sterne and the Stanford Publishing group), followed by complete strangers who happened to be interested in the topic of "Web analytics."

Cost-per-Acquisition / Cost-per-Click

Cost-per-acquisition is one of the first metrics discussed in *Web Analytics Demystified* that tie Web analytic data to return on investment. One of the reasons this book was written is to help marketing managers understand how spending money online translates into either making money back—or at least not throwing money away. Cost-per-acquisition is critical to help ensure you are not paying too much for leads or prospective customers.

How to Calculate

Cost-per-acquisition is the dollar amount spent on the campaign divided by number of unique prospects acquired.

```
COST OF CAMPAIGN / CAMPAIGN RESPONDENTS = COST PER ACQUISITION
```

It is important to calculate this metric for a specific timeframe, for the day, the week, the life of the campaign, and to use campaign costs that are as accurate as possible. It is also important to use *respondents* not *responses* for this calculation since you are working to determine not the simple cost-per-click but rather the cost of acquiring people that you can further market to and that, hopefully, will ultimately convert.

If you wanted to calculate the cost-per-click you would simply make the same calculation using the number of campaign *responses*:

```
COST OF CAMPAIGN / CAMPAIGN RESPONSES = COST PER CLICK
```

Dependence

Depending on the type of campaign, costs can be more or less difficult to determine. In general, for campaigns that have a fixed delivery cost (CPM banner advertising, some partnerships) you can simply divide the total cost by the number of days under examination to get the cost of campaign for the calculation. Variable delivery cost campaigns (cost-per-click, pay-per-click) are slightly trickier in that you need to sum the cost for each day in the timeframe under examination.

This calculation also depends on having tools to allow you to measure responses and respondents to a given campaign.

Usage

Cost-per-click and cost-per-acquisition are major factors in helping the online business understand which campaigns are cost effective for the organization. While not the final word in whether a campaign is a success or not, used in combination with response rate, conversion rate and cost per conversion, these metrics will help smart business managers determine which campaigns to keep and which to drop.

Ideally you will be able to have or create a view of these important campaign metrics—open rate, response rate, cost-per-acquisition, conversion rate, cost-per-conversion and campaign return on investment—that allow for the easy comparison of active campaigns.

Interpretation

Cost-per-click and cost-per-acquisition are monetary metrics describing the individual cost for each. A cost-per-click of $2.50 means that for each response to the campaign in question you are paying $2.50. A cost-per-acquisition of $0.49 means that each person you acquire via this campaign costs you $0.49. Taken alone these numbers are less interesting than when you compare them to the predicted value of the campaign overall. If you are paying $2.50 for each response to the campaign but the ultimate goal is to sell a product for which you only make $25.00 per sale, the campaign will need to convert at 10 percent just to break even:

- 100 responses costing $2.50 each = $250.00
- 250.00 divided by $25.00 order value = 10 conversions to break even
- 10 conversions divided by 100 responses = 10 percent conversion rate to break even

With all of the above, this campaign will not be profitable at a two-time or three-time expenditure target unless the campaign converts at 20 or 30 percent (which in most instances is unlikely).

The best way to back into the answer to "What is a good target for cost per acquisition?" is to do the following:

1. Figure out the total amount you'd like to make from the campaign (be realistic)
2. Make sure you know your average order value (AOV) or average value per conversion
3. Figure out what multiple you'd like to enforce for your campaigns
4. Divide the total amount you'd like to make (step 1) by your target multiple (step 3) to get your maximum campaign spend
5. Figure out your campaign conversion rate, either from an average or from previous similar campaigns
6. Divide your earning target for the campaign by your AOV to get the number of conversions required to make your earning target
7. Multiple the number of conversions by your conversion rate to determine how many respondents you need
8. Divide the maximum campaign spend (step 4) by the number of respondents required (step 7) to get the maximum spend per respondent (cost-per-acquisition)

As an example:

1. We'd like to make $10,000 from the campaign
2. Our AOV is $100.00
3. We like our campaigns to produce at a 5x multiple
4. We'd like to spend no more than $2,000 on the campaign
5. Our conversion rate is 5 percent
6. We need 100 conversions to make $10,000
7. With a conversion rate of 5 percent we need 2,000 respondents
8. With a target spend of $2,000 and needing 2,000 respondents, we can spend no more than $1.00 per acquisition on the campaign

In the example above, if your conversion rate were double (10 percent) you could also afford to spend twice as much ($2.00 per acquisition) on the campaign. With this information in mind you can use your response rate to determine whether you can actually afford to run a cost-per-click or cost-per-acquisition campaign or not.

Example

For an example of cost-per-acquisition in action, take another look at the author's marketing campaign strategy described earlier in this chapter. Part of this strategy was buying relevant keywords through Google's AdWords program where the author was paying for each click to www.webanalyticsdemystified.com from Google (Figure 37).

☐ Keyword	Status	Max. CPC	Clicks	Impr.	CTR	Avg. CPC ▼	Conv. Rate	Cost/Conv.
Total — search			178	33,891	0.5%	$0.06	13.48%	$0.41
Total — content targeting			15	16,538	0.0%	$0.06	13.33%	$0.44
☐ web analytics	Strong	$0.10	12	711	1.6%	$0.08	16.67%	$0.44
☐ web analysis	Strong	$0.10	56	7,086	0.7%	$0.06	16.07%	$0.37
☐ traffic analysis	Moderate	$0.10	6	1,976	0.3%	$0.06	16.67%	$0.34
☐ log analyzer	Moderate	$0.10	10	1,680	0.5%	$0.06	20.00%	$0.28
☐ traffic statistics	Strong	$0.10	13	1,394	0.9%	$0.06	0.00%	$0.00
☐ web logs	Moderate	$0.10	26	3,912	0.6%	$0.06	26.92%	$0.19

Figure 37: Cost-per-acquisition ("cost-per-conversion" in Google-ese, which is technically correct, although the author treated conversion differently in this campaign) for a handful of keywords that the author was purchasing in the last half of 2003 (data provided by Google AdWords).

As you can see in Figure 37, the author was paying between $0.19 and $0.44 per visitor acquired, with the act of acquisition being a lead generated when the respondent submitted their email address to get a copy of *Web Analytics Demystified*. Based on the calculations presented above the author was losing money, as there was no money made on the "free" download. The value of each lead, however, was predicted to be somewhere between $5.00 and $9.00, depending on how well this book ultimately sells online. With this in mind, the Google program was working quite well for the author (perhaps you even found this book via a paid placement on Google or a related Web site).

Referring Sources and "Marketing Mix"

Much like campaigns and campaign analysis, understanding which referring sources are sending you traffic is critical to developing a clear picture of how you acquire visitors with an eye towards converting them. Keeping track of which referring domains, URLs, search engines and search keywords drive the greatest volume of traffic to your site is an important first step in being able to develop new online marketing programs and partnerships. Unlike most campaigns, referring traffic from domains is often free and simply a function of how the Internet is designed to work—Web sites link to other Web sites.

When you are considering the source of traffic there are two major incoming sources—sites that somehow link to your Web site and people who type your URL directly into a browser. Within each of these there are subtypes. For sites linked to yours these subtypes are search engines and those sites that are not search engines (such as your partners and the online media). For people who type your URL directly into a browser there are those who enter the URL each time and those who have your site "bookmarked" (listed as a "favorite site").

The relationship between "directly referred traffic," "search engines" and normally referred traffic is a function of your overall marketing program (your "marketing mix"). The more offline marketing you do that prominently displays your URL the greater the effect on your "directly referred traffic." The more energy and money you spend on search engine optimization and placement programs the greater the effect on your "search engine" referrals. The greater the effort you put into online marketing and partnerships the greater the effect on normally referred domains/URLs. The particular blend of these three areas that is right for your business depends entirely on your brand, your focus and the amount of money you have to spend. Most small businesses find that it is easiest and least expensive to focus on the latter as, comparatively speaking, online marketing is much less expensive than offline marketing. Most truly large businesses (think Fortune 500) find it easiest to focus on the former, having built their businesses on "old world" advertising and marketing. Everyone struggles, more or less, with search engine optimization, although the recent addition of cost-per-click/pay-per-click and paid placement programs from the major search engines have allowed businesses to enter into search results in a way that make it easy to calculate return on investment.

Regardless of your particular marketing mix there is always room for improvement and optimization. Understanding the relationship between traffic driven by marketing campaigns and otherwise referred traffic is the first step in the optimization process. Making sure you understand the concepts presented in *Web Analytics Demystified* is critical to optimizing you marketing mix because, as the old adage states, you cannot change what you do not measure and you should not measure what you will not change.

Referring Domains

The referring domains discussed in this section fall into the broad category of those Web sites that are not search engines that link directly to your Web site and thereby drive traffic to you. There are many reasons these links have been created, including:

- The referrer is a partner of yours and you have worked directly with them to create the link.
- The referrer is a list of some kind and they've included you in the list.
- The referrer is a content site of some kind and they have written about you.
- The referrer is unhappy and they have included a link to create headaches for you.

In actuality the list of reasons, both good and bad, that a Web site may link to yours is endless. The advantage of closely watching referring domains as they help you acquire visitors is that it may allow you to capture an opportunity—or head off a liability.

Referring domains, at least the top three to five, are an excellent addition to an acquisition KPI report.

How to Calculate

All known Web analytics applications have some type of referring domain reporting included and typically report either the number of visits or visitors from the referring domain. Please consult your application's documentation for specifics on how to generate this report.

Dependence

The only dependence for an application to report on referring domains is the presence of a referring URL in the header of the document request. In most instances where there is no referring URL in the header of the request, the request has been made directly (a visitor typed in the URL or used a browser bookmark). Occasionally this is not the case—some forwarding applications and methods for redirection strip the original header when the URL request is passed along. The most common culprit is an "HTTP 3xx redirect request" (see http://www.w3.org/Protocols/rfc2616/rfc2616-sec10.html) or a custom, server-side redirect script that, rather than passing along the original referrer now includes the redirect script as the referring source.

In instances where the referrer is incorrectly removed the only recourse (known to this author) is to attempt to either insert the original referring URL back into the HTTP request or to pass the URL along to the application after the redirect. Failure to do so will result in skewed data regarding referring domains and URLs, sometimes dramatically so, often completely invalidating the information contained in a referring domains or referring URLs report.

Usage

The primary use for a referring domains report is to ensure that you know *why* another Web site is sending you traffic. Any time a Web site sends you traffic you have the opportunity to establish a relationship with the visitors as they arrive. Technically you are already acquiring them but, as you have already read, simply acquiring these visitors is not enough. If you understand what it was that brought the visitor to you, you can work to continue to connect with the visitor along those lines, and perhaps drive the visitor to convert.

Most Web analytics packages will report two related metrics when discussing referring domains—referring URL and entry page. The referring URLs are the exact pages on the referring Web site that contained links to your site, the entry pages are the pages on your Web site that the referring URL sent traffic to. The general strategy is to examine the referring URLs to understand what the traffic partner is saying about your Web site that would compel a visitor to click the link to your site, and then make sure that the content on the associated entry pages is consistent with what the partner is saying. The worst-case scenario is where you have worked with an online partner to craft a message that drives a large volume of visitors to your Web site but you send those visitors to a page that has nothing to do with the message. Situations like this create confusion in the minds of online visitors and decrease the likelihood that those visitors will convert.

Ideally you are always working to create a message in your marketing materials and program that is consistent when visitors arrive at your Web site. Regardless of whether it is email, banner ads, text in cost-per-click/pay-per-click advertising, language on partner sites, listings in search placements, and so on. that you are using to reach people, acquisition only leads to conversion when the message is consistent (or at least not *inconsistent*) with the information you present when the visitor arrives at your Web site.

Interpretation

Most analytics packages report on the referring domain and the number of either visits or visitors that come from each. Typically a referring domain report will include line items for "Directly Referred Traffic" and "Search Engines" and also perhaps "Internal Traffic" depending on the exact package you use. In most cases, "directly referred traffic" refers to visits or visitors arriving from people typing your URL into a browser directly or using a bookmarked link in their Web browser. Often this "directly referred traffic" can be thought of as a measure of the overall strength of your brand and your offline brand awareness marketing.

It is worthwhile to watch the traffic from referring domains for large spikes or dips in the volume of traffic your top domains are sending. A large increase can indicate a change in placement or message, a large decrease can mean the same. Either way, any changes should be investigated by drilling down into the associated referring URLs and entry pages these URLs are driving traffic to.

Example

BackcountryStore.com pays close attention to its incoming traffic to keep track of the effect of its search engine optimization (SEO) programs, brand awareness and the business relationships it has established. To this end, they watch a "% Change" report that is provided by their Web analytics application frequently, watching for sites that exhibit a high degree of movement, either up or down (Figure 38).

	Name	% Change
1.	Search Engines	7.54% ⬆
2.	Bookmarks or directly referred URLs	-14.50% ⬇
3.⊙	thenorthface.com	10.34% ⬆
4.⊙	backpackreviews.com	13.61% ⬆
5.⊙	northface.com	-5.32% ⬇
6.⊙	bizrate.com	-4.65% ⬇
7.⊙	dealtime.com	3.80% ⬆
8.⊙	msn.com	34.74% ⬆
9.⊙	epinions.com	4.00% ⬆
10.⊙	arcteryx.com	3.40% ⬆
11.⊙	com.com	4.41% ⬆
12.⊙	shopping.com	5.26% ⬆

Figure 38: Domains referring traffic to BackcountryStore.com and the percent change from comparable timeframes. WebSideStory, BackcountryStore.com's Web analytics vendor, refers to visitors who have typed the URL directly into the browser as having come from "Bookmarks or directly referred URLs."

In the report shown in Figure 38 you can see traffic volumes decreasing quite sharply from three domains ("winternext.com," "tgoemall.com" and "hot-deals-online.com") and increasing dramatically from "store4outdoors.com." While the marketing group at BackcountryStore.com would most certainly look at what may have changed with these domains, they will also work to understand why traffic from search engines and visitors who know their URL are down 9.9 percent and 6.1 percent respectively. Especially for the search engine traffic, BackcountryStore.com depends on visitors being able to find them online when they are looking for outdoor gear.

Related Metrics

As mentioned, referring URLs, search engines and entry pages are all closely tied to referring domains, being either a peer data type (as in the case of search engines) or an associated data type useful for drilling down (as in the case of referring URLs and entry pages). Additionally, referring domains often include those domains that you are running online marketing on and so many of the campaign analysis metrics are closely related as well.

Referring URLs

Referring URLs are similar to referring domains in that referring URLs are the source of data from which referring domains are derived. Referring domains are typically presented something like Figure 39:

	Search Engines	Visits
1.	Google	2,952
2.	Yahoo	1,596
3.	MSN	1,113
4.	CNET Search.com	295
5.	AOL NetFind	285
6.	Google Canada	151
7.	AltaVista	94
8.	Ask Jeeves	88

Figure 39: Sample of traffic from major search engines to BackcountryStore.com.

For any line item, these entries are usually derived from something like Figure 40:

	Name	Visits
1.	www.google.com/search?hl=en&ie=UTF-8&oe=UTF-8&q=patagonia	340
2.	www.google.com/search?hl=en&ie=UTF-8&oe=UTF-8&q=burton	299
3.	www.google.com/search?hl=en&ie=UTF-8&oe=UTF-8&q=burton snowboards	257
4.	www.google.com/search?hl=en&ie=UTF-8&oe=UTF-8&q=shaun white	239
5.	www.google.com/search?hl=en&ie=UTF-8&oe=UTF-8&q=the north face	221
6.	www.google.com/search?hl=en&ie=UTF-8&oe=UTF-8&q=backcountry store	211
7.	www.google.com/search?hl=en&ie=UTF-8&oe=UTF-8&q=leatherman	191

Figure 40: Example referring URLs that are the basis for the referring search engines shown in Figure 39.

As you can see, the referring domain is simplified from the original referring URL and aggregated. In some instances you will need to get back to the referring URL, most often to see the message or link that drove traffic to your Web site as described under referring domains. A referring URL report is the most common way to access this information.

How to Calculate

All known Web analytics applications have some type of referring domain URLs included and typically report either the number of visits or visitors from the referring URL; please consult your application's documentation for specifics on how to generate this report.

Dependence

Referring URLs have the same dependence as referring domains. Please see the discussion of "dependence" under referring domains.

Usage

Typically when faced with the choice between examining referring domains and referring URLs you should start with referring domains. In many examples, especially search engines, there are an infinite number of possible referring URLs for any single referring domain. Rather than sift and sort through hundreds of individual referring URLs it is better to examine the information at the highest level (the domain) and delve deeper if necessary.

As described under referring domains, the primary use for a referring URL report is to determine exactly what marketing message visitors were responding to when they decided to click to your Web site. You would want to drill-down on this to ensure that the message is consistent with the information you provide when a visitor actually arrives at the site. Inconsistency in the message from the click to the visit is one of the places where abandonment most frequently occurs. You get the "nope, that's not it…" syndrome, where a visitor clicks to your Web site but does not immediately see what they are looking for and so they click back and keep searching.

Interpretation

Similar to referring domains, referring URLs are reported in visits or visitors. This metric tells you the exact number of visits or visitors coming to your site from each individual URL. Referring URLs are usually used as a diagnostic tool rather than a regularly observed performance indicator.

Navigation Path by Referring Source

Navigation path (or "click stream") by referring source is a metric offered by some analytics packages and is often referred to in a variety of different ways. The gist of "paths from referrer" is that you have some way to search the exhaustive set of navigational paths followed by each visitor in each session and relate those paths to the original referring source (be it a domain or search engine). The value of doing so is that you can, without any type of campaign identification, begin to quantify the value of a particular referring source.

How to Calculate

Navigation path by referring source is a metric that some Web analytics packages have and others simply do not and those that do have wide variations in their sophistication. Ideally your application provides a simple interface to search or specify which pages you are interested in and which referrers you'd like to examine. If your particular application does not support this functionality but does support campaign analysis of some kind you should be fine. If your application supports neither you may want to consider switching applications.

Dependence

Aside from a dependence on the application supporting this functionality the only major dependence is on the "completeness" of the dataset supporting the analysis. If the application you use does not keep an exhaustive list of all navigation paths traversed by visitors you run the risk of making decisions based on incomplete data. There are many reasons that this dataset may be incomplete—log files may have been rotated out or you may be missing data from servers in a clustered environment, your ASP may not keep "all paths," the data may be too large to analyze completely, and so on.

Before undergoing an analysis using this type of tool it is a good idea to make sure you know how complete the supporting data model is so you can estimate the accuracy if you are working from a sample.

Usage

Providing you have access to a complete set of data you can begin to examine which referring sources drive traffic to key pages on your Web site. As an example, you could search a report like this for all "referred" navigational paths that traverse a key page, perhaps the "purchase confirmation" page on a commerce site. This would allow you to quickly determine which referring partners are sending you the most qualified traffic in the absence of commerce analysis tools like those discussed in Chapter 9.

You can also search these paths for a particular referring source and work to understand the most common paths and goals for these referred visitors, providing you the opportunity to look for trends and patterns that may inform future marketing activities with that partner or site.

Interpretation

Most often navigation path by referring source is reported in visits and aggregates similar paths. So if 30 people came from "yahoo.com," landed on "page A" then clicked to "page B" and "page C" you might see something like Figure 41:

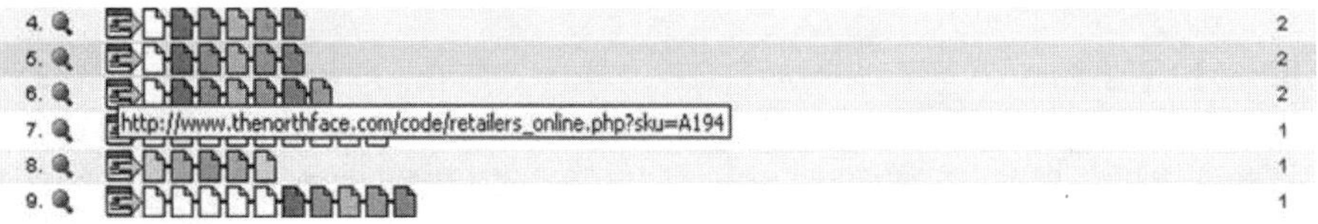

Figure 41: Example of navigation path from referring source from the BackcountryStore.com Web site.

A common problem with any navigational path or "click-stream" reporting is visualization and aggregation. The most common paths to multiple visitors are very short, say three-page paths. When paths get longer it is much more likely that these paths will begin to become unique. While it is reasonable to mine click-stream data for short paths and path fragments it is often unclear how much value there is in knowing about detailed activity for a small number of visitors. In most applications the response to this issue is to provide a "process analysis" toolset similar or same as that described in Chapter 6.

Search Engines

Search engines are another large category of referred traffic (not "directly referred") that is coming specifically from those Web sites commonly referred to as "search engines." While this list is potentially very, very large, it commonly includes the major search engines such as Google, MSN Search, Yahoo! Search, AOL, AlltheWeb, Ask Jeeves, HotBot and Lycos (a more complete list can be found at SearchEngineWatch.com). Companies commonly spend large sums of money in an attempt to increase and improve their ranking in these search engines, often referred to as "search engine optimization" or "SEO," and the desire to have optimized placement in search engines has evolved pay-per-click and pay-for-placement options from the major engines. Clearly traffic from search engines is tremendously important to online marketing and the Internet in general.

Because of the advent of pay-per-click and pay-for-placement options from the major search engines it is important to consider the mix of traffic when you examine the traffic from a given search engine. Years ago we considered all traffic from search engines to be "organic" and resulting from normal indexing as opposed to be from a paid placement. Organic placement was optimized by either making good Web pages that were well indexed by the search engine "robots" or by somehow tricking the search engine "robots" into thinking that your pages were good/relevant/and so on. Now, nearly all of the popular search engines offer some type of paid placement, either pay-per-click or pay-for-placement. The issue is that traffic from each type of program (organic or paid) is grouped together in a search engines referral report.

Because, hopefully, the Web analytics application you are using supports the types of campaign analysis tools described in Chapter 8, you should definitely be tagging or identifying any paid search engine placement to help you isolate paid placement from organic. Doing so will allow you to determine how well indexed you are normally in the search engines. Knowing this helps you understand how much traffic you can likely expect from this piece of your "marketing mix."

How to Calculate

Most known Web analytics packages automatically report on traffic from search engines by engine based on visits or visitors.

Dependence

Search engines have the same dependence on data described under referring domains. Additionally, the individual engines that are included in a "search engines" traffic report must be determined and maintained somehow. An important question to ask your analytics provider is how the list of known search engines is generated and who maintains this list.

Usage

The major reason for understanding search engine traffic is to ensure that any money you spend on search engine optimization and paid inclusion is paying off. While a search engines report won't tell you what visitors are doing when they land on your Web site it will help you understand the total volume of traffic you get from each engine. Knowing that conversion is a function of the pool of visitors you have to potentially convert, monitoring the volume of traffic is important.

Interpretation

Similar to referring domains, watching traffic volumes from search engines is important to ensure that you are getting visitors from these important sources of traffic and to make sure that you understand why any large spikes or dips are occurring. Any time you spend time, money or energy to optimize your site's placement in a search engine (or all search engines) you hope and expect to see an increase in the volume of traffic coming from this source. Similarly, if you are seeing a decrease, either sudden or gradual, in the volume of traffic from any engine that had been sending you traffic previously, it is worthwhile to explore the reason for this decrease and the potential effect this will have on your online business.

Example

As shown in Figure 38, BackcountryStore.com pays close attention to the volume of traffic referred to its Web site from search engines and engages actively in search engine optimization (SEO) activity. Regularly, the marketing staff at BackcountryStore.com will use a report similar to that shown in Figure 42 to make sure that they know how changes in traffic volumes from the major search engines affect their revenue stream.

Search Engines	% Change
1. Google	17.07% ⬆
2. Yahoo	5.74% ⬆
3. MSN	-2.11% ⬇
4. AOL NetFind	30.40% ⬆
5. CNET Search.com	19.35% ⬆
6. Google Canada	18.98% ⬆
7. Google Germany	11.60% ⬆
8. Netscape	18.54% ⬆
9. Ask Jeeves	23.43% ⬆
10. AltaVista	4.80% ⬆
11. Lycos	7.03% ⬆

Figure 42: Traffic to BackcountryStore.com from some of the major search engines showing the "% Change" in visits from each.

Without question, the report shown in Figure 43 provides much more important information to BackcountryStore.com about the traffic they get from search engines.

		Search Engine	Orders ▾	Revenue	Customers *	Visits	B/B%	Items	Shipping	ASP	%
1.	⊙	iwon	5		5		1.33%	10	$9.74	$124.15	0.23%
2.	⊙	Excite	5		5		0.84%	8	$67.30	$193.27	0.23%
3.	⊙	CompuServe	3		3		0.71%	3	$21.70	$148.11	0.14%
4.	⊙	alltheweb	3		3		0.94%	5	$114.46	$295.25	0.14%
5.	⊙	Google Switzerland	3		3		0.52%	6	$99.75	$221.38	0.14%
6.	⊙	LookSmart	2		2		1.55%	5	$11.20	$174.20	0.09%
7.	⊙	AOL UK	2		2		2.25%	4	$69.65	$208.42	0.09%
8.	⊙	Google Italy	2		2		0.26%	10	$112.35	$228.85	0.09%
9.	⊙	MetaCrawler	1		1		0.29%	1	$5.40	$56.21	0.05%
10.	⊙	Mamma	1		1		0.85%	2	$7.30	$51.90	0.05%
11.	⊙	efind	1		1		2.86%	1	$5.48	$164.95	0.05%

Figure 43: Search engine traffic to BackcountryStore.com that drives visitors to purchase (data provided by HitBox Commerce™). The "B/B%" column is the "browse-to-buy" ratio, an indicator of how likely visitors from each search engine are to purchase. The "Revenue" and "Visits" columns have been blurred to protect BackcountryStore.com's privacy.

By closely watching both the traffic volume and revenue driven by search engines, BackcountryStore.com is able to make the best use of search engine optimization and understand which activities work well and which do not.

Search Keywords and Phrases

The traffic that comes from each of the search engines carries important information about the intentions of the visitor you are hopefully about to acquire—the word or phrase that the visitor searched for just before they clicked to your Web site. Carried in via the referring URL, this text provides a great deal of insight into the information that the visitor hopes to find on your site. Ideally the page that the visitor lands on has information relevant to the word or phrase they used to find your site; if not you run the risk that the visitor will immediately back up to the search engine and find what they are looking for somewhere else.

Search keywords and phrases, at least the top five to ten, are an excellent addition to an acquisition KPI report.

How to Calculate

Most known Web analytics packages report on search keywords and phrases by visit or visitor. Ideally your analytics package will report on the entry pages to which each search engine is sending search keyword traffic, to provide insight into the quality of fit between the search and the resulting page.

Dependence

Search keywords have the same dependence on data described under search engines and referring domains. Additionally, the individual engines that are included in a "search engines" traffic report must be determined and maintained somehow in order to determine which URLs will contain keywords and phrases. An important question to ask your analytics provider is how the list of known search engines is generated and who maintains this list.

Usage

Search keywords and phrases are useful in that they are a direct reflection of what your visitors are thinking about or looking for when they click to your Web site. Depending on how your site is indexed in the major search engines and whether you are paying for placement via a pay-per-click program your site will appear at some location in each of the search engines. If you appear high enough in these listings you will inevitably acquire visitors from search engine listings. In an ideal world people would be searching for words and phrases that are consistent with your marketing messaging and goals; unfortunately this is not always the case. Often when you are reviewing a report on the top search terms and phrases driving traffic to your Web site you will likely think, "Now why did someone search for that?!"

Words and phrases that will appear in this list will typically fall into three categories: your brand name and URL, words you expect and words you do not expect. People search for your brand name and Web site URL for mysterious reasons—perhaps they are lazy and they have a search engine for a home page (Google, MSN, Yahoo!) so it is easier to type in your name or URL and hit "Search" than it is to type your URL into a browser directly. Without extensive focus groups it is likely that we will never know why visitors do this so you should simply know that this happens.

The second category, words and phrases that you do expect, typically includes the names of your products or brands that you sell, the kinds of services you provide, the type of information you offer, and so on. These are the words that you sincerely hope will help you acquire visitors because it means that your marketing programs are working and that when people think about "X" they are willing to consider you as a provider of "X." Too few or no visits from these words and phrases indicates that your site is poorly indexed and you should consider some kind of search engine optimization. Search engines have become a driving force in Internet marketing over the last few years and not being indexed or listed in search engines will put you at a severe disadvantage (considering that your competition is likely listed).

The third category, words and phrases you do not expect, are a source of opportunity and insight into how your visitors think. This group of terms can provide some insight into how you tell people about your company and offerings and how potential customers receive that message. Mining this list can help you to refine your message and future marketing materials to capitalize on emerging trends or changes in the competitive landscape.

Interpretation

Keyword and phrases reporting is typically done on a "per visit" or "per visitor" basis, much like each of the other referring source reports. An important factor to keep in mind when interpreting this report is that if you are making keyword purchases through one of the popular search marketing programs (Google, Overture) most likely your search results contain *both* the words and phrases you are purchasing and those that you simply get "organically" (without purchase). In most instances this is a good thing, allowing you to quickly see which words and phrases are driving the greatest volume of traffic to your Web site regardless of how those words show up in the search engines. If you do have mixed paid/organic search results it is a good idea to track the keywords and phrases you are purchasing using campaign analysis tools (see "Campaign Response Metrics" in this chapter and "Campaign Conversion" in Chapter 13).

Similar to other referring source metrics the important thing to watch for are dramatic changes in the volume of traffic being driven by search terms. A dramatic upward movement for a word or group of words can mean that you have been re-indexed by one or more search engines and that your new placement is more favorable. It can also mean that someone in your marketing group has started aggressively purchasing those words and phrases. The first example is good news since there is little or no cost with most search engine optimization (when done properly). The second example is potentially good news, providing visitors responding to those keyword purchases are doing something on your Web site that is making you more money than was spent on the keyword buys.

One strategy for interpretation is to take advantage of any search tools that your analytics package may have to group similar terms and phrases. Doing so can help you visualize any trends that may be emerging.

Example

In early 2002 the nice folks at BackcountryStore.com had noticed that a number of searches that were bringing visitors to their Web site implied that visitors were looking for paddleboats, kayaks and related gear. While they had some small items of this type available in their product selection they had not really considered stocking kayaks and paddle boats since they were A) expensive to purchase and ship and B) space-intensive to keep in stock. Still, there appeared to be a trend and so being the smart analytics users they are they started to monitor their internally executed searches for a similar trend.

Name	Page Views
Search for kayak	3,000
Search for kayaks	1,237
Search for kayak storage	194
Search for tandem kayak	163
Search for kayak wheels	158
Search for paddle	143
Search for kayak cart	133
Search for paddles	126
Search for sand paddle tires	109
Search for paddle boat covers	101
Search for kayak seat	100
Search for kayak rudder	99
Search for best price on kayak	95
Search for KAYAK	92
Search for kayak dolly	92
Search for kayak rack	91
Search for paddle tires	77
Search for inflatable kayak	73

Figure 44: Search terms from BackcountryStore.com's internal search that suggested that visitors were interested in buying paddle boats and gear from them online.

What they found was that significant numbers of visitors were in fact looking for these types of items (Figure 44), large enough numbers that a relatively modest conversion rate would yield a fairly profitable business selling paddle boats and gear through BackcountryStore.com. After working out the details, BackcountryStore.com was able to stock paddle boats and currently enjoys a healthy revenue stream from this line of business (Figure 45).

Figure 45: BackcountryStore.com's paddleboat category, prompted by referring search keyword and internal search activity.

Related Metrics

Search keywords and phrases are closely related to both search engines and referring domains/URLs in that they all share the same primary source of information (the referring URL). This metric should also be compared to campaign analysis metrics of response and conversion if you are purchasing cost-per-click/pay-per-click search results.

Notes on Search Engine Marketing and Search Engine Optimization

Search engine optimization and search engine marketing are big business, especially lately. At the time this book was being written, Jupiter Research had pegged the paid search market at $1.6 billion in 2003 after having grown almost 50 percent from 2002 (cyberatlas.internet.com). They also predict that online spending for search engine marketing will grow 20 percent year-over-year until 2008, at which point it will be a $4.3 billion dollar business accounting for roughly 30 percent of all online advertising. This, coupled with Yahoo!'s purchase of Overture (www.overture.com)—the organization that pioneered pay-for-performance search marketing in the late 1990s as GoTo.com—for more than $1.6 billion (ironically the same amount as Jupiter estimates for the entire market, www.seoconsultants.com), points to a long and very lucrative life for companies that provide pay-for-performance search engine marketing.

Why?

The answer, at least anecdotally, is that search engine marketing works. It is easy to buy, easy to understand and, thanks to Web analytics applications that support campaign analysis, easy to measure return on investment. Go ahead and Google the phrase "case study on search engine marketing" and you will get pages of results discussing why search engine optimization and search marketing is an effective tool for growing an online business. Or, take a look at what the folks at Marketing Sherpa have to say on the subject (http://library.marketingsherpa.com). Essentially what you will find is that the pay-for-performance model of search engine marketing is an extremely valuable tool for connecting people's needs with the companies that can help them—it's that simple.

Moreover, because you can easily measure the response and conversion rate for any word or phrase you bid on and purchase using most popular Web analytics applications you can essentially remove all of the guesswork from this type of online marketing; words and phrases either make you more money than they cost you or you simply bid less. The folks at HitBox have nearly completely automated this system. You simply identify the traffic as coming from a "keyword network" and the application does the rest, measuring the response and conversion rate for all purchased keywords automatically. The final step in this process is to tie conversion information to a commerce measurement package to allow online marketing managers to know exactly how much revenue each individual term drives and the distribution of products actually sold (to calculate margins on product sales).

So assuming you have tools to measure which words bring you visitors who ultimately provide some kind of return on investment, why would you not invest in keywords at Google, Overture or a similar program? The unfortunate answer may ultimately be that you cannot afford to bid on words that bring you enough traffic to be worth your while. Consider the calculation outlined under "cost-per-acquisition / cost-per-click" in this chapter. If you run numbers through the equations described in that metric you will learn that there is an upper limit on the amount you can afford to pay for each click. As search engine marketing continues to become more popular the likelihood is that many of the terms relevant to your online business, especially generic terms, will simply be priced out of your reach by companies that are willing to pay more. Much like in the time of banner advertising, when some "deep pocket" companies drove the cost-per-thousand (CPM) up on popular destination and portal sites, the same is likely to happen on search engines as we approach the saturation point.

The only recommendation the author has on this point is to get in now and start figuring out which words work for you and which ones do not. Capture as much market share from those terms as possible, convert those visitors and retain them as best you can. Then, as terms are slowly priced out of your reach, use your analytics tools to explore other, less expensive terms and focus your energies there. By continually watching the acquisition, conversion and retention metrics for search engine keywords you can easily determine where your money is best spent (essentially, to quote the great bard Kenny Rogers, "know when to hold, know when to fold 'em …")

Key Performance Indicators Recommended for Measuring Acquisition

While the majority of the key performance indicators recommended for measuring reach are simply percentages and ratios, within acquisition we start to see the emergence of what are often referred to as "string statistics," such as referring domains and search keywords and phrases, as valuable indicators.

The following are excellent acquisition performance indicators and should be considered for inclusion in regular reporting regardless of business model:

- Percent new visitors to alert you to significant changes in your new visitor acquisition programs and their effect on your overall traffic.
- Average number of page views per visit for all visitors to ensure that your content consumption stays relatively stable. Stability in this metric is an indirect measurement of the user experience on your Web site.
- Page "stickiness" for your home page and key entry points into the site to watch for dramatic changes in "stick" and immediate bailout.
- Response rates for all active campaigns to determine when a campaign has effectively run its course and needs to be replaced, refreshed or simply ended.
- Cost-per-acquisition and cost-per-click for active campaigns to ensure that you are not paying more than you can afford for any campaign. You should create a column for "maximum CPA/CPC" so that you can clearly see if you have exceeded that limit.
- The top three to five referring domains and volume of traffic you receive from each to watch for changes in referring traffic patterns.
- The top five to ten search keywords and phrases and the volume of traffic you receive from each to watch for changes in visitor interest as expressed by external search.
- Average time spent on site and percent of visits under 90 seconds should be watched closely and correlated to any inbound marketing activity.

Keep in mind that each of these will not be necessarily interesting as raw numbers; the most important aspect of any performance indicator is the relationship between the current and previous measurement. Simply a leading indicator of changes happening, each of these KPIs is designed to alert you to the fact that some aspect of your visiting traffic has changed and more research is warranted.

CHAPTER 13 MEASURING CONVERSION

"Every Web site is different, and nobody is selling exactly the same thing in the same way to the same audience. We've found over 1,100 variables that affect conversion rates on a Web site, and those variables can be broken down into even more detail."
Bryan Eisenberg in *Converting Search Engine Traffic*

For most businesses with an online presence that is used to help grow the overall business—especially those businesses that exist solely online—getting a visitor to somehow "convert" is the *rasion d'etre*. Regardless of what the act of conversion actually is, it is this act that keeps the business growing and moving towards profitability (or increased profitability). While many Web sites express that they seek to reach and acquire traffic in order to "build brand" it is the author's opinion that this is A) not enough and B) not likely to be a successful long-term goal for one's online marketing programs unless the company has extremely deep pockets. The customer life cycle is applicable to many, if not all, business models for a good reason and conversion is the critical step in this process.

Measuring conversion is really about measuring abandonment, the people that start any given activity but for whatever reason do not complete it. Abandonment, described in greater detail below, is an expression of a visitor's lack of commitment to or understanding of the process you are trying to get them to complete. Online visitors, except in very special situations (such as where the offer is simply too good to pass up), will seize nearly any opportunity to bail out of a process and seek fulfillment elsewhere. Even though published conversion rates are creeping upwards as Web site operators become more adept at using analytics data like that described in this book to improve online processes, industry average "site-wide conversion rates" still hover around 3 percent (Shop.org). Assuming that your online business exists to either sell something or provide some kind of valuable information, if you are "average," is making a sale to three in a hundred people good enough for you?

The issue of industry average comparisons brings up a very important point on the topic of conversion—you should only compare your conversion rate to itself in an effort to increase said rate. While it is very tempting to try and determine what your competitors' conversion rates are and then beat that rate it is most likely an exercise in futility. First, you'd be lucky to be able to figure out what your competitors' conversion rates are as smart businesses keep these numbers secret and only share vague information about increases or decreases. Second, unless you market the exact same way to the exact same audience, have the same products at the same prices, and so on, there is no reason to make this comparison. Smart business managers will focus on making use of the continuous improvement process as described in Chapter 2 to design, implement and measure changes with the goal of increasing key conversion rates without regard to published averages and competitive information.

Which Conversion Rates Should Be Measured?

As stated in Chapter 8 there are many different conversion rates that can be measured and they exist for every Web site regardless of business model. The most obvious activity to measure to completion/conversion is the online purchase process. Whether you are selling shoes, CDs or airline tickets, applying the continuous improvement process to the online purchase process is one of the fastest paths to achieving return on investment for your investment in any analytics application. That being said, there are three major categories of conversions that can and should be measured online:

- Activities leading to an online purchase
- Activities leading to the collection of "valuable" information, such as registration
- Activities leading the visitor to information that will reduce operational costs, such as calls to your technical support group, and so on

Each of these activities can be easily defined as a series of discreet steps, although any single step may contain more than a single page. This definition in tandem with the process measurement tools described in Chapter 6 will enable accurate measurement of abandonment and conversion rates help you improve these rates.

With the categories above in mind, there are a handful of common activities that are worth discussing regarding abandonment and conversion.

Site-wide Conversion Rate

The site-wide conversion rate, also commonly referred to as the "order conversion rate," or "purchase conversion rate," is the standard conversion rate that is often used in conversion rate studies. Calculated as orders (or appropriate goal) divided by total site-wide visits or visitors, this conversion rate will give you a feel for how well you convince visitors to complete goals regardless of their entry point on your Web site.

Home to Purchase

The home page to purchase rate is the number of orders taken divided by the number of visitors (or visits) to a site's home page. For an online store this would indicate visitors traversing the following rough path:

1. Home page
2. Product or category page(s)
3. Shopping cart
4. Checkout
5. Order complete

Between the home page and the completed order there can be any number of pages visited in any order. Essentially what this activity captures is the number of visitors who enter the site via the "most common" entry point and the abandonment rate for those visitors through the generalized purchase process.

Search to Purchase

Search to purchase is a variation on the "home to purchase" activity for those sites that rely heavily on internal search to guide visitors towards online purchases. This is essentially the same as the "home to purchase" activity except that the first step would be a "search results" page:

1. Search results
2. Product or category page(s)
3. Shopping cart
4. Checkout
5. Order complete

The reason you'd start measuring this activity at the "search results" page and not a search form is that most sites now offer search forms on most, if not all, pages. If you have a single dedicated page for search that visitors need to intentionally click to in order to search you would make that the first page in a six-step process.

Measuring "search to purchase" and comparing that to A) your "home to purchase" process and B) your overall "all visits to all orders" conversion rate will help you assign value to search on your Web site. It is not uncommon for sites having robust, accurate and well-presented search results to have a higher conversion rate for "search to purchase" than "home to purchase" and the site-wide average (keeping in mind that this activity contributes orders to the site-wide average).

"Special Offer" to Purchase

"Special offer to purchase" is again nearly the same as "home to purchase" and "search to purchase" except that here you would be measuring the effect of different merchandising and pricing options. The rough path describing this activity:

1. Special offer or pricing page(s)
2. Shopping cart
3. Checkout
4. Order complete

This activity as described assumes that you have an "add to cart" option on the pages in step 1. If you don't you'd likely want to add a step to capture that information, helping you to see how likely visitors are to be interested enough in your special offers or pricing to actually put an item in the shopping cart.

Lead Generation

The attempt to entice visitors to provide your business with some type of personal information is arguably the most popular activity on the Internet. This process is essentially the measurement of abandonment from the point where you tell the visitor why they should provide this information to the point where you have successfully gathered that information. The shortest version of this process is:

1. Provide form and incentive to fill it out
2. Thank the visitor for providing the information

In reality this process is more often something like:

1. Tell the visitor why they should complete the process
2. Form 1
3. Form 2
4. Form 3
5. Thank the visitor for providing the information

You can see the value in measuring abandonment through this activity, especially for longer processes. Imagine in the second example above that you implement your particular Web analytics package's version of process measurement and discover that you have 50 percent abandonment between "form 2" and "form 3." If you are practicing continuous improvement you will immediately re-examine "form 2" to make sure that you really *need* each piece of information you ask for. If the answer is "no," you should redesign the form to only ask for information you *must have*, deploy the changes and measure the effect on abandonment at this step and on the overall conversion rate.

Web Analytics Tip: How to Ask Visitors for Information and Get Results

In the author's experience, the single most common reason that visitors abandon lead generation processes is the request for intrusive or seemingly irrelevant information. Regarding the former, unless you are a financial institution you should never ask a visitor for their social security number or mother's maiden name, ever. With reports of identity theft on the rise the likelihood that a stranger will provide this information willingly is extremely low. Regarding the latter, consider that visitors understand that nothing good comes for free on the Internet—they are likely to provide some information to get something that has perceived value. That being said, there appears to be an anecdotal correlation between the number of form fields you ask a visitor to complete and the likelihood they will abandon the form. Marketers always seem to want to ask questions like "How did you hear about us?" and "How many people do you supervise?"—questions that are very easy to answer with garbage and may simply make the form look too long to bother completing.

In general, unless you are offering some amazing deliverable that a visitor is unlikely to be able to get elsewhere, following these simple rules will help you improve completion for this type of activity:

- Do not ask for any information that is not *absolutely required*, period.
- Unless you are a trusted brand and a financial institution, never ask for any personally identifiable information that could lead to identity theft. If you are a financial institution only ask for this information if the visitor has intentionally started a process.
- If the number of required fields is especially large, consider breaking the form up into a small number of logically grouped questions over a number of pages. Try and ensure that each of these pages is quick to load and clearly identify for the visitor how much of the process they have completed (such as "Step 2 of 4").
- If possible, perform client-side form validation rather than forcing the page to reload to display any problems with the information the visitor has provided. Client-side form validation saves visitors time and reduces the risk that other required form fields will be cleared (password fields are the most common problem).
- Do not ask for any information that is not *absolutely required*, period.

As you can see, the most important thing is to not ask for "optional" information unless you're offering the most amazing thing ever and it is absolutely free of charge. Following these simple rules should help you increase your registration and form completion rates significantly.

Navigation to Important Information

The process of navigating to important information is the most generic activity of all since you can easily classify a purchase confirmation page as "important information." Still, it is worth treating this process as special for the legions of Web sites that exist to help visitors find information in frequently asked question (FAQ) documents. In this model, the visitor is likely following a flow similar to:

1. Support site home page
2. Page containing lists of support categories
3. Page containing lists of commonly asked questions
4. Page containing a specific answer to an FAQ

While your site may have a completely different series of pages the idea is to measure the flow of visitors moving along sequential, required steps towards specific information. The reason you'd measure abandonment and conversion along a path like this is that theoretically there is some advantage to your visitors finding this information. While there are many estimates for the operational costs associated with maintaining support staff nearly every analyst agrees that self-service via the Internet is the most cost-effective solution for providing support. This statement is only true if visitors can actually find information on your Web site, hence the need to measure flow from less to more specific information.

Using Process Measurement Tools

With all of the above in mind the only challenge that remains is to identify A) which processes on your Web site you need to measure and B) how the particular Web analytics application you have allows you to do that. Some questions you may want to ask when deciding which processes you need to measure include:

- When visitors complete the process does your business make money?
- If visitors fail to complete the process might they pick up the phone and call you instead?
- When visitors complete the process do you know more about them and can you market directly to them in the future?
- If visitors fail to complete the process might they complete a similar process on your competitor's Web site?
- Have you spent money on an enabling step in the process for which you need to quantify your return on investment?

If you answer "yes" to any of these questions that process is an excellent candidate for active measurement. Once you have made the decision to measure a process the next step is to setup your application to do so. The best advice the author can give you regarding setup is to contact your application vendor and explain to them what you are trying to measure. Make sure they understand you would like to be able to measure visitor flow through a sequential process and make measurements based on visits (best) or visitors (second best).

Metrics to Help Measure Conversion

Once you have decided what processes to measure and how to measure them, the following metrics will help you understand visitor success and failure in each.

Conversion Rates

The conversion rate for any process is the critical measurement of how likely visitors are to complete the processes. From conversion rate you can estimate visitor satisfaction, the overall effect of your marketing campaigns and the likelihood that your online business will be successful.

Conversion rates are one of the most valuable performance indicators that should be tracked on a regular basis

How to Calculate

For any multi-step process you are measuring, the conversion rate for the process is simply:

```
COMPLETIONS / STARTS = CONVERSION RATE
```

Keep in mind that there are macro conversion rates, such as ratio of all orders to all visitors to the Web site, and micro conversion rates, such as the number of leads generated from respondents to a single campaign or campaign component. It is very likely that you will measure a number of different conversion rates on your Web site.

Also keep in mind that when you are making a conversion rate measurement you want to use "like" metrics, that is, visits for both the numerator *and* denominator, and not visits for the numerator and page views for the denominator.

Dependence

The major dependence for measuring conversion rate is being able to get accurate and similar numbers for both the number of "completers" and "starters." Some examples of similar data types for conversion rate measurements include:

- Visits to final step / visits to first step
- Visitors to final step / visitors to first step
- Orders / Visitors
- Orders / Visits (both visits and visitors are unique measurements)
- Registrations / Visitors or Visits

Conversely, some examples of dissimilar data types include:

- Visits to final step / page views to first step
- Visits to final step / visitors to first step
- Orders / page views
- Registrations / page views

In general if is not recommended to use page views for any conversion rate measurement because page views are easily inflated (page reloads inflate page view stats). Unless page views are the *only* metric available to your analytics program they should not be used.

Usage

Conversion rate measurements are most frequently used to determine the rolling success of both the Web site and individual processes contained in it. As one of the most valuable key performance indicators, conversion rates should be watched daily to ensure that marketing activities continue to reach qualified visitors and bring them to the Web site. Any dramatic change in conversion rates should be immediately researched to determine what caused a rise or a fall in the rate.

Interpretation

Conversion rates describe the percentage of people who successfully complete a designed process. So if the conversion rate for a process is reported as 10 percent this tells you that one in ten visitors completed the process.

Abandonment Rates

Abandonment rates for any process describe the number of visitors who fail to move along successive required steps in that process, typically measured on a step-to-step basis. Measuring the number of visitors lost from step to step is extremely important to the continuous improvement processes—knowing which steps in any process visitors bail out at high rates is the single best way to focus resources towards improving overall conversion for that process.

How to Calculate

The calculation for abandonment rate should be made for each step in a multiple-step process. So if you are measuring the conversion rate for a five-step process you should also be using the process measurement tools that your Web analytics package to measure four different abandonment rates; between steps one and two, steps two and three, steps three and four, and steps four and five. Depending on whether you are using visits or visitors to make process analysis measurements, the calculation is (using visits as an example):

```
1 —(NUMBER OF VISITS AT CURRENT STEP / NUMBER OF VISITS AT
PREVIOUS STEP) = ABANDONMENT RATE FOR CURRENT STEP
```

As you can see there is no abandonment rate for the first step in any multiple-step process since there is no "previous step."

Dependence

Abandonment rates have similar dependence as conversion rates, using similar types of data measured over same timeframes.

Usage

For any multiple-step process abandonment rates are critical to know how to improve the processes conversion rate. It is one thing to know what the conversion rate is for an activity or processes, it is another to know at which point visitors are deciding to no longer move along in the process. Knowing which pages or steps in a process contribute most significantly to loss is the first step in stemming that loss and increasing the conversion rate. Abandonment rate measurement is critical to the continuous improvement process, as described in Chapter 2.

In general, when you are able to accurately calculate abandonment rates for any given step in a process you want to ask yourself whether there are marketing or process changes that you could make to pages in that step to encourage more visitors to move to the next step. Important questions to ask include:

- Are there forms in this step that may be asking for too much, unnecessary or personal information?
- Is the action or activity you are asking the visitor to complete at this step easy to identify? Are buttons obvious?
- Is the marketing material clear and compelling so that visitors are likely to begin or continue the process?
- Is the page quick to load and consistent in look and feel to previous pages in the process?

In a situation where you are using the continuous improvement process you may also want to run an A/B test on the existing site and the changed site to ensure that any changes you make have lower abandonment than the current site. See Chapter 6 for more information on how A/B testing makes use of abandonment and conversion rates.

Interpretation

If an abandonment rate between two steps is reported as 85 percent this tells you that 85 in 100 visitors failed to move from step to step. But with an 85percent abandonment rate, you know that 15 in 100 visitors *did* successfully move from step to step.

Campaign Conversion Metrics

As discussed in Chapter 12, measuring campaigns as they drive traffic to your Web site is extremely important. Perhaps more important is measuring how these acquired visitors convert from simply being browsers to being "connected" to your online business. The following are conversion metrics specific to marketing campaigns you may be running to drive traffic to your site:

Campaign Conversion Rate

The conversion rate for a campaign is the same as the general conversion rates discussed above but is specific to a single source of traffic to your Web site. Recall from Chapter 8 that any marketing vehicle that drives traffic to your Web site as a "campaign" and employ campaign analysis tools to measure the effect of that traffic. Measuring campaign conversion rates is critical in that, hopefully, you are trying to reach and acquire visitors to your Web site *not only* to build brand or name awareness but also to entice those visitors to complete a specific goal or series of goals. You should be measuring what campaign respondents are doing on your site in terms of their completion or conversion through those named goals.

Much as your Web site has many different processes that can be measured using the process measurement tools described in this book, a given campaign can have multiple goals. If you have a typical online business that is selling products and services on the Internet you likely have the following named goals somewhere on your Web site:

- Purchase process complete
- Item added to shopping cart
- Shopping cart checkout initiated
- Registration process complete
- Newsletter signup process complete
- "Send to a friend" functionality has been used

You may also have some "softer" goals on your site including:

- Three or more product views in a visit
- Five or more minutes spent browsing in a visit
- Two or more visits in a day, three or more visits in a week, and so on

When you are setting up your online marketing campaigns you want to be sure to give careful thought to what named goals you want to measure for your campaigns. Some vendors provide functionality to allow conversion through specific goals; others provide functionality to measure conversion through all named goals. Ideally the vendor you use will provide at least the ability to measure conversion through all named goals, as having only a single goal available to a given campaign is limiting and will not paint the complete picture about how visitors respond to your campaigns.

Campaign conversion rates are excellent conversion performance indicators, at least for actively running campaigns.

How to Calculate

The campaign conversion rate calculation is simply the number of visitors completing specific goals on your site divided by the number of respondents for visitors responding to a specific campaign:

```
CAMPAIGN COMPLETERS / CAMPAIGN RESPONDENTS = CAMPAIGN
CONVERSION RATE
```

It is important to note that you should only make this measurement for visitors responding to a specific campaign unless you are attempting to generate an "all campaigns" conversion rate.

Dependence

The major dependence in calculating campaign conversion rates is ensuring that your analytics application is able to provide you both the number of completers and the number of respondents to an individual campaign. You need to be careful not to mix and match campaigns and also be careful not to mix and match metrics, that is, do not use "completions" divided by "respondents" as the former is a non-unique metric, the equivalent of a page view, and the latter is a unique metric, the equivalent of a visitor.

Usage

The use of campaign conversion rates is similar to that of generalized conversion rates in that you should work towards improving these rates through judicious use of the continuous improvement process. Campaign conversion rates go one step further, however, and you should calculate the minimum conversion rate for any campaign you are paying for, using the strategy described in Chapter 12 under cost-per-click/cost-per-acquisition, and consider eliminating or ending campaigns that do not meet minimum performance requirements.

When you have multiple named goals, it is important to examine how visitors responding to a given campaign flow through these multiple goals. It is not uncommon for a marketing group to design a campaign intended to attract visitors who are likely to complete "goal A," and then actually attract visitors who complete "goals B and C." Having visibility into this activity allows marketers to learn from their mistakes and better understand the audience they reach and acquire from different marketing outlets.

Interpretation

Interpretation of campaign conversion rates is similar to that of generalized conversion rates, but specific to an individual campaign. If your campaign conversion rate is 2.5 percent this tells you that 25 visitors in 1,000 completed one or more of the different named goals you have established on your Web site.

Example

As mentioned in Chapter 12, the author engaged in online campaigning in the last half of 2003 in an attempt to drive visitors to the *Web Analytics Demystified* Web site and download the preview copy of this book. Email, vanity URLs and search keyword buying through Google were all employed to create leads.

	ID	Description	Responses	Leads	Conversion Rate
1.	KNL-Google	KNL-Google	237	29	12.23%
2.	EML-Updaters	EML-Updaters	39	17	43.58%
3.	OTL-Open Preview	OTL-Open Preview	105	11	10.47%
4.	OTL-Stanford	OTL-Stanford	11	6	54.54%

Figure 46: Campaign conversion rates from the author's Web site. The act of conversion at the time was the download of a preview copy of Web Analytics Demystified.

As you can see in Figure 46, most of the methods that the author used to generate leads were effective from a conversion rate standpoint. Even though very few visitors came through the "Stanford Publishing group" vanity URL (the "OTL-Stanford" campaign), more than half of these respondents downloaded a copy of the book. Even the Google campaigning, for which the author spent out-of-pocket against future returns on book sales, was effective, converting at more than 12 percent.

Cost-per-Conversion

Cost-per-conversion is a simple, yet important, calculation that helps marketing managers know their campaign money is being spent wisely. Much like cost-per-click and cost-per-acquisition, cost-per-conversion is a key performance indicator for campaigns.

How to Calculate

Cost-per-conversion is simply the running cost of the campaign to date divided by the number of conversions in the same timeframe:

```
COST OF CAMPAIGN TO DATE / CONVERSIONS TO DATE = COST-PER-
CONVERSION
```

It is important to be careful to ensure that you are using numbers from the same timeframe, so if the campaign has been running for 10 days and you have agreed to pay $30,000 for the month you would use the number of conversions from the last 10 days as a denominator and $10,000 as the numerator. If you were to use the full value of the campaign ($30,000) you would be artificially inflating the cost of the each conversion.

Dependence

The primary dependence for cost-per-conversion is using data from the same timeframe. Also, for some types of campaigns, cost can be difficult to calculate. In cost-per-click (CPC) campaigns you would need to calculate the total cost for the timeframe by multiplying the number of clicks by the cost-per-click unless you are able to get a daily summary of costs from some administrative interface.

Usage

Cost-per-conversion is used in conjunction with your marketing goals and known values for conversion and customer acquisition. Imagine the scenario where in the course of a month (30 days) you get 1,000 conversions and your average order value is $10.00. In this case the total (estimated) value of the campaign in the month is $10,000. Next imagine that the total advertising costs for the campaign were $30,000 for the month. The measured cost-per-conversion would be $30.00 per conversion, three times your average order value!

Interpretation

Since cost-per-conversion is a straightforward calculation it is perhaps more useful to look at a way to back into an appropriate cost-per-conversion:

1. Determine the average value of a conversion.
2. Determine the multiple you'd like to make from the campaign.
3. Divide the results from step 1 into the results from step 2. This is the maximum cost-per-conversion you should pay for this campaign.

For example:

1. Our average value of a conversion is $30.00.
2. We like to make a 5x multiple on our campaigns.
3. The most we can afford to pay for each conversion is $6.00.

If, when you calculate your cost-per-conversion for the campaign over time, you are paying more than $6.00 per conversion you know that you are paying more than your target spend on the campaign. If this is the case you can either A) decide to end the campaign or B) decide that the multiple you have picked is too aggressive and scale that back. If, in the example above you only wanted a 2x multiple you could pay up to $15.00 per conversion.

Example

The author of *Web Analytics Demystified* used Google's AdWords program to generate leads for the book, collecting names and email addresses for people whom he hoped would ultimately purchase a copy of the book. Although this data has already been presented in the example in Chapter 12 for cost-per-acquisition, in the context of the author's campaigns the data is interchangeable with cost-per-conversion.

Keyword	Status	Max. CPC	Clicks	Impr.	CTR	Avg. CPC ▼	Conv. Rate	Cost/Conv.
Total — search			178	33,891	0.5%	$0.06	13.48%	$0.41
Total — content targeting			15	16,538	0.0%	$0.06	13.33%	$0.44
web analytics	Strong	$0.10	12	711	1.6%	$0.08	16.67%	$0.44
web analysis	Strong	$0.10	56	7,086	0.7%	$0.06	16.07%	$0.37
traffic analysis	Moderate	$0.10	6	1,976	0.3%	$0.06	16.67%	$0.34
log analyzer	Moderate	$0.10	10	1,680	0.5%	$0.06	20.00%	$0.28
traffic statistics	Strong	$0.10	13	1,394	0.9%	$0.06	0.00%	$0.00
web logs	Moderate	$0.10	26	3,912	0.6%	$0.06	26.92%	$0.19

Figure 47: Cost-per-conversion information for a sample of keywords the author purchased to drive leads to www.webanalyticsdemystified.com (data provided by Google AdWords).

As you can see in Figure 47, the Google AdWords application automatically calculates cost-per-conversion ("Cost/Conv.") for those keywords that were successful in driving visitors who converted into leads. While at the time the value of a lead was technically $0.00, the author estimated that each lead generated would ultimately be worth between $5.00 and $9.00. Based on this information, the reported costs-per-conversion of between $0.19 and $0.44 were well within the author's budget for lead acquisition and conversion.

Campaign Return on Investment (ROI)

Compared to other campaign metrics described in this book, campaign return on investment is perhaps one of the most important measurements you can make if you are doing any online marketing. While it is important to measure your cost-per-acquisition and cost-per-conversion it is the relationship, between the total amount you spend and the total amount you make that will help you determine the overall value of your online marketing.

How to Calculate

Campaign return on investment is very simple to calculate for any given timeframe but there are two variations:

```
AMOUNT MADE BY CAMPAIGN TO DATE / AMOUNT SPENT ON CAMPAIGN TO
DATE = "ROLLING" CAMPAIGN RETURN ON INVESTMENT

AMOUNT MADE BY CAMPAIGN TO DATE / AMOUNT SPENT ON CAMPAIGN IN
TOTAL = "TOTAL" CAMPAIGN RETURN ON INVESTMENT
```

The "rolling" campaign ROI is simply an expression of how well you are doing so far in the campaign, likely to become a positive number more quickly than the "total" campaign ROI. The two are differentiated to help you understand both how the campaign is currently performing and when you can expect the campaign to break even if the campaign performs at a roughly linear rate.

Again, the amount made by the campaign would simply be the gross profits the campaign has delivered; the amount spent on the campaign would be the cost-per-acquisition times the number of responses for the "rolling" number, or the total cost of the campaign (or a suitable estimate or upper-limit). Keep in mind that the former can be an estimate based on the average value of a customer times the number of converters in the campaign if you are not actually selling online.

Dependence

The only real dependence for campaign ROI is having accurate numbers to work with, which should not be so difficult—or should it? Depending on who controls the flow of campaign spending and campaign conversion these numbers can be difficult to come by. In cases like this it is worthwhile to work with an average cost-per-acquisition and an average value-per-conversion. With these numbers and access to the number of respondents and number of converters you can make a rough estimate of your campaign ROI, which is better than nothing.

Usage

Campaign return on investment should be used to ensure that you are not losing your shirt on a campaign on a daily or weekly basis, to predict at what point the campaign will begin to become profitable for the online business and to determine when you believe you will start to see the multiples of return that you are looking for.

Interpretation

The best way to think about return on investment is to think, "For every dollar I have spent I have made back X." If the "rolling" calculation yields a number like "0.50" this tells you that for every dollar you have spent in the timeframe you are looking at you have made back $0.50. If the "total" calculation yields the same value this tells you that for every dollar you have committed to spending on the campaign you have made half of that dollar back. In this example the "rolling ROI" calculation is not great news; unless something pretty dramatic changes a loss like this will make it very difficult to realize a positive ROI on the entire campaign. In the same example the "total ROI" calculation is not bad in and of itself since all campaigns start off in the red and (hopefully) move towards the black.

The interpretation of the total ROI case is that you are halfway towards break-even on the campaign, which tells you roughly how long you will need to run the campaign. Unfortunately you cannot just say to yourself, "Ok, if we're halfway there then we'll just run the campaign for three more similar time periods and we'll make a 2x return." Reality dictates that campaign performance decreases over time so unless you are providing continuous input you cannot be sure the response and conversion rates will be linear. That being said, if the inputs remain roughly the same you will be able to generate a relatively accurate picture of when the campaign will contribute positively to your online business.

Segment, Commerce and Search Related Conversion Metrics

The visitor segmentation and commerce tools described earlier in this book have conversion-related attributes. For visitor segments it is the rate at which a visitor moves from a lower-value segment ("browsers") to a higher-value segment ("buyers"). For commerce there are a number of different metrics that are important and nearly all revolve around the key conversion activity of making a purchase.

Segment Conversion Rates

One of the components cited as important in the chapter on visitor segmentation was the ability to measure the movement from one segment to another. This measurement is essentially the conversion rate for groups of visitors completing any set or number of activities, depending on how you assign visitors to segments. Depending on your particular Web analytics package's support for segments you can perform more or less complex segmentations. Some examples of segment conversions that are commonly tracked include:

- "Unregistered" to "Registered" visitors
- "Browsers" to "Buyers" in an online store
- "Anonymous" to "Known" visitors
- Those visitors referred from a particular source to "Customers" or "Registered" visitors
- Visitors from a particular geographic region to "Customers" or "Registered" visitors
- "Light" content users to "Heavy" content users
- "Infrequent" visitors to "Frequent" visitors
- "Campaign Responders" to "Directly Referred" visitors (and vice versa)

The list is nearly as infinite as the number of online businesses. The most important things to consider when setting up visitor segments are A) does the segment you are creating make sense and B) will you be able to reasonably act on the information once you have collected it.

How to Calculate

Those Web analytics packages that support this type of analysis automatically calculate segment conversion for you. If you have the ability to segment but not convert segments you may be unable to measure this metric. If you are unsure about how your particular analytics package supports segment conversion please consult your vendor directly.

To generate a segment conversion rate you would simply divide the number of segment converters into the number of visits or visitors in the lower-value segment during the timeframe being analyzed:

```
SEGMENT CONVERTERS / VISITORS TO LOWER VALUE SEGMENT = SEGMENT
CONVERSION RATE
```

It is important to use the same metric for both the numerator and denominator; if the segment conversions are measured in visits use visits, if the segment conversions are measured in visitors, use visitors, and so on.

Dependence

Segment conversion depends entirely on the analytics package's ability to record and present this information. Because, for the most part, visitor segmentation occurs behind the scenes, either in cookies or in query strings passed around in Web server log files, you depend on the application's ability to track segment conversions. Some applications, particularly some outsourced solutions, provide the ability to denote segment conversions in the page tag; other applications provide the ability to perform an *ad hoc* analysis of previously collected data to report on segment conversion.

Usage

Segment conversion is typically used to keep track of process conversions occurring over longer periods of time than just the "visit" or the day. Because visitor segmentation is designed, in most cases, to keep track of visitors over the lifetime of their visits (once you are segmented you stay in that segment until the application or analysis is told otherwise), these tools allow us to observe visitors over long periods of time.

Interpretation

Your application will hopefully provide at least two of three useful metrics for tracking segment conversion. These are:

- Number of converters from "segment A" to "segment B"
- Average amount of time it took for the segmentation to occur in days, hours, minutes and seconds
- Average number of visits between the time the visitors entered "segment A" and when they entered "segment B"

While we refer to the averages for the second or third items above it would probably be more useful to have the distributions for these numbers but, as is often the case in Web analytics, you take what you can get.

Having the information mentioned above available to you will allow you to assess how effectively and how quickly you move visitors from lower- to higher-value segments. If you were to see that you were converting visitors from "segment A" to "segment B" at a rate of 20 percent but the average time to conversion was 20 days and the average number of visits was 30 you may reasonably assume that you have a fairly complex conversion process or that marketing materials encouraging visitors to convert is not entirely clear. See Chapter 7 for an example of how BackcountryStore.com used segment conversion to improve its checkout process.

Example

An excellent example of how segment conversion metrics can help in the continuous improvement process is presented in Chapter 7 under the heading "Examples of Uses for Visitor Segmentation Tools." Essentially, BackcountryStore.com's staff questioned whether they should require registration in their purchase checkout process. To validate whether visitors wanted to register or not, they created an "anonymous" test checkout process. They then let visitors go through the registration whichever way they desired, segmenting and converting visitors as they did so.

	Segment Name	Avg Visits	Avg Time Spent	Segment Conversions
1.	Unregistered ⇒ Customer	1.01	0:20:52:44	78
2.	Unregistered ⇒ Registered	0.97	1:02:46:54	28
3.	Searcher ⇒ Customer	1.15	2:03:55:53	23
4.	Sale Items ⇒ Customer	1.36	3:11:14:43	18
5.	Registered ⇒ Customer	0.67	0:13:57:46	7

Figure 48: Segment conversion report for BackcountryStore.com. Of interest is the difference in conversions from "Unregistered => Customer" and "Registered => Customer."

As you can see in Figure 48, a clear majority of visitors were opting to go through the purchase checkout process anonymously, following the "Unregistered => Customer" path. Based on this information, BackcountryStore.com kept the anonymous checkout process in place. This streamlined checkout process was in part responsible for BackcountryStore.com increasing its site-wide conversion rate by nearly 30 percent, a notable accomplishment for any online business.

Average Order Value (AOV)

Average order value is a commerce metric that should be watched with the same religious fervor that is most often reserved for conversion rates if you sell anything on your Web site. Depending on the number of different items you sell, this value can help you understand how your business is doing from a 10,000-foot view. Average order value can be calculated at both a macro and a micro level, that is, you can calculate the AOV for all orders taken online, AOV for a category of items and AOV for a single product or line of products.

At a minimum, if you sell online, AOV should be calculated at the site level as a key performance indicator for the health of the online store.

How to Calculate

Very simple to calculate, the site-wide AOV is the total revenue generated divided by the number of orders taken.

```
TOTAL REVENUE / TOTAL ORDERS = AVERAGE ORDER VALUE
```

If you are interested in the AOV for a product category or a single product you would make the same calculation for the orders and revenue taken for that particular group.

Dependence

Average order value only depends on having an accurate and timely way to determine how many orders have been taken and for how much revenue—fundamental data for any store, online or offline.

Usage

Average order value is best used as a key performance indicator and for making simple conversion rate calculations. An example of the latter would be to quickly determine the effect of a 10 percent increase in your site-wide conversion rate, so if your current conversion rate is 5 percent and your AOV is $100.00, if you increase your conversion rate by 10 percent to 5.5 percent you stand to make an additional $500.00 per 1,000 visitors to your site.

Interpretation

Average order value is simply the average sales for the items you have sold through your Web site. If you only sell one item for one price the AOV for your site will be the same as the price of that one item. If you sell two things for two different prices, the closer the AOV is to one price or the other the greater the number of either of those items you are selling.

Related metrics

Average order value is related to a number of different commerce metrics that are, hopefully, core functionality in your online commerce tracking toolset, including number of orders, the number of items that were sold, site-wide conversion rate and total online revenue. See Chapter 9 for additional information on common commerce metrics.

AOV for New and Returning Customers

In addition to calculating the average order value for all items sold online, both overall and by product or category, it is useful to make this same calculation for new and returning customers. Doing so will help you to better understand the value of visitor and customer retention. If you sell online, these calculations are very important conversion performance indicators.

How to Calculate

Both are calculated in the same way as average order value except the data used is for either new or returning customers. See average order value (AOV) for the calculation.

Dependence

Being able to make these calculations depends on your analytics application's commerce package being able to differentiate "new" and "returning" customers. Often done via the passing of a unique customer ID during the purchase process, the accuracy of these calculations is entirely dependent on knowing how many orders and how much revenue should be attributed to each of these customer segments.

Usage

New and returning customer AOV is extremely useful in determining the overall makeup of your marketing programs. Were you to discover that your new customer AOV was $100.00 but your return customer AOV was only $75.00 you could reasonably justify focusing your marketing efforts on new customer acquisition. But if your site's new customer AOV is $50.00 and your return customer AOV is $500.00 you would immediately fly into customer retention mode and attempt to lure as many previous customers back to your Web site as possible.

Interpretation

See average order value (AOV).

Example

Average order value is an excellent metric to watch in your key performance indicator report, one that can tell you a great deal about your online business. An example of how AOV should be reported is presented in Figure 49.

Key Performance Indicators	This Period	Last Period	% Change	Warning
Average Order Value	$128.54	$109.20	17.71%	
AOV - New Visit Customers	$123.96	$112.57	10.11%	
AOV - Repeat Visit Customers	$130.56	$107.83	21.07%	
Revenue per Visitor	$3.55	$2.20	61.12%	
Revenue per Visit	$3.11	$1.94	60.03%	
Percent Orders from New Customers	30.55%	28.79%	6.10%	
Percent Orders from Repeat Customers	69.45%	71.21%	-2.47%	WARNING

Figure 49: Key performance indicator worksheet for an anonymous online business showing AOV for all, new and repeat visiting customers.

Based on the numbers presented in Figure 49 you can reasonably assume that something has changed for the better between reporting periods, with all AOV metrics up between 10 and 21 percent. This information would easily validate any marketing activity, especially retention marketing activity that the online business was engaged in at the time.

Percent of Orders from New and Repeat Customers

If your Web site is focused on selling more than a single product and your hope is that visitors will purchase and then return to purchase again, it is useful to keep an eye on the percent of order you are receiving from new and repeat customers. Complimentary to AOV for new and returning customers, these calculations will help you better determine how much effort you should be putting into various customer acquisition and retention programs and whether they are paying off or not.

How to Calculate

The percent of orders from either customer type is simply the number of orders from new or returning customer divided by all orders.

```
NEW CUSTOMER ORDERS / ALL ORDERS = PERCENT ORDERS FROM NEW
CUSTOMERS

RETURN CUSTOMER ORDERS / ALL ORDERS = PERCENT ORDERS FROM
RETURNING CUSTOMERS
```

Dependence

These calculations have a similar dependence as AOV for new and returning customers, your analytics package's commerce tools ability to determine and report on whether a customer is new or returning. See the "dependence" discussion under "AOV for New or Returning Customer" for additional information.

Usage

Percent of orders from new or returning customers is useful for helping determine whether new customer acquisition marketing programs or customer retention marketing programs are being effective. If you spend 50 percent of your marketing budget on retention marketing but only 30 percent of your orders are coming from return customers something is not working. Conversely, if you spend 50 percent of your marketing budget on retention marketing and 65 percent of your customers have purchased previously you are doing better than average for retention but having problems with new customer acquisition.

Ideally these percentages are pretty close to your marketing spend on new versus return customer acquisition, providing you separate out your marketing that way.

Interpretation

This measurement provides a strict percentage of the distribution of orders between new versus returning customers. Similarly, you could make the same calculation based on revenue to see percentage revenue by new versus returning customers.

Example

In Figure 49 we can see that the AOV for repeat customers is increasing more than 20 percent while the percent of orders from repeat customers is down roughly 2.5

percent. While the marked increase in AOV is good news, it is slightly less so in the context that the overall percentage of orders taken from repeat customers is down. Were this anonymous online business actively engaged in retention marketing they would likely view these results as a "qualified success"—they had increased AOV, likely through merchandising efforts, but failed to attract significantly increased numbers of return visitors.

New and Repeat Customer Conversion Rates

Closely related to AOV for new and returning customers and the percentage distribution of orders along the same lines, online stores should calculate the differential conversion rates for new and returning customers, if possible. As a measurement of the efficacy of new versus return customer acquisition marketing programs, these rates will often surprise you in how different they are and these differences are telling when trying to understand barriers to purchase on a Web site.

If they are easily calculated, these conversion rates are key conversion performance indicators and should be watched closely.

How to Calculate

This metric is calculated in the same way as a normal site-wide conversion rate (orders/visitors) only for only new or returning customers and visitors:

```
NEW CUSTOMER ORDERS / NEW VISITORS = NEW CUSTOMER CONVERSION
RATE

RETURN CUSTOMER ORDERS / RETURNING VISITORS = RETURNING
CUSTOMER CONVERSION RATE
```

Dependence

It is important when making these calculations to ensure that you have accurate measurements for both the orders and visitors components. Any mixing will necessarily affect these numbers and potentially skew one calculation or the other.

Usage

Perhaps more than any other metric described in this book, these two conversion rates have the potential to help you understand barriers to making purchases on your Web site. Aside from their comparative value, each are interesting in their own right as they help you gain insight into how compelling your products or services are and how good a job you do at the overall sales and fulfillment process.

Interpretation

If these two conversion rates are relatively far apart you can determine that there may be a learning curve to your purchase or checkout process, so that when visitors complete the process once they are willing to come back and purchase again more freely. Consider if you had 100,000 new and returning visitors and your new visitor conversion rate was 0.5 percent, yielding 500 customers, while your returning visitor conversion rate is 2.0 percent, yielding 2,000 customers. In this situation, it is reasonable to assume that there is some barrier to making the first purchase but once the visitor has done that they are more likely to purchase if they return.

Sales per Visitor

Sales per visitor, according to Eisenberg and Novo in *The Guide to Web Analytics,* is a simple metric for measuring your marketing efficiency. Similar to the purchase conversion rate, sales per visitor is a measurement of the amount of revenue you receive, compared to the total number of visitors to the Web site (not only visitors who purchase). As a comparative point with your purchase conversion rate, sales per visitor can be a useful conversion performance indicator.

How to Calculate

Sales per visitor are exactly that, gross sales divided by the number of unique visitors in the same timeframe.

```
GROSS SALES / VISITORS = SALES PER VISITOR
```

Dependence

Any online business should have easy access to both of these numbers so sales per visitor should be easily calculated. You should be careful to use de-duplicated unique visitors, not a sum of daily visitors that may include repeat visitors.

Usage

Sales per visitor is a simple metric for measuring marketing efficiency and also as a check-and-balance against any changes in your purchase conversion rate. Ideally if your conversion rate increases your sales per visitor is increasing at roughly the same rate. If it is not, then you are converting more browsers into buyers but you are doing so at the expense of your average order value (AOV).

Interpretation

Sales per visitor is a simple dollar value, such as "$10 sales per visitor." This number, by necessity, will always be much smaller than the average order value, which uses the same numerator (gross sales) but a much smaller denominator, in most cases. Sales per visitor will vary widely from business to business depending on the average order value and site-wide conversion rate.

Searches Yielding Results to Search No Results

The ratio of searches yielding results to those searches yielding no results can be tricky to calculate, especially if you are using Web-server log files as a data source. But if you can calculate it you can learn interesting things about your internal search engine. Essentially this is a ratio that quickly describes if visitors are successfully finding the products or information they are looking for and whether that pattern is changing over time. This ratio makes a good conversion performance indicator providing you have internal search and the ability to measure whether searches yield results or not.

Figure 50: Searches yielding results (above) and one yielding no results (below) from BackcountryStore.com.

How to Calculate

This calculation is relatively simple as long as you have a way to count page views (or visits or visitors) to search "results found" and "no results found" pages.

```
PAGE VIEWS TO "RESULTS FOUND" PAGE / PAGE VIEWS TO "NO RESULTS
FOUND" PAGE = RATIO SEARCH RESULTS TO NO RESULTS
```

Dependence

This calculation depends on your analytics package's ability to count the number of searches that are successful in yielding a set of results versus the number of searches that yield a "no results found" message. Many client-side data collection solutions can be tricked into doing this via either a page name or custom variable that simply counts page views, visits or visitors to a page called "results" or "no results."

Usage

This ratio is a quick performance indicator telling you whether more "no results found" pages are being served up from timeframe to timeframe. The closer this ratio is to 1.00—God help you if it is greater than 1.00—the more likely visitors are searching for terms that are not indexed in your search engine or simply looking for stuff you don't have. Ideally you have a way to see what people are searching for when they get these "no results found" pages and can evaluate whether to make changes to your search engine, your site or your product line to provide better search results in the future.

If you are using this ratio as a regular performance indicator, large changes can also indicate technology problems with your search engine. It is not unheard of for search engines to return empty or error results sets when they are under particularly heavy load, especially around the holidays. Watching this metric closely can help you better respond to emerging issues surrounding your internal search functionality.

Interpretation

If the calculation tells you that the ratio of results found to no results found is "0.10" then you know that one in ten searchers is not finding any results. It is more likely, depending on your business model, that these numbers will be more like "0.001" or thereabouts, especially if you have a well-indexed site, a search engine that is good at interpreting query requests or a large catalog of products that your visitors understand.

Web Analytics Tip: How to Increase Your Purchase Conversion Rate

Perhaps the question I get asked most often from owners of online stores is, "How do we increase our conversion rate?" Fortunately I have developed some experience in this realm and have discovered the "low hanging fruit" that many people often overlook. By checking whether you are making some of these common mistakes, and then using the continuous improvement process to implement, test and measure the effects of correcting the mistakes you find, you can be well on your way to increasing conversion rates.

Here are three of the lowest-hanging fruit, and thanks to Bryan Eisenberg for validation from his book, *The Marketer's Common Sense Guide to Converting Web Site Traffic*:

Don't Require Registration

Forced registration is perhaps the single most common impediment to any conversion process. I often refer to this as "the Amazon.com'ification" of the checkout process, that is, "Amazon.com does it and they're the best in the business so it must be the right thing to do..."

Not necessarily.

Online businesses require registration in the checkout processes for a variety of reasons— the marketing people want the information, the company believes that registration will simplify the purchase process the next time the visitor returns, the transaction application requires a unique user record for the transaction, our competitors (or Amazon.com) require registration (but see below)—none of which are good reasons to *require* registration. In fact, in my opinion, there are no good reasons to require registration, period. Registration is an action that should either occur silently during the purchase process or that your visitor should opt-in to based on their desire.

There is nothing more annoying for a new online visitor than to find the products that they want, to add them to the shopping cart, to click "checkout now" and to be taken to a page telling them, "You must first register with our site." This is essentially saying, "We require you to provide us personal information that appears to be unrelated to the purchase process before we'll let you spend your money with us online, and, if you are unwilling to provide this information we'd rather not have your money..." Sounds ridiculous when it's stated that way but consider that the new visitor has no vested interest in your online business until you've actually successfully and pleasantly shipped the items they want. All of the data I have ever seen strongly indicates that given the choice between registering in a purchase process or simply walking away and finding a different site to purchase from, the majority of visitors will walk away.

To continue beating a dead horse—which is strangely necessary since nearly every Web site I try to purchase from requires registration—consider this. Imagine that you owned a grocery store and that you were really good at inviting people in, providing well-lit aisles, a wide variety of products at competitive prices, well-oiled grocery carts and helpful employees that encourage you to fill your shopping cart. Requiring registration on your Web site is just like letting each of these full shopping carts wait in line, only to be met by a cashier telling them "before I can check you out I first need you to fill out this page of information." It would never work! Customers would be flabbergasted. Carts would be abandoned where they stood. Customers would vow "never to return," and so on.

Crazy, huh?

So what can you do? You want (or need) to collect certain types of information from your visitors but it sounds like I'm telling you not to. Not true. What I'm telling you is to do it elegantly. Consider what Amazon.com actually tells people when they begin the checkout process (Figure 51)—"you'll create a password later." This is an elegant, behind-the-scenes way to collect the information they need to process the transaction *and* get the visitor to register. The very next step after you provide your email address is to provide shipping information, which is exactly what the potential customer expects—I click "checkout" and then provide my shipping information.

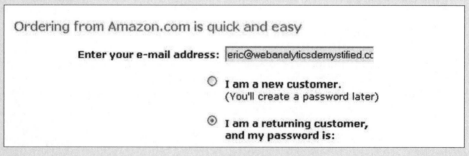

Figure 51: Amazon.com's method for starting a checkout for new visitors. All that is required is an email address and you are told that eventually they'll want you to add a password.

Here are three things I recommend you consider regarding registration and the purchase process:

1. **Don't require registration, period.**

Consider the popularity of Google and the tools they provide for the Internet. One of these tools is the Google Toolbar (toolbar.google.com). The Google Toolbar is an ingenious application that lives inside your browser that allows search from your browser, blocks annoying pop-up windows, and, germane to this discussion, provides an easy way to automatically fill in most forms. As long as you ensure that your forms are "Google Toolbar compliant," that is, all of the fields are named such that the toolbar will be able to auto-complete them, then you can rest assured that your visitors have handled the "how to simplify the next purchase" question.

2. **Don't require registration, but provide an optional registration process that visitors can opt into.**

By simply allowing for anonymous checkout you provide the simplest process possible. Visitor clicks "checkout" and you ask them where they want the product shipped—no email address, no password, nothing. If you're still dead-set on getting the visitor registered, provide them an optional path and bribe them. Offer the visitor "10% off" or "free shipping" on their *next order* if they take the time to register with you. If you do this, consider having a slightly more involved registration process and ask them everything you would ever want to know. However, make sure you do this *after* you have processed the current transaction.

3. **Register the customer silently during the checkout process and send them an email telling them that you've done this and how to take advantage of it.**

This is perhaps my personal favorite because it is the best of both worlds. The customer gets to check out quickly and easily and the marketing group gets to feel like they are creating loyal (registered) customers. If you just create a temporary password for the visitor and then send them an email telling them how to change the password and the advantages of doing so you will likely get some percentage of visitors actually changing their password and some larger percentage of visitors at least coming back to your site, thus creating additional opportunities to sell to them.

Think about Your Buttons

Make sure that your buttons are easy to see, easy to read and that the most important button stands out like a sore thumb! This may seem, well, obvious, but you don't have to look very hard at the Internet to find examples of Web sites failing to follow this guidance. Often the culprit is the graphic designer, wanting every element on the page to blend together in visual harmony, showing off their imagistic prowess. The problem is that most of your customers are not graphic designers; they are most likely regular people who are simply trying to figure out what to do next. Consider the two buttons shown in Figure 52:

Figure 52: Example buttons from an anonymous European Web site (left) and BackcountryStore.com (right).

Most people will agree that the "Add to Shopping Cart" button found on BackcountryStore.com is much easier to see than the "Add to basket" found on an anonymous European shopping site. Even in the context of the entire page the "Add to Shopping Cart" button stands out and is an easily seen "next step" (Figure 53).

Figure 53: Whole screen from BackcountryStore.com, note the "Add to Shopping Cart" button on the right side of the page. Note also the "Send Email" button near the lower-right portion of the screen, consistent in look but less pronounced.

If you do a good job at designing buttons you will easily be able to create a small palette of options with optional, required and *really* required button types. Your graphic designers may cry and complain about "but adding buttons that big and ugly will positively ruin the aesthetic appeal of the entire page and undo all of the work that I've done!" If this is the response you get, I highly recommend that you smile, nod and go find graphic designers who are as committed to your businesses success as they are to their portfolio.

Include a Progress Indictor

Progress indicators in the checkout process are just one of those things that you really have to have to make visitors feel comfortable, at least the first time they purchase. The problem with progress indicators is that some of them lie. You may see a three-step process but not realize that there are three sub-steps at each step and actually you're about to engage in a nine-step process. When you do this to a visitor you are essentially creating doubt in their minds about your integrity, increasing the likelihood that they will bail out on the purchase process prior to completion.

Because my family taught me it's better to say nothing at all if you have nothing nice to say I will refrain from providing examples of large, well-known online businesses that have extremely misleading progress indicators. Rather, I would refer the reader to Figure 54 which has two examples of nice-looking and accurate progress indicators from BackcountryStore.com and Amazon.com.

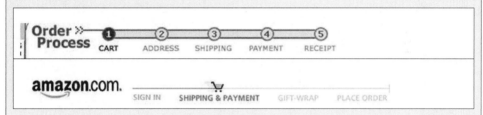

Figure 54: Progress indicators from BackcountryStore.com (top) and Amazon.com (bottom), both of which are easy to read and are accurate in terms of describing the number of pages you'll have to get though to complete your purchase.

For an excellent example of how the purchase process *should* work for any Web site selling durable goods, check out what the folks at BackcountryStore.com are doing (www.backcountrystore.com). Additionally, Bryan Eisenberg's book, *The Marketer's Common Sense Guide to Converting Web Site Traffic,* which was not available in its final form as of the writing of this book, has a more complete list of the "low hanging fruit" and is definitely worth reading. Look for it at Mr. Eisenberg's Web site, www.futurenowinc.com.

Key Performance Indicators Recommended for Measuring Conversion

The key performance indicators discussed in this chapter are some of the most important you will measure and monitor, if you choose to do so. Because conversion rates are easy to measure and relatively easy to influence, the online business should watch these numbers very closely and make sure there is a response plan in place should key conversion rates dip suddenly and dramatically. Which conversion rates you watch depends entirely on what kind of Web site you have and which multiple-step processes are most critical to your visitors' success.

With that in mind, key indicators that should be tracked regardless of your particular business model include:

- Conversion rates for any processes that can make or save you money or that are critical to your customer's experience on your Web site
- Campaign conversion rate for any active campaigns, or if you have too many to reasonably watch, for your most expensive active campaigns
- Cost-per-conversion for the campaigns you have decided to track
- Segment conversion rates for key or critical segment conversions

Additionally, if you are selling online you should also be watching the following:

- Your site-wide conversion rate, all purchases to all visits or visitors
- New and repeat site-wide customer conversion rates
- Percent of orders from new and returning customers
- Site-wide average order value and that for new and returning customers
- Sales per visitor, for comparison to your site-wide conversion rate

Again, keep in mind that it is not the numbers but changes in these numbers that you are watching for.

CHAPTER 14
MEASURING RETENTION

"To get repeat business you have to do more than satisfy your customers, you have to delight them. If you do, they'll not only come back, they'll recommend your site to colleagues, friends and families. The result: more sales with zero additional marketing expense."
Eisenberg and Novo, *The Guide to Web Analytics*

It is a rare, rare Web site that would go through all the work described in the last three chapters to reach, acquire and convert visitors and not want these visitors to remain loyal and return to convert again. While your particular Web site may not be actively running campaigns, have clear conversion goals or sell anything online, the desire to have visitors return is nearly universal. Whether it is studies that tell us that current customers are much easier to sell to and more profitable or just the good feeling you get when someone takes the time to write you and tell you they enjoy your Web site and will tell their friends about you—and this does happen—customer retention is important to any Web site.

That being said, retention is easily the most difficult of all the metrics described in this book to measure. Because every business model is different, and every visitor is roughly different (barring the concept of the "average visitor" described in Chapter 10), the span of time over which visitor retention should be measured can vary from days to months to years. Consider two examples, one site that provides news and another that sells cars. The first site will likely be able to measure visitor retention over the span of a month—it is likely that a visitor that had a good experience getting their news at that site will return at least once a month to read more news. The latter may not see a visitor who researched the buying decision for a car on their site again for three to five years, if ever—easily longer than the average lifespan of a Web analytics product on any given Web site.

There will always be attrition and churn; this is just a fact of life. Even if you are the best at what you do online today that may not be the case tomorrow. In a world where your competition is only a mouse-click away retention can be difficult, if not nearly impossible. When you are making the measurements listed in this chapter be sure and A) be reasonable about the amount of time you give visitors to return to your site and B) use the loyalty, frequency and recency measurements described in this chapter to help you hone and refine that period of time.

Metrics to Help Measure Retention

The following metrics and ratios will help you better understand how good a job you do at visitor retention. Of course, ideally you would have a consistent unique user identifier (UUID) written to every visitor's browser so you could track them personally when they return, but just in case you are not that far these metrics will help you develop at least a picture of how good a job you do.

Number of Returning Visitors

Just like the measurement of the number of new visitors described in Chapter 11, measuring the number of returning visitors in a given timeframe will help you understand how well your retention marketing programs are doing. While the raw numbers can be misleading if not compared to overall traffic volumes, the number of returning visitors is an important metric to understand.

How to Calculate

Most, if not all, Web analytics packages will measure some kind of returning visitor metric for you automatically. The returning visitor measurement usually depends on a timeframe, such as "daily returning visitors," "weekly returning visitors" or "monthly returning visitors," to put their return in context. If you are interested in how many times a visitor is likely to return you should see the "frequency of return" metric described in this chapter. If you are interested in the percentage of returning visitors, simply divide the number of returning visitors into the total number of unique visitors in the timeframe.

Dependence

Getting an accurate number for the returning visitor measurement depends on having a system to identify that a visitor has been to the Web site previously. You should employ a system that uses cookies to keep track of returning visitors, as IP addresses are subject to change as how your visitors connect to the Internet varies widely for mobile users or business travelers. Obviously a system built on cookies is not foolproof (see disadvantages of page-tagging data collection described in Chapter 3), but cookies are the standard for keeping track of visitors and will likely continue to be so for some time.

Usage

The number of returning visitors should, in general, be used in conjunction with a ratio, such as "acquisition mode," or the ratio of returning visitors to all visitors, in order to put the number in context. It would be great to know that your Web site had 100,000 returning visitors last month unless you had 100,500 total visitors to the site, in which case you acquired nearly no new visitors, or unless you had 100,000,000 total visitors to the site, in which case those 100,000 returning visitors was a relatively small group.

Interpretation

The number of returning visitors for a timeframe is exactly that, the number of visitors who had been to your site at least one time previously and returned in the timeframe you are looking at. If your analytics package offers "daily," "weekly" and "monthly" returning visitors, as many do, then "100 daily returning visitors on Monday" would tell you that 100 visitors came to your site on Monday and all of these people had been to your site at least one time before.

If your analytics application supports returning visitors for odd timeframes this can be very helpful to help you understand how visitors return during events, such as the NFL football season or between Thanksgiving and Christmas, or whether you are likely to get more returning visitors on weekdays versus weekends. Consult with your vendor to see if this is possible with your specific package.

Example

The normal pattern of monthly returning visitors to the BackcountryStore.com Web site is loaded more heavily toward visits earlier in the month (Figure 55).

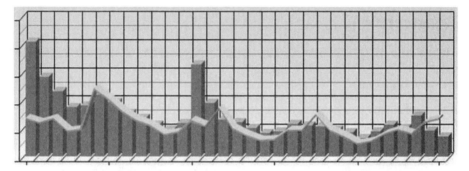

Figure 55: Monthly returning visitor pattern for BackcountryStore.com. Note the spike in returning visitors mid-month, attributed to retention marketing activities.

The interesting piece of information in Figure 55 is the second spike near the middle of the month. This spike is tied directly to BackcountryStore.com retention marketing activities and this graph provides quick visual evidence that the campaign had some success. Of course, to truly determine the success of the campaign, BackcountryStore.com would need to drill-down into its campaigns and commerce measurements to see how many of these returning visitors actually made purchases.

Average Frequency of "Returning" Visitors

Once you have learned how your analytics package presents returning visitors, you are faced with having to make sense of what this metric is telling you. As with reach, acquisition and conversion, many retention metrics are ratios and percentages. The ratio of daily to monthly returning visitors will give you an idea of the average number of times visitors return in a month and how that number changes month-over month.

How to Calculate

As long as your analytics package provides you with daily and monthly returning visitors this ratio is simply:

```
DAILY RETURNING VISITORS / MONTHLY RETURNING VISITORS = RATIO
OF DAILY TO MONTHLY RETURNING VISITORS
```

Dependence

Calculating this ratio is only dependent on your Web analytics package providing you with both daily and monthly returning visitors. If you application does not have a "monthly returning visitor" specifically, but you can calculate de-duplicated returning visitors for custom timeframes you can simply generate the monthly metric on your own.

Usage

The ratio is useful in understanding whether changes in your site or marketing affect the average number of times visitors are likely to return in a given month.

Interpretation

This number represents the average number of days in the month that visitors are likely to return, so if the ratio calculated is "4.5" this tells you that the average visitor returns to the site over more than times. Keep in mind the concept of the "average visitor" described in Chapter 10—not all visitors are average but when you have enough of them the frequency of return visits is believed to have a normal distribution.

If yours is a business model that depends on having visitors return with increasing frequency—as is the case with the online commerce model as visitors build purchase momentum, or if you provide news and information as visitors build brand loyalty—the higher this number the better. Conversely, if your site provides some kind of product support higher numbers could indicate that either visitors are having increasing difficulty with your products or simply that they are not finding the support information they are looking for and so have to return to the site repeatedly.

Related metrics

This measurement is closely related to the average frequency of return for "retained" visitors, described in this chapter under "Visitor Segmentation Metrics for Retained Visitors."

Ratio of Returning Visitors to All Visitors

Much like the calculation of percent new visitors ("new visitor reach") calculated in Chapter 11, the ratio of returning visitors to all visitors is an easy-to-read metric describing how you are doing at retaining visitors. The percent of returning visitors is an excellent retention KPI for any Web site.

How to Calculate

Percent returning visitors is calculated easily:

```
RETURNING VISITORS / ALL VISITORS = PERCENT RETURNING VISITORS
```

Dependence

Making this calculation properly depends on having numbers from identical timeframes and having de-duplicated numbers for each. If the longest timeframe for which you can get unique returning visitors and unique visitors is a month, then a month is the longest period of time for which you should calculate percent returning visitors.

Usage

Monitoring the percent of returning visitors on a regular basis can help you understand if something has changed about your visitors or your retention marketing, in which case more research is warranted.

Interpretation

As an example, if 40 percent of your monthly visitors are returning visitors for three months in a row and then suddenly that number decreases to 20 percent then one of two things has happened. Either you have suddenly increased your new visitor acquisition programs or you have experienced significant attrition in your already converted audience. In the first case you simply need to be sure you understand which marketing programs are responsible for the sudden increase in new visitor acquisition, in the latter you need to attempt to understand what might have changed in the relationship with your existing audience.

Loyalty metrics

Loyalty on the Internet is a measurement of how many times a visitor returns to your Web site over time. Typically measured in "number of visits per visitor," loyalty metrics provided by most Web analytics applications simply inform you on the number of times visitors have returned since you first implemented your particular analytics solution. Some categories of loyalty measurement make good retention performance indicators.

How to Calculate

Fortunately, most analytics applications measure and present loyalty automatically, removing the need for you to count and aggregate visits by visitors over time. You should consult your Web analytics vendor or their documentation to understand how your application reports on loyalty metrics.

Dependence

The major dependences for loyalty are A) your particular application's ability to measure loyalty accurately and B) the length of time you have been using your current application. Because the loyalty measurement nearly always depends on a cookie for determining uniqueness, the measurement also depends on using a single application consistently over time. So if you change your Web analytics application then you need to start over again in making the measurement.

This perhaps makes more sense if you consider that when you implement a new analytics application every visitor is a "new visitor" with their first return. Even if they have been coming to the Web site every day for a year, once you change measurement techniques they will be counted as a new visitor (see the definition of new visitors in Chapter 4 and about their use in Chapters 11 and 12). With this in mind, it is a good idea to pay only cursory attention to loyalty and frequency measurements until you are confident your previously retained visitors have had enough chance to return to the Web site at least once after you implement the new solution, so that they have been counted as "new."

Usage

Loyalty measurements are used to better understand how good a job you do overall in retaining visitors. The major groupings in any loyalty measurement are "1st visit" and "more than one visit" with the former grouping describing all new visitors and the latter describing all "retained" visitors. By understanding how the percentage of new versus returning visitors change over time, especially in groups that may be considered "sweet spots" for your online business, you will be able to better understand how well you retain visitors.

Interpretation

Again, most Web analytics packages present loyalty as the number of visitors coming to your Web site for the "nth" visit in some type of table (Figure 56).

Number of Visits	Visitors	%
1	273,161	77.13
2	39,660	11.19
3	14,471	4.08
4	7,179	2.02
5	4,332	1.22
6	2,772	0.78
7	2,040	0.56
8	1,515	0.42
9	1,148	0.32
10	874	0.24
11	719	0.20
12	606	0.17

Figure 56: Loyalty measurement taken from BackcountryStore.com showing the number and percentage of visitors who come to the Web site "n" times.

The example in Figure 56 shows that 14,471 or 4.08 percent of all visitors returned for the third time in the timeframe in question (row highlighted in blue). This is interesting to the folks at BackcountryStore.com in that they can see that the majority of visitors who came to their Web site in this timeframe were new visitors (coming for the 1st visit) and that after that the majority of returning visitors had returned five or less times (roughly 18.5 percent of the total number of site visitors).

Again, as is a recurring theme throughout *Web Analytics Demystified*, it is not necessarily these numbers that are interesting but how these numbers change over time. BackcountryStore.com would be smart to keep track of the percentage of visitors who return between two and five times month-over-month and watch for increases or decreases in this number. It may choose to build a key performance indicator out of the number of "1st visit" visitors and the aggregate of "2nd through 5th time" visitors to monitor for any large changes.

Frequency of Visit

Closely related the loyalty of visitors you reach, acquire and convert is the frequency at which they return to your site throughout this process and then after they have been converted. Specific business models drive the ideal frequency of return for visitors; online stores typically desire that visitors return and purchase monthly whereas software vendors may want visitors to return and upgrade their applications once yearly. The ideal frequency of return for your Web site will be determined ultimately by what you are trying to get your audience to do and how you are trying to get them to do it.

How to Calculate

Much like loyalty and recency, frequency is most often calculated for you by your analytics package. Most often frequency is calculated as the "average number of days between visits" and is calculated for visitors returning in the timeframe in question but considers all lifetime visits ("lifetime" meaning "since you implemented the application you are currently using").

The calculation is typically something like:

```
(DAYS BETWEEN 1st AND 2nd VISITS) + (DAYS BETWEEN 2nd AND 3rd
VISITS) + (DAYS BETWEEN "N - 1"th AND "N"th VISITS) / (N -1) =
FREQUENCY OF VISIT
```

So you sum all of the numbers of days between visits for the lifetime of measured visits and then divide by the number of visits minus "1" to get the average number of days between visits. You will be looking for the package to report back to you the number of visitors who return in a timeframe who have an "average number of days between visits" of "n" days (or half-days).

Dependence

Frequency has the same dependence as loyalty, your application's ability to accurately measure the number of days between visits as well as the amount of time you have used your current application. As with loyalty it is a good idea to give your visitors time to establish their retention patterns before placing too much emphasis on what frequency measurements are telling you. The author typically recommends waiting six months to measure frequency of visit.

Usage

Once your frequency measurements have had a chance to normalize, these numbers can be used much like loyalty, to better understand how you connect with your audience. Consider the data from BackcountryStore.com, presented in Figure 57, demonstrating graphically the frequency of return for visitors.

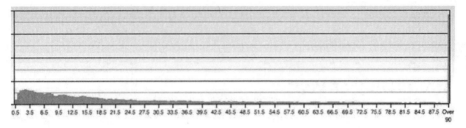

Figure 57: Example of average frequency of return for BackcountryStore.com.

As you can see in the figure most visitors are returning roughly every three weeks (from 0.5 to 21.5 days between visits). It should be noted that the largest single category is for "over 90 days" as represented by the large red bar on the right.

Interpretation

Average frequency of visit can help you to understand how often you should expect visitors to return to your Web site given all the marketing you do. In general you want to look for groups of returning visitors, the percent of visitors who return, on average, every seven days (weekly on average) or less versus the percent that return between seven and 14 days (every other week on average). Knowing at which frequency the majority of your retained audience is returning is very helpful in planning for marketing activity and site-wide changes.

One useful example is that if you determine that the majority of your visitors are returning every two weeks on average you should consider updating your home page at least every two weeks. One common method for keeping visitors engaged is to keep presenting new information that they may find compelling. By the same token if you have allocated resources to make changes to your home page on a daily basis, but you can determine that only a small percentage of your audience returns daily, you may save money by scaling back the frequency with which you update your Web site.

Example

As you can see in Figure 57, BackcountryStore.com can reasonably expect that most visitors will return at least once a month but that a large part of their audience will return perhaps only two or three times a year. This helps the BackcountryStore.com marketing group plan for outbound marketing programs like opt-in email campaigns, bi-annual storewide sales and timing of catalog printing and mailing.

Recency of Visit

Recency is closely related to frequency in that it is about the time that elapses between visits to the Web site. The difference between frequency and recency, however, is that recency is the measured amount of time elapsed since the last visit a visitor made to the Web site. So if your application reports that 1,000 visitors had a recency of "3 days," then you know that these 1,000 visitors had been to your site three days ago and have returned on the day under examination.

How to Calculate

As with loyalty and frequency, recency is a metric that is calculated and reported automatically by your analytics application. It is unclear to the author how many of the currently available Web analytics offerings support recency measurement but it is likely that over time this will become a widely supported metric. One valuable reason for supporting recency in a Web analytics application is the online business' desire to be able to segment one's customer base using the recency, frequency, monetary value (RFM) model. For a good explanation of the RFM model see either Jim Sterne's book on *Web Metrics*, or this article at ClickZ by Mark Sakalosky: http://www.clickz.com/res/analyze_data/article.php/961901.

If you are selling products online, it is best if your analytics application supports recency measurements (and frequency and loyalty for that matter) from both a non-commerce and commerce perspective.

Dependence

Recency has the same dependence as loyalty and frequency, albeit slightly less so. Because recency is only dealing with the current and previous visits a visitor made to your site you can likely begin using recency measurements much more quickly than those for frequency and loyalty.

Usage

According to Jim Novo, recency is the most powerful predictor of future behavior, based on the reasonable assumption that the more recently a visitor or customer has done "something" on your Web site, the more likely they are to return and do that thing again. With this in mind recency can be a valuable ally, especially if you are able to determine the recency for different visitor segments and campaign respondents. The greater the number of recent visitors on your Web site, the higher the likelihood that actions will occur in the short term. If you have an online business, and the "actions" are purchases, you can see where recency can be a valuable metric.

If you are selling products on your Web site you may want to establish recency KPIs to keep track of the percentage of visitors who had visited in the last three days. Theoretically as that percentage increases your total online revenue is increasing as well.

Interpretation

Recency is easily interpreted. If your application reports that 500 visitors have a recency of "20 days" you are being told that these 500 visitors had visited your site 20 days ago. Relating recency into an RFM model, or performing useful segmentations based on recency measurements, can be slightly more difficult. The author recommends reading what others in the Web analytics space, such as Jim Sterne, Jim Novo and Mark Sakalosky, have to say on using recency.

Visitor Segmentation Metrics for Retained Visitors

One of the most practical strategies for learning about your retained visitors is to segment them as such—as having been successfully acquired and/or converted—so that you can monitor their activity as they return to your site. Knowing why visitors come back is paramount in successfully converting and retaining. Being able to see where retained visitors are coming from, what pages or content they are consuming and what activities they are engaging in will allow you to create better content and navigation systems for this group. The following are metrics that you should be looking at if you are able to segment visitors as "retained" using your particular analytics package.

Activity of "Retained" Visitors

The activity of retained visitors is really a group of measurements similar to those we've looked at in previous chapters. Metrics like page views, visits and visitors will help you to determine what percentage of your total audience is retained and how much content they are likely to consume.

The typical metrics that are important to watch for retained visitors include:

- Number of page views
- Page view distribution by day of week
- Number of visits
- Number of visitors
- Average time spent on the Web site per visit
- Frequency and recency of return to the site
- Any campaigns that they may be responding to
- Any commerce activity they may be engaged in
- The pages and content that they are browsing

It is important to differentiate between "returning" visitors and "retained" visitors, if possible. A returning visitor, as measured by most Web analytics applications, is simply a visitor who has been to the Web site at least one time previously—this measurement has no regard to the activities they engaged in during previous visits. But a retained visitor is someone who has completed an activity on your Web site and continues to return to the site. It is this distinction that dictates that you segment these retained visitors and measure them as separate from all returning visitors.

The interpretation of all of the aforementioned metrics differs greatly by business model; some businesses, such as those selling products online, desire retained visitors return with great frequency. Other businesses expect that retained visitors will only come back sporadically, especially if the retention piece is technical support for a product. You should create a series of performance indicators around the activity of retained visitors and set thresholds as appropriate to your online business.

Views of Key Pages and Contents

One of the most practical visitor retention metrics to watch is which pages and content groups this segment of visitors is interested in and how these page views differ from those for your global and "unconverted" audience. By keeping track of the sections of your Web site that this visitor segment is visiting most often you will be able to learn a great deal about their specific interests. Knowing about retained visitor interests will enable you to modify your Web site and marketing materials to better speak to this class of visitor.

Example

As an example, the folks at BackcountryStore.com keep track of their "customer" visitor segment, people who have purchased with them at some time in the past and that they consider retained when they return to the Web site. Based on this data, they are able to mine the most popular pages for both the retained and un-retained segments and look for differences (Figure 58).

Figure 58: Page activity for BackcountryStore.com's retained "customer" segment (left) and "all visitors" segment (right).

As you can see, there are tangible differences in preferences for the retained visitor segment when compared to that of all visitors. The first thing you notice is that retained visitors are logging in ("/Grow Community/Customer Login") and tracking their purchases ("/Educate Customers/UPS Tracking"), activity that BackcountryStore.com expects.

One thing they do not necessarily expect is that the general audience is interested in skiing and snowboarding ("/Sell Products/Ski/Ski" and "/Sell Products/Snowboard/Snowboard") but retained visitors are not. This information potentially has an impact on BackcountryStore.com's marketing and merchandising, suggesting that visitors are initially attracted to the Web site looking for ski and snowboarding gear but that attraction is not translating well in terms of repeat purchases. Even if BackcountryStore.com does not make any changes to its outward marketing and messaging, having this information helps to set expectations internally in regards to the likelihood that retained customers will be purchasing expensive skis and snowboards during repeat visits.

Retained Visitor Conversion Rate

There are a number of studies outlining how much less expensive it is to market to existing customers, although these numbers seem to be changing all the time. It is, however, not a great stretch to imagine that your likelihood of success in getting someone who has already converted or purchased to repeat the process is high, especially if the visitor had a pleasant experience the first time through. Most online businesses that measure the difference in conversion rates for new and retained customers see radically different numbers—one site that the author has had the pleasure of working with in the past converted new visitors at a rate of roughly 10 percent when the visitor added an item to the shopping cart. This same site had an 80 percent conversion rate for returning customers adding an item to the cart (see "a note about why repeat and retained customers purchase at a higher rate than new visitors," below).

Measuring your retained visitor conversion rates, the approximation for how likely retained visitors are to repeat and convert again, is a key retention performance indicator. Much like the "return customer conversion rate" described in Chapter 13, understanding the impact retained visitors have on conversion is very important to developing and refining your marketing programs. This rate is an important retention performance indicator if you are trying to get retained visitors to convert again.

How to Calculate

This metric is calculated the same way as a normal site-wide conversion rate (orders / visitors), only for retained customers or visitors:

```
RETAINED VISITOR CONVERSIONS / RETAINED VISITORS = RETAINED
VISITOR CONVERSION RATE
```

Dependence

It is important when making these calculations to ensure that you have accurate measurements for both the retained visitor conversion and retained visitors components. Any mixing will necessarily affect these numbers and potentially skew one calculation or the other.

Usage

Being able to determine the differences in how retained visitors convert through any important activity on your Web site will help you make determinations regarding how much emphasis to place on retained visitors in your Web site design and outbound marketing programs. The differences in conversion for new and retained visitors, along with your acquisition costs will help to drive your overall marketing strategy. As an example, if you are able to determine that while retained visitors are much less expensive to market to they also have a much lower conversion rate through key processes, you are unlikely to spend as much money on retention marketing as you would if you determined that retained visitors converted at a rate four times the new visitor conversion rate.

Interpretation

As long as you are careful in making your calculation (see "Dependence" above) then this measurement is a simple conversion rate that can be compared to other conversion rates on your Web site.

Customer Retention Rate

The customer retention rate is, according to Eisenberg and Novo, the ability of your site to generate repeat business. A simple calculation and important retention performance indicator, the customer retention rate is a "must measure" number for any online business.

How to Calculate

For an online business, the customer retention rate is simply the number of repeat customers divided by total customers for a timeframe.

REPEAT CUSTOMERS / ALL CUSTOMERS = CUSTOMER RETENTION RATE

This rate can be extended easily for any retained visitor and used to generate a "visitor retention rate":

RETAINED VISITORS / ALL VISITORS = VISITOR RETENTION RATE

You should note that the second calculation is simply the "percent returning visitors" described elsewhere in this chapter.

Dependence

These calculations depend only on your application's ability to supply the necessary metrics, either via commerce measurement or visitor segmentation tools as described earlier in this book.

Usage

The customer retention rate is used to determine how good a job you are doing at attracting repeat business or repeat conversions if that is a goal of your business. Hopefully you are able to establish a baseline for this metric and then use the continuous improvement process to slowly but surely increase your customer retention.

Interpretation

Eisenberg and Novo comment that "to get repeat business you have to do more than satisfy your customers, you have to delight them." If you subscribe to this line of thinking, as does the author, you can think of your customer retention rate as a measure of "delight" expressed by your online visitors. Eisenberg and Novo go on to point out that a key factor for an online business to be successful and profitable is to increase the customer retention rate. This, in tandem with the notion that existing customers are less expensive to market to than new customers, will effectively lower your customer acquisition costs (Chapter 13).

Average Frequency of Return for "Retained" Visitors

One valuable metric for understanding how effective your site is at visitor and customer retention is the frequency of return for this online visitor segment. Some Web analytics packages will calculate frequency of return for visitor segments automatically; others will provide frequency metrics for "customers" specifically (those visitors who have placed orders online). If, for some reason your application does not support this measurement, but does provide unique visitor measurements for segments, you will still be able to calculate an average frequency of return.

How to Calculate

Providing your analytics package provides at least daily and monthly unique visitor metrics for segmented visitors you can simply divide the number of daily visitors into the number of monthly visitors to get an approximation of the average number of visitors or visits per month.

```
SUM OF DAILY VISITORS / MONTHLY VISITORS = AVERAGE VISITS PER
MONTH FOR THE SEGMENT
```

Dependence

This metric only depends on your application's ability to provide the sum of daily or weekly visitors as well as monthly unique visitors for a given visitor segment.

Usage

The resulting calculation will help you to understand whether your retained visitors (or any visitor segment for that matter) are returning to your Web site once or several times a month on average. Depending on your business model you may desire that retained visitors return several times a month, perhaps to consider additional purchases or to interact with a visitor community.

Interpretation

The resulting calculation will tell you essentially the number of days in a month the average retained visitor is returning to your Web site. Say, for example, that the sum of daily visitors for the retained segment was 1,000 and the measurement for the monthly visitors for the same segment was 250. This tells you that 250 unique visitors came to the site in the month, on average, four times (1,000 daily visitors / 250 monthly visitors = 4 days/month).

Again, based on your particular business model, higher or lower numbers are better. Depending on how important visitor retention is to you, you may want to consider making this measurement part of your retention performance indicators and watching for dramatic changes in the number.

Related Metrics

This measurement is related to the generalized frequency measurement discussed in this chapter but, whereas frequency is generally reported directly by Web analytics packages, you should keep in mind that this metric is a calculation of the average frequency of return over a shorter timeframe.

Web Analytics Tip: How to Retain Customers

After your online business has gone through all the trouble of getting a customer to make the first purchase you then need to actually retain that customer and get them to come back and purchase again. This chapter contains all the great metrics you can use to measure retention but doesn't really address how to get them to return and purchase again. You need to keep in mind that the most critical factor in making a subsequent purchase is the act of making the first purchase.

In my opinion, the decision to make a first purchase depends on a handful of both tangible and intangible factors. These factors include:

- How your prices compare to those of your competition
- How well you market your Web site on and off the Internet
- How well your company or brand is known in the marketplace
- How good a job you do at actually moving visitors to the first purchase
- What others say about you (BizRate, ePinions, Pricegrabber, and so on)

As you can see, most of these factors are within your control but some are more malleable than others. You can probably lower your prices, but most profitable online businesses would rather not compete on price. You can spend more money on marketing, but marketing budgets are typically finite and your competition is often able to spend more. You can have a perfectly designed purchase process, but never move every visitor who starts a shopping cart through to purchase. You can do the best job possible at getting products to people, and still some people will have problems and complain. It never ends.

Provided, then, that you are able to get a visitor to make the first purchase, you now have a great opportunity. If you are able to absolutely delight your new customer you will have likely gained a customer for life.

Some of the things that delight customers include:

- Products that are promptly shipped and that arrive on time
- Products that show up "as ordered"
- Follow-up mailings or emails to make sure that the product was shipped properly and that the customer is satisfied
- Coupons for future purchases that magically appear shortly after the first purchase
- Courteous and prompt customer service if there is anything wrong with the order, which is followed up by quick resolution to the problem

All of these items are essentially "Duh! Of course we do that …" items, but the reality is that this is not always the case. If every online business did everything right there would be no need for BizRate to help potential customers ensure that you're a merchant they want to do business with (www.bizrate.com).

Regarding the events that occur after the visitor has clicked the "process my order" button and committed to making the purchase, it is my strong opinion that you cannot overdo a commitment to excellence. Making sure that the product will ship on time and contacting the customer proactively if it will not, providing your customers the ability to track their purchase after it has been shipped, making sure you have friendly, knowledgeable support staff in case your customers have questions about the product and gladly taking any returns without question should be the bare minimum. Going the extra mile and sending coupons or discounts, following up to ensure that the product was well-received and is everything the customer hoped and more—activities like this will only reinforce in your customer's mind that they made the right decision.

You may be saying to yourself, "Yeah, that's easy for you to say but much harder to do." I agree, not all businesses will be able to delight their customers after the first purchase has been made, and I simply assume that over time these businesses will fail, clearing the competitive landscape for those companies that are willing to work to satisfy and retain their customers. Now you may be saying, "Harsh. This guy is harsh!" And you're right, I am harsh. So is your competition and they are always only a click away.

Key Performance Indicators Recommended for Measuring Retention

Not everyone reading *Web Analytics Demystified* is necessarily focused on visitor and customer retention in a traditional sense. Some business models don't necessarily expect a customer to make a second purchase in the near future (car dealers, real-estate Web sites, some subscription-based content sites). Still, very few Web sites are designed to only have a visitor come to the Web site a single time, never to return.

With that in mind, key retention indicators that should be tracked regardless of your particular business model include:

- The ratio of daily to monthly returning visitors, as a quick measurement of the average frequency of return for all visitors. If you are tracking "retained" visitors you should then track this KPI for the retained visitor segment as well.
- Percent returning visitors to ensure that your new/returning visitor mix is in line with your new/retention marketing spend.
- Loyalty measurements for groups of returning visitors such as "2nd through 5th return ever" to monitor for large changes in visitor loyalty.
- Activities of "retained" visitors (differentiated from "returning" visitors using visitor segmentation tools) including number of page views, number of visits and number of visitors. It is also worthwhile to track the average time these retained visitors spend on your site.
- Retained visitor conversion rate, which is important for all of the reasons that conversion rates are important.
- Customer retention rate, to keep track of how many customers or visitors you are attracting back to your site.

CHAPTER 15
BRINGING IT ALL TOGETHER USING KEY PERFORMANCE INDICATORS

"Without clear goals, there's no need to measure anything; without measuring there's no way to know if the work you're doing is helping to achieve your goals."
Jim Sterne in *Advanced Email Marketing*

Perhaps the most common complaint about Web analytics data and the applications that provide said data is that there is simply "too much information"; too many graphs, too many charts, too many options, too many variables—too much for the average user to understand and make use of. It is surprisingly likely that you will hear someone complain, "I have 400 reports to choose from in my analytics package and I'm not sure which to use so I just don't use any of them …"

Counter this complaint with the plight of the Web analytics vendor and the need to present *all* of the latest and greatest information to the customer because of the competitive nature of business. Vendors that only have a small number of well-presented data are often marginalized as "niche players" in a larger market. While it would be ideal to have small, useful modules of information, perhaps compartmentalized to inform well about a specific activity of interest, none of the vendors known to the author have adopted this approach.

So, in order to ensure that you are able to make the most use of the information provided in *Web Analytics Demystified*, you should do two things. First, make good use of the continuous improvement process as described in Chapter 2. If you are able to focus your goals for change on your Web site around a small number of changes, the metrics that support those changes become much more reasonable and easy to manage. Instead of looking at everything, you can focus on a specific conversion rate for the process you are trying to improve.

The second strategy the author recommends is to make good use of key performance indicators (KPIs). Realistically, key performance indicators are simply metrics or ratios, all of which have been described in the last few chapters of this book. Conceptually, these metrics are powerful and easy-to-understand indicators of A) how well your Web site is doing and B) whether anything has changed dramatically and needs additional attention. Key performance indictors are usually built with comparisons of previous reporting periods and percent change indicators to highlight any monitored metrics that have significant movement up or down, applying warnings if necessary (Figure 59).

Key Performance Indicators	This Period	Last Period	% Change	Warning
Average Order Value	$128.54	$109.20	17.71%	
AOV - New Visit Customers	$123.96	$112.57	10.11%	
AOV - Repeat Visit Customers	$130.56	$107.83	21.07%	
Revenue per Visitor	$3.55	$2.20	61.12%	
Revenue per Visit	$3.11	$1.94	60.03%	
Percent Orders from New Customers	30.55%	28.79%	6.10%	
Percent Orders from Repeat Customers	69.45%	71.21%	-2.47%	WARNING

Traffic Metrics

	Today	One Week Ago	% Change	
Page Views:	13,814,892	12,347,523	11.9%	▲
Visits:	6,030,778	7323112	-17.6%	▼
Unique Visitors:	3,663,210	3235998	13.2%	▲

Figure 59: Samples of Key Performance Indicator (KPI) reports.

How Do I Build a KPI Worksheet?

For the most part, all of your KPI monitoring can be done in a simple spreadsheet application, such as Microsoft Excel™. Excel offers the opportunity to easily manipulate numbers to create the necessary ratios, create graphs, generate warnings and is arguably the world's most popular analytics application. This popularity imparts a familiarity and comfort to data presented in Excel spreadsheets and this comfort often promotes action—if people understand the data and the format they are less likely to simply discard the data as "unreadable." Excel also offers the ability to easily annotate data via text or the "notes" functionality, allowing you to improve communication about what the data means. The author strongly recommends building your KPI reporting around Microsoft Excel, or a similar application.

The basic idea you want to keep in mind when you are building a KPI worksheet is this:

The numbers on their own are less interesting and less informative than changes in the numbers over time.

Raw numbers are great and they can say a lot about the success of one's Web site. Even some of the complex ratios presented throughout Chapters 11 through 14 of *Web Analytics Demystified* are interesting as simple indicators of success or a lack thereof. However, a key performance indicator worksheet is most valuable to the online business when it is prompting action, and the greatest driver for action online is seeing that you are doing much better or much worse than you were yesterday. If you are doing much better, you need to understand what it was that you did that created that success; if you are doing much worse you need to figure out what is going wrong and work to correct the problem.

See Figure 60 for a general example of how the author builds KPI worksheets, emphasizing the relationship between data from "this period" and "last period."

E38	▾	fx =(C38-D38)/D38					
C	D	E	H	I	J	K
4.00	4.08	-2.02%	136,854	34,249	101,060	24,781
This Period	**Last Period**	**% Change**	*S.A.*	*Entries*	*S.A.*	*Entries*
9.06%	10.53%	-13.95%	74,258	819,942	67,805	644,211
16.50%	17.74%	-6.98%	6,516	39,484	5,194	29,278
22.14%	23.70%	-6.58%	1,429	6,453	1,166	4,919
81.24%	83.34%	-2.52%	4,842	5,960	3,382	4,058
18.34%	20.11%	-8.77%	894	4,874	873	4,342

Figure 60: General strategy for building KPI worksheets, highlighting data collected in "this period," "last period" and the percent change between the two. The data in yellow is the raw data used to generate the KPI.

The "percent change" calculation is perhaps the most critical on any KPI worksheet as it provides a visual representation of the change in the values from period to period. This calculation is simply:

```
(THIS PERIOD — LAST PERIOD)/LAST PERIOD = PERCENT CHANGE
```

Additionally, because Microsoft Excel offers the ability to apply conditional formatting to values, the author often applies colors to the percent change values depending on whether they are moving in a positive or negative direction. Keep in mind that negative values are not always bad and should not, by default, be colored red. In many instances the desired change in a KPI is a decrease, hence a negative value, and so these instances should be colored as appropriate.

Here are some specifics that the author recommends for building a KPI worksheet for your online business:

Use the Right Measurements

As will be discussed in the next section, there is likely a core group of indicators that make the most sense for your online business to be watching on a daily or weekly basis. You want to try and focus your energy on understanding and being able to act upon this group of KPIs. These numbers are intended to be drivers, prompting you to drill down more deeply into the primary data, not be end-all-be-all comprehensive reporting. Be careful about what you put in these reports and make sure that the data is meaningful but not dense. Meaningful data prompts people to ask related questions about the information contained in the KPI; dense data prompts people to skip over the KPI and not consider the information it may have contained.

Think about Presentation

Remember that in many instances the presentation is as, or more, important than the data you present. This statement sounds odd but this is proven true over and over again, poorly presented data will be overlooked or mistrusted. When you build your KPI report the first thing you want to consider is what data will be included and what that data will be able to tell you about your Web site. The very next thing you want to consider is "how should we present this data in a visually pleasant way that will not turn the intended audience off?" Simple things like headers that have your company logo or colors, the use of lines and cell color and shading, consistent use of fonts and font sizes are all important to how a report is perceived by an audience.

Allow for Annotation

While it is an excellent idea to automate the delivery of KPI reports throughout the organization, often the numbers and their meaning can be confusing to users "less invested" in the data. The worst-case scenario is where a marked decrease is presented in the report, causing top-to-bottom panic within the organization, when the decrease was expected by a small group of individuals who simply "forgot" to tell everyone else.

If you provide a space in your reports, ideally at the top, for annotation and interpretation of the data you will likely avoid panic situations. By routing the KPI report through a small group of individuals who are vested in understanding the data and able to drill down on any KPI that warrants more investigation, the report can be annotated prior to wider delivery, making the report more efficient when it is received.

Automate Delivery

Key performance indicator reporting for the online business is very important and, in the author's opinion, the next "big thing" in Web analytics that will truly get businesses to act upon the data that they are already collecting—as long as these reports can be generated in a timely fashion and shared out to the organization. Often the answer to the question, "Why don't you provide regular reporting to your entire organization on Web analytic data?" is, "It just took entirely too much time to copy and paste all the data from the application into the spreadsheet and we gave up."

Fortunately Web analytics vendors are waking up to the need for automated, customized reporting in a format other than their particular application, and allowing for automated reporting. Some vendors offer customized HTML reports that can be generated and emailed out on a scheduled basis, others allow data to be exported directly to a SQL environment, where reports can be generated through internal tools and processes. Finally, at least one vendor has created an application that allows data to be directly imported into Microsoft Excel for report generation, also allowing generated reports to be scheduled for automation via email. Regardless of which vendor you use, if KPI reporting is important to you (and it certainly should be), you should ask your vendor how they enable this type of reporting and how customizable and flexible data export formats are.

Once you have decided that you are going to build a KPI report and automate its delivery to your organization, the next step is to decide which metrics listed in *Web Analytics Demystified* to include in your report. While the author is unable to personally help you decide exactly which metrics to include, experience shows that you will be successful if you start with KPIs that are most relevant to you particular business model.

The Four Broad Business Models

While the author recognizes that every online business is different, or at least every online business desires to be recognized as being different, experience shows that there are four fundamental online business models: Online commerce, advertising, lead generation and customer support.

Online Commerce

The online commerce model is perhaps one of the most well understood of the four business models, simply because this is where the majority of the money is spent and made. Any Web site that sells products, services or information fits into this model and each of these sites have similar challenges. While the specifics of how online commerce works differs slightly between sites selling products (such as consumer electronics or books), those selling services (such as airline tickets or hotel rooms) and those selling information (such as news or stock information), fundamentally the challenges are the same—attract visitors to the Web site, show them the value proposition and get them to convert. The online commerce model is typified by a focus on all four stages of the customer life cycle (Chapter 10); new customers need to be reached and acquired, the act of purchasing is the conversion and obviously it is strongly desired that these customers are retained.

Advertising

The advertising business model is one typified by attracting visitors to a Web site who will read content and at the same time, theoretically, view and respond to advertising. News and sports Web sites, such as CBSNews.com, CNN.com and ESPN.com all have this business model. The basis for making money on advertising sites is the ability to sell electronic advertising in cost-per-thousand (CPM), cost-per-click (CPC), cost-per-acquisition (CPA) or sponsorship models.

In the cost-per-thousand (CPM, from cost-per-milli, Latin for "thousand") model, the advertiser agrees to pay the Web site for every 1,000 impressions of the ad served. Rates for CPM advertising vary widely depending on the type of site serving the advertising and the qualification of their audience in relation to the advertisers needs. Most news and sports Web sites sell advertising in a CPM model.

In the cost-per-click (CPC) model, the advertiser agrees to pay the Web site for each click on an advertising unit, not for the individual impression. The CPC model is relatively new and took off slowly until Overture and Google started selling advertising on search Web sites using this model. Now, anyone (even the author of this book) can advertise on a number of different Web sites and only pay for the traffic that is actually acquired.

In the cost-per-acquisition (CPA) model, the advertiser works out an agreement with the Web site that specifies that they only pay for the visitors that they truly "acquire," which in most instances means they have been converted. The CPA model can be more intensive to set up initially, depending on the strategy used to determine that a customer has actually been acquired but, if a strategy can be agreed upon, this is often the most financially beneficial model for the advertiser because they are no longer playing the odds regarding conversion rates, they have actually acquired a customer.

Sponsorship is typically a customized payment model where an advertiser agrees to pay a Web site a fixed amount for preferred placement throughout the site. While the author has never seen a solid return on investment case for the sponsorship model of advertising, there are surely many out there as this model is based on saturation and is often used to build brand awareness as much as it is to reach and acquire visitors.

While it is very important for advertising Web sites to reach and acquire new visitors on a near constant basis in order to have an expanding audience to serve advertising to, the act of conversion is typically less clear on these Web sites, often limited to the act of signing up for a newsletter or email list. Perhaps the most important component of the customer life cycle for the advertising business model is retention, keeping audience members coming back time and time again.

Lead Generation

The lead generation business model is typified by the presentation of information about a product or a business in the attempt to gather contact information for the visitor. The general idea is that, if the visitor is interested enough in the content the Web site provides, and if the value proposition is clearly presented, the visitor is more likely to provide personal information such as name, email address, and so on. Important performance indicators for the lead generation model mostly focus on the reach, acquisition and conversion end of the customer life cycle as retention is usually driven via external (email, phone) contact after the lead is generated.

Customer Support

The customer support business model is typified by a Web site designed to help visitors answer questions about a product or service without having to pick up the telephone and generate a costly phone call to a support department. For the most part, customer support is integrated into one of the other models already discussed—rare is a Web site that focuses solely on customer support after a product has been purchased without also trying to get the visitor to purchase additional products (online commerce model) or to generate some kind of lead (lead generation). Still, because the customer support model focuses mostly on the retention phase of the customer life cycle it is worth differentiating. Also, while the other business models are driven financially by the idea that "more page views are usually better" the customer support model tends to be the opposite, the more quickly the visitor can find the information they are looking for the better.

Key Performance Indicators by Business Model

As previously discussed, each online business will need to monitor different performance indicators depending on their specific online goals. It is impossible for the author, in the context of this book, to describe to you, the reader, exactly which metrics you should be paying attention to. In the author's experience, however, there are a handful of KPIs that make sense for businesses to watch depending on their overall business model. The following sections cover those KPIs and the rationale behind their use.

Online Commerce Key Performance Indicators

Because it is as important to retain customers as it is to acquire and convert new visitors, the online commerce model draws performance indicators from each phase of the customer life cycle. Please see the description of the original metric in previous chapters for additional information about the indicator's calculation.

Metric	Rationale for Inclusion
Ratio of New to Returning Visitors Page 112	The ratio of new to returning visitors, called "acquisition mode" by the author, is a fast reference to describe the effect of your marketing mix on driving visits.
Percent New Visitors Page 114	Because the online commerce model depends on the near-constant input of new visitors, monitoring the percentage of new visitors to your site is extremely important.
Page "Stickiness" Page 132	For key landing pages on your Web site (home page, marketing response pages), you want to ensure that visitors are responding to your marketing materials but getting no further than the first page.
Referring Domains Page 150	Keeping track of the top 10 or so Web sites that are sending you traffic will help you determine whether online business partners are performing as expected.
Search Keywords and Phrases Page 158	Keeping track of the top search engine words and phrases that are driving traffic to you will help you ensure that your featured product mix is one that inbound visitors are actually looking for.
Percent of Visits Under 90 Seconds Page 141	Dramatic changes in this percentage can indicate either much better or much worse reach in your marketing campaigns. Either should be responded to proactively.
Key Conversion Rates Page 165	Any and all key conversion rates, such as home to purchase, search to purchase, shopping cart and checkout completion should be monitored closely.
Average Order Value Page 180	Watching for significant movement in your average order value can identify changes in either your customer or available product mix, both of which should be responded to proactively. Also monitor AOV for new and returning customers.
New and Repeat Customer Conversion Rates Page 184	Again, here you are watching for dramatic changes that may indicate changes in your customer base or product and marketing mix.
Sales per Visitor Page 185	A good point of comparison with your conversion rate, helping you ensure that as your incoming traffic increases your site-wide conversion rate stays roughly the same.
Percent Returning Visitors Page 194	Much like monitoring the percent of new visitors to the site, watching how the percent of returning visitors changes will help you keep track of visitor retention.

| Customer Retention Rate Page 204 | Again, similar to keeping track of your returning visitors, monitoring the percentage of returning customers is useful in determining how effectively your retain customers. |

Table 5: Recommended key performance indicators for the online commerce business model.

You will probably find it worthwhile to have a separate worksheet in your KPI reporting for campaign-related metrics, one that allows you to see the important effects of campaigns in a single, easy-to-read view. If you have too many campaigns to monitor easily, consider having individual reports for "top campaigns by response rate" and "top campaigns by conversion rates," as these are the fundamental measurements of campaign success.

Metric (Page in Book)	Rationale for Inclusion
Open Rates Page 122	As you work to reach visitors, making sure that open rates for HTML mailings stay high will help you determine whether your message is being well received.
Response Rates Page 144	You want to make sure that you know at any given time what campaigns are working hardest for you to attract visitors. While response rate can be slightly more involved to calculate, monitoring response rate will help you control marketing spend.
Cost-per-Acquisition Page 146	Monitoring your acquisition costs for campaigns is perhaps the best way to control your marketing spend on campaigns.
Campaign Conversion Rates Page 172	For your top campaigns, keeping track of their conversion rate is again critical to ensuring that your marketing efforts are focused on your most successful campaigns.

Table 6: Recommended key performance indicators for tracking campaigns within the online commerce business model.

It is important to keep in mind that these performance indicators are only a subset of all available metrics discussed in this book. Your online business may have different specific reporting needs and you should work to include those indicators that are most useful to you.

Advertising Key Performance Indicators

The advertising model for online businesses dictates that new visitors are acquired and that they view as many different pages and pieces of content as possible in order to generate advertising views for the Web site's "customers." The recommended performance indicators reflect this focus. Please see the description of the original metric in previous chapters for additional information about the indicator's calculation.

Metric (Page in Book)	Rationale for Inclusion
Overall Traffic Volumes Page 106	Because advertising views are so closely tied to page views it is worthwhile to keep track of changes in overall traffic volume to the Web site.
Number of Visits Page 108	Similar to overall traffic volumes, watching for changes in the number of visits to the Web site can help predict whether more or fewer advertising views will be available.
Ratio of New to Returning Visitors Page 112	The ratio of new to returning visitors, called "acquisition mode" by the author, is a fast reference to describe the effect your marketing mix has on driving visits.
Percent New Visitors Page 114	Because the advertising model depends on the near-constant input of new visitors, monitoring the percentage of new visitors to your site is extremely important.
Percent Returning Visitors Page 194	Much like monitoring the percent of new visitors to the site, watching how the percent of returning visitors changes will help you keep track of visitor retention.
Page "Stickiness" Page 132	For key landing pages on your Web site (home page, marketing response pages) you want to ensure that visitors are responding to your marketing materials but getting no further than the first page.
Referring Domains Page 150	Keeping track of the top 10 or so Web sites that are sending you traffic will help you determine whether online business partners are performing as expected.
Search Keywords and Phrases Page 158	Keeping track of the top search engine words and phrases that are driving traffic to you will help you ensure that your content is what inbound visitors are actually looking for.
Percent of Visits Under 90 Seconds Page 141	Dramatic changes in this percentage can indicate either much better or much worse reach in your marketing campaigns. Either should be responded to proactively.
Average Pages Viewed per Visitor Page 131	Knowing how many pages, and advertising views, you can expect the average visitor to see is helpful when selling advertising units. Monitoring for changes in this number is important to ensure advertising delivery.
Average Number of Visits per Visitor Page 128	Important for understanding how attracted your visitors are to your content and worth monitoring for large changes.
Entry Pages and Content Page 115	Keeping track of the top 10 pages and content areas that visitors are most likely to begin their visit will help you identify key pages advertisers may be interested in.
Heavy User Share Page 136	Depending on how you define "heavy user" this can be an important KPI to keep track of the percentage of your online audience that is likely to see a larger number of advertising units.

Average Time Spent on Site Page 143	Longer visits typically mean greater interest in content and more advertising views, so large changes in average time spent should be monitored.
Key Conversion Rates Page 165	Any conversion rate on your Web site that will lead to increased retention and loyalty should be monitored closely. Examples include newsletter sign-up, alert features and chat or newsgroup application sign-up.
Activity of "Retained" Visitors Page 202	If you have the ability to determine the number of page views, visits, visitors and average time spent for returning visitors it is worthwhile to separate that reporting out to watch for changes in the activity of your retained audience.

Table 7: Recommended key performance indicators for the online advertising business model.

Additionally, if you are actively spending money on campaigns to drive visitors to your Web site you should consider monitoring campaign metrics as described in Table 7.

Lead Generation Key Performance Indicators

The lead generation business model is focused on having visitors view information that prompts them to submit some kind of personal information (the "lead"). The recommended performance indicators reflect this focus. Please see the description of the original metric in previous chapters for additional information about the indicator's calculation.

Metric (Page in Book)	Rationale for Inclusion
Overall Traffic Volumes Page 106	Because the likelihood of generating a lead is tied to the number of page views it is worthwhile to keep track of changes in overall traffic volume to the Web site.
Ratio of New to Returning Visitors Page 112	The ratio of new to returning visitors, called "acquisition mode" by the author, is a fast reference to describe the effect your marketing mix has on driving visits.
Percent New Visitors Page 114	Because the lead generation model depends on the near-constant input of new visitors, monitoring the percentage of new visitors to your site is extremely important.
Percent Returning Visitors Page 194	Much like monitoring the percent of new visitors to the site, watching how the percent of returning visitors changes will help you keep track of the volume of visitors who have learned to use your support systems online.
Page "Stickiness" Page 132	For key landing pages on your Web site (home page, marketing response pages) you want to ensure that visitors are responding to your marketing materials but getting no further than the first page.

Referring Domains Page 150	Keeping track of the top 10 or so Web sites that are sending you traffic will help you determine whether online business partners are performing well.
Search Keywords and Phrases Page 158	Keeping track of the top search engine words and phrases that are driving traffic to you will help you ensure that your content is what inbound visitors are actually looking for.
Entry Pages and Content Page 115	Keeping track of the top 10 pages and content areas that visitors are most likely to begin their visit will help you identify the type of information visitors are most interested in.
Lead Conversion Rate Page 166	The lead conversion rate is likely the most important KPI you will track. You should always work to understand why this number is increasing or decreasing.
Top Pages and Content Requested by New Visitors Page 137	Knowing what first-time ever visitors are looking for on your Web site can help you to tailor content and drive visitors towards the lead generation process more quickly. Changes in these patterns should be responded to proactively.

Table 8: Recommended key performance indicators for the lead generation business model.

Additionally, if you are actively spending money on campaigns to drive visitors to your Web site you should consider monitoring campaign metrics as described in Table 8.

Customer Support Key Performance Indicators

The customer support business model is mostly focused on a visitor's ability to find specific kinds of information, with fewer clicks being better as this likely indicates that visitors are finding the information are looking for quickly. The recommended performance indicators reflect this focus. Please see the description of the original metric in previous chapters for additional information about the indicator's calculation.

Metric (Page in Book)	Rationale for Inclusion
Overall Traffic Volumes Page 106	Because visitor desire for support is tied to the number of page views it is worthwhile to keep track of changes in overall traffic volume to the Web site.
Percent New Visitors Page 127	New visitors are those who may struggle more to find information as they learn your information architecture and support system. The greater the volume of new visitors, the more likely you are to have inbound support calls if visitors are unable to find information online.
Page "Stickiness" Page 132	For key landing pages on your Web site (home page, product support pages) you want to ensure that visitors are not becoming confused and simply leaving the Web site.

Search Keywords and Phrases Page 158	Keeping track of the top search engine words and phrases that are driving traffic to you will provide insight into what support issues visitors may be experiencing most commonly.
Percent of Visits Under 90 Seconds Page 141	It is unlikely that a visitor can do much on a customer support site in less than 90 seconds other than find a phone number to call. This indicator should be watched and correlated to call volume (if possible).
Entry Pages and Content Page 115	Keeping track of the top 10 pages and content areas that visitors are most likely to begin their visit will help you identify the type of information visitors are most interested in.
"Information Find" Conversion Rate Page 168	If you track the process of visitors moving from your home page to specific information you can generate an "information find" conversion rate. You should always work to understand why this number is increasing or decreasing.
Top Pages and Content Requested by New Visitors Page 137	Knowing what first-time ever visitors are looking for on your Web site can help you to tailor content and drive visitors towards the most common support topics. Changes in these patterns should be responded to proactively.

Table 9: Recommended key performance indicators for the customer support business model.

Do keep in mind that each of the performance indicators listed above for each business model are simply recommendations and that you may need to follow more, or different, metrics depending on your specific needs. The most important thing to consider when deciding which metrics to watch as KPIs is the answer to the question, "Is the information actionable?" If the KPI does not have the potential to drive action and make you look more deeply into your analytics reports or make some critical change to your Web site or marketing programs, the metric is likely *not* a good key performance indicator for you.

CHAPTER **16**
ADVANCED TOPICS

"Leveraging information and capabilities throughout the corporation, these integrated [Web analytics and e-Business] applications can deliver sustainable competitive advantage by helping corporations present a unified—rather than fragmented—front to the customer."
Guy Creese and Mark Veytsel, the Aberdeen Group

Congratulations! If you are still reading and you have made it this far you now understand more about Web analytics than most people know, want to know, or even know that there is to know. Everything contained in *Web Analytics Demystified* in the preceding chapters was about core functionality that is, or should be, provided by Web analytics applications—the basics that everyone should understand in order to make the best use of whatever analytics application they have purchased to help them run their online business. If you have read the previous chapters and they have made complete sense to you then you are likely well on your way to a significant upgrade in your Web analytics reporting—which will, hopefully, translate into a better visitor experience online, more profits, less abandonment, and so on.

Still, when the author sat down and planned *Web Analytics Demystified* there were a small number of topics that were important, but outside of the concept of "a Marketers Guide to Web analytics." Data integration—or the combining of the aforementioned Web analytics data with related data about the customer, the performance of the Web site, information about advertising, and so on, is a topic of some import to online businesses that are a bit further along in their understanding of the Web Analytic process. Conversely, the use of personas when architecting Web sites and Web-based applications can be a powerful tool in making sure that your design is consistent with both your site's business objectives and the goals of your most important customers. These topics are treated in this final Chapter of *Web Analytics Demystified*.

Data Integration

While every metric presented in the preceding chapters of *Web Analytics Demystified* should be available from your analytics application regardless of price or complexity, some online businesses will inevitably be further along and need additional information about their visitors. One of the first topics to arise when businesses begin to move towards a more advanced Web analytics program is that of data integration.

Data integration is built around the idea that the Web traffic data you are collecting and analyzing in your analytic program is only a subset of the data that you actually have about your online visitor or customer. There are typically a number of different but related data sources that are components that the author considers "information about the customer"—especially for businesses doing some type of online commerce—including:

- Customer specific data, such as the customer's name, address and business title
- Marketing information, such as the campaigns you have exposed the customer to in the past and those they have favorably responded to
- Survey information, such as data collected from exit surveys or external sources such as BizRate.com
- Customer complaints and questions, logged in a customer support system

In addition, many online businesses that are part of larger, multi-channel enterprises have the desire to integrate data from other parts of the enterprise into their analytics reporting to create a single-view environment of how the overall business is performing. Data often integrated when businesses are looking to create enterprise-wide views that the author considers "information about sales" include:

- Order specific data, such as the customer's order history, frequency of returns, types of purchase
- Point-of-sale order information from individual stores
- Order information taken from kiosks in stores
- Order information taken from customer service representatives (CSR) via telephone
- Orders originating from catalogs and offline advertising, including television, radio, newspaper and direct mail

Finally, some online businesses want to have the tightest integration possible and combine information about online sales with enterprise resource planning (ERP) information, which the author considers "information about the business," including:

- System-wide availability of products
- Cost and margin information about products
- Shipping information
- Overall health-of-business as measured against online sales or traffic

Early in the history of Web analytics there was a sense that eventually this work will lead to a "360-degree view of the customer," meaning you would be able to see everything they did, beginning to end, as they interacted with your business online and offline. Back-end data integration was ultimately going to be the conduit through which this holy grail of customer knowledge would be enabled because information about the customer was truly disparate. Because different systems were used to track point-of-sale, telesales, catalog sales, online sales and customer support, a single customer identifier was unlikely to be found. Without a single customer identifier, the integration of these disparate, but related, data appeared to be unlikely at best.

Several years have now passed, giving software engineers plenty of time to work on this problem but the author is disappointed to report that little progress has been made in this area. On the contrary, most analysts and vendors are proclaiming that the "360-degree view of the customer" was simply psychobabble and is unlikely to ever be available, no matter the price. While the author tends towards the pessimistic side regarding promises made by the vendors and analyst community, he does believe that there is value in attempting to build a wider view of the customer, but that it should be done as makes sense and where the data is easily combinable.

To this end, some of the vendors are currently establishing partnerships with companies that have different, but related, views of the customer. Some notable examples include:

- Coremetrics partnerships with email providers like CheetahMail and Digital Impact, enabling direct email marketing integration, as well as their partnerships with BeFree for affiliate marketing integration and ForeSee Results and BizRate.com for customer survey integration
- WebSideStory's partnership with SalesForce.com enabling one-to-one online marketing integration
- Omniture's partnership with Speedera to provide integrated application performance measurement
- WebTrends/NetIQ's partnership with Hyperion to enable OLAP integration of multiple data sources

The general trend you can see above is that vendors are forging strategic partnerships around their individual technologies to allow visitors and customers to be tied together using a common customer identifier. While these particular partnerships only help you if you have no analytics solution in place—or are willing to scrap what you have, choose new vendors and start over—it is worthwhile to know that analytics vendors are working on solving the problem of data integration.

Depending on the particular stage your online business is in regarding analytics and reporting, the integration of disparate data will be either absolutely irrelevant or absolutely critical. If data integration is a priority for you there are two broad strategies for making this happen, custom data collection and back-end data integration.

Custom Data Collection

One of the quickly emerging solutions for data integration is the idea of custom data collection and reporting via the existing analytics application interface. Instead of limiting what can be tracked and reported on to the core Web analytics data points (views, visits, visitors, referrers, and so on), many Web analytics applications are opening up their data collection architectures to allow any data point to be collected and analyzed. By allowing you, the customer, to define specifically what data you want tracked and reported on, "light" data integration is made available. While the author believes that more and more Web analytics vendors will be providing custom data collection in the future, this strategy is not without its advantages and disadvantages.

Advantages of Custom Data Collection

The major advantage of using custom data collection to enable "light" data integration and reporting is that most known vendors offer reporting on custom data directly from within their existing interface. Why this is an advantage will become more clear after reading about back-end data integration, but suffice to say being able to easily tie custom data directly to the more traditional Web analytic data discussed in this book is desired. Custom data collection can facilitate many of the most common data integration needs expressed by online businesses, especially for vendors who have solved the problem of being able to tie normal analytic data directly to custom fields using some type of cross-tabulation or drill-down functionality.

A related advantage of custom data collection is that, because this collection and reporting happens within the existing analytics interface it typically costs less. Again, this will be clearer in the context of back-end data integration, but unless your vendor supports direct import of non-standard data into their reporting module there will likely be some reporting costs incurred internally by your business.

Disadvantages of Custom Data Collection

The major disadvantage of custom data collection is the limitation on what types of data can be collected and how the data is tied to other data within the interface. In this regard, some vendors are able to collect custom variables in the form of strings and simply report back on the number of times each string was collected (analogous to a page view). Other vendors are able to collect complex, two-dimensional strings in a "parent-children" relationship and report back on the number of views generated for each. Yet other vendors are able to tie custom-collected data back to other events in a visit, such as a purchase or an internal search. Depending on what kind of custom information you are trying to glean about your visitors you will need different reporting abilities from your analytics application. Before you commit to using custom data collection to satisfy your data integration reporting needs you should contact your analytics vendor to determine what can be collected and how this data is tied to other data within the application.

Back-End Data Integration

Conceptually, back-end data integration involves tying together disparate, but related, data sources after the fact in order to develop a more clear or refined picture of "what happened." The most common case of this type of data integration is the "who was that" model, tying Web Analytic data to your company's customer relationship database in such a way you can stop saying "10 visitors looked at our pricing page yesterday" and start to say "Bob and Ted and Alice and Ramona looked at our pricing page yesterday and here are each of their email addresses so we can follow up with them individually." Marketers much prefer the latter, to the point that at least one vendor in the analytics marketplace has made considerable investment in making this type of data integration easy and accessible.

The fundamental challenges in this type of data integration are, "What application will be used to analyze the data?" and, "How will the records be tied together?" For the first challenge, there are a variety of tools—business intelligence tools, OLAP applications, data warehouses, databases and even the Web analytics vendors' own toolsets—that are able to bring the data together in a common environment, prerequisite for analysis. The best application to use for data integration really depends on what kinds of questions you are trying to answer. Regarding the second challenge, this is the $64,000 question, how to tie these data sources together in a meaningful way.

What Application Should Be Used to Integrate Data?

The answer to this question is, unfortunately, "It depends." It depends on what kinds of questions you are trying to answer. It depends on your internal expertise with databases and data warehouses. It depends on whether your Web analytics application supports the direct import of non-traffic data. Each of the different kinds of applications listed above will likely create as many problems as they are able to solve when attempting to integrate data, so the best guidance that the author can give you in this regard is as follows:

Have Well-Defined Questions

The more defined your questions are the more clear the strategy for combining data will become. "We want a list of the names of known visitors who saw pricing and demo pages in the month of August," will be easier to determine than "We want to know everything about all the visitors who have ever been to the Web site."

Integrate Slowly, if Possible

By keeping the scope of individual integration projects reasonable and then building on your knowledge you are more likely to be successful than if you just jump in, head first. Keep in mind that the continuous improvement process applies everywhere, not just to making changes to your Web site.

Don't Become Frustrated

Remember, hindsight is 20/20 and nobody is perfect. If you really get involved in data integration projects you will quickly run into questions that cannot be answered for any number of reasons. Some data is not available, some data sets are not combinable, some data sets are too large to be analyzed in a reasonable amount of time. The best practice here is to make note of the questions you wanted answers for but could not get and revisit them next time you are shopping for a Web analytics application.

Garbage In Means Garbage Out!

Another universal truth: crappy data combined with good data yields crappy data, not the other way around. When you have worked out a strategy for data integration you should consider spending significant time making sure that the data sets are as clean as possible prior to their final integration for analysis. Vigorous scrubbing is necessary to ensure that the combined data will be meaningful, especially when attempting to integrate CRM data collected primarily via the Internet.

Choose a Data Integration Tool Carefully

Because data integration is relatively new it is not uncommon that people will use new applications or applications they are unfamiliar with to attempt to combine data. The problem with this is that you may very well end up banging your head against a wall to solve a problem that would be easily solved with enough information about the application. By integrating in an environment that you or someone in your company knows well or by integrating in a well-known environment (such as SQL, which is well-supported on and off the Internet) you increase the chances that the integration will go smoothly. Alternatively you could outsource the integration through your Web analytics vendor, provided they offer integration services, and rely on their expertise.

How Should Different Data Sets Be Tied Together?

Once you have decided on an application or process for integrating the data you still have to work out how the data sets should be related to each other. Depending on the kinds of questions you are trying to answer this can be more or less difficult. Say, for example, you are simply trying to tie Web traffic to the volume of inbound calls to your customer support center on a daily basis. This integration will likely be very easy since the key that ties the two data sets together is simply the date/time stamp on the records in each set. Likely you have granularity to at least the level of the minute, allowing you to slice-and-dice the data from each set and answer questions like:

- When call volumes go up, was there a related increase in traffic to our support site immediately prior, suggesting that visitors are not making effective use of online support materials?
- Do we see a correlation between calls on a certain subject and traffic to that subject's support area online?

But what if you want to know the exact pages that a visitor was looking at in your customer support section just prior to making a call to your customer support center? Having this information would be great for your support staff, no doubt! They could ask insightful questions of the caller about the information they had recently viewed and perhaps save the caller time in diagnosing any problem they may be having. Unfortunately, this type of integration has a strong dependence on A) a unique user identifier (UUID) that is common to both your Web environment and your customer support management system and B) real-time, integrated reporting based on the UUID.

Let the author assure you that while "A" above is quite possible given a great deal of thought when designing your Web site, the combination of "A" and "B" is quite difficult to attain, perhaps impossible (for the time being).

Again, the best the author can do is to provide the following guidance when attempting to tie data sets together:

Consider the UUID

If you are able to pass in a UUID of your choosing, either via a variable in your page tag or the query string to your log files, you will be much more likely to be able to tie your Web data back to internal information. Because every system generates its own unique ID for a customer, visitor, and so on. your best bet is to tie the Web data to another system's UUID at the time the data is generated. This way, providing the analytics application is able to provide you some type of data export, you will already have a UUID that is "yours" contained in the data.

Carefully Research Your Data Export Options

Unless you have knowingly purchased a Web analytics application that allows you to import data from other sources you will most likely end up exporting data for analysis in some other environment. If this is the case you want to understand as much as possible about export formats in order to determine what fields may be available to facilitate data combination. While most applications support some type of export to Microsoft Word™ or Microsoft Excel™ these formats are typically too limiting for data integration projects. A comma- or tab-delimited file (CSV) is getting better but the ideal formats are direct exports to a database or XML. Each of the latter two formats will come with an established schema describing the relationship between Web analytics data.

Choose Your Vendor Carefully

Not all Web analytics vendors have built the same support into their applications for data import and export. As of the time of this book's writing, some vendors provided robust support for importing and exporting data, either directly or via OLAP tools provided by business partners. Other vendors had worked quite hard on establishing partnerships with companies that have frequently integrated data sets (email, advertising, marketing, CRM, performance data). Still other vendors provide little or no support for data integrations projects.

It is best to ask your existing vendor how they A) currently support data integration projects and B) plan on doing so in the future. If they look at you with a blank stare when you ask this question, buy them a copy of *Web Analytics Demystified* and get a new analytics vendor.

Advantages of Back-End Data Integration

The major advantage of back-end data integration is that, when properly done, the information quality of Web analytics data is significantly increased. The difference between knowing that "100 visitors" did something, and knowing who each of those "100 visitors" were and what they had done on previous visits to your Web site is, well, like the difference between *knowing about* money and actually *having* money. The more you know about your online visitors and customers the better off you are. Being able to directly market to prospects based on their online habits is surely part of the future of Web analytics.

Disadvantages of Back-End Data Integration

Aside from the difficulty involved in setting up a back-end data integration, the major disadvantages of back-end data integration revolve around privacy concerns. There have been a few cases of Web analytics vendors getting in trouble with privacy groups for passing information deemed to be "private" using only semi-secure protocols (HTTPS is semi-secure, at best). You should be careful to A) protect your customer's data as much as possible and B) have a clearly posted privacy policy stating exactly what you are doing and why you are doing it, especially when outsourcing the integration of data, which typically involved passing of information via the Internet. While it is amazing to this author what the popular media and general public will become agitated about, cookies being the most popular subject for alarm, woe is the online business that attracts the wrath of the "privacy concerned" on the Internet. More than any other aspect of Web analytics measurement, the combination of related but separate data sources is the most likely to attract unwanted attention and so should be monitored closely and administered closely.

Use of Personas in Design and Architecture

A strategy that is becoming more common in the Web design process is the use of personas and persuasive architecture. Personas, first described by Alan Cooper in his 1999 book, *The Inmates Are Running the Asylum,* are a tool used to focus designers and design decision makers on the real needs of their customers. These personas are essentially fictitious people with real goals that they want to accomplish on your Web site. The use of personas allow designers and decision makers to easily choose to include or drop pages and content based on the answer to the question, "Would this information help one of our personas complete their task on our Web site?" If the answer is "no," or "probably not," then the page can be left out of the final design. These tools, when used properly, can provide your design team a great Ocham's razor to simplify your Web design.

How Personas Are Used

Harley Manning of Forrester Research does a good job of describing how personas are best defined in his 2003 report, *The Power of Design Personas.* In this report Manning cites that studying individual users in the business' target market develops effective personas. The descriptions are then used to tell a story about a real person, their motivations, goals and behaviors. An example persona that BackcountryStore.com may have used in their design process may be described as such:

Name:	Bobby Backcountry
Goals:	Buying high-end outdoor gear at the best price; feeling like he's a contributing member of an elite community.
Motivations:	Bobby is motivated by a need to be perceived as an elite outdoor athlete, one that can afford the very best gear and knows how to use it. Bobby wants to shop on a Web site that also has a community, because he believes himself to be a knowledgeable "gear head" and he wants to share that knowledge. Bobby is always looking for the best deal on gear because his financial situation does not allow for exorbitant spending.
Description:	Bobby is in his early 30s and earns less than $30K per year working an information technology job that affords him the opportunity to escape into the backcountry at a moment's notice. Bobby has always "made due" with whatever gear he could afford or find but since turning 30 he yearns to be perceived of as successful. Bobby is not married and does not have a girlfriend right now; he finds companionship both among other outdoor enthusiasts and also, because he is a technocrat, online at Web sites frequented by backcountry experts.
Actions:	Research gear; Purchase sale items; Register; Post to community forums.
Frequency of Visits:	Frequent – up to once per week
Frequency of Purchase:	Infrequently – typically around sales activity
Keywords:	(All high-end brands); sale; sale items; specials; discounts; on sale; savings; cost savings.

Table 10: A fictitious persona that may have been useful for the owners of BackcountryStore.com when designing their Web site. It is worth noting that the addition of "motivations" to a persona is a patent-pending invention of Future Now, Inc.

This description of Bobby's persona will help designers greatly in making design decisions. Imagine that Bobby is BackcountryStore.com's primary persona—the key user type that BackcountryStore.com is trying to serve. If designers were faced with the following design and marketing decisions, understanding Bobby would make the decision process very easy.

1. Do we feature our most high-end gear, regardless of the price?
2. Do we hide our clearance and discount gear since the margins are much lower on these items?
3. Do we de-emphasize the role of community, assuming that anyone who comes to BackcountryStore.com already has enough friends to hang out with?

Clearly, with Bobby in mind the answer to each of these questions would be "no." Bobby is looking for deals on gear and wants to spend time on a Web site that creates and fosters a sense of community. With a small number of "Bobby's" used carefully to focus design decisions, Web site owners can streamline the process of having to decide which pages should and should not be included in the final version of the site.

Personas Used in Persuasion Architecture

Bryan Eisenberg and the smart people at Future Now, Inc., have incorporated personas into their design framework, one that they have termed "persuasion architecture." The main tenet of persuasion architecture is that the goal of any commercial Web site is to inform and *persuade*—persuade the visitor to provide a lead, make a purchase, click more deeply into the site or not pick up the phone and place a costly telephone call. The way you persuade a visitor to do something is to create a series of micro-actions that, when considered collectively, constitute a macro-action. The macro-action is the business objective that we discussed in Chapter 5—make a purchase, submit a lead, and so on. The micro-actions are the individual steps in the process of completing the business objective, steps that can be measured using any number of the tools and metrics described in this book.

Persuasion architecture essentially asks these three critical questions of every page a visitor would see in a macro-action:

1. What action needs to be taken at this point?
2. Who, or which persona, needs to be taking that action?
3. How do we persuade the person or persona to take the action?

By answering these important questions you are again able to use personas in a very valuable way. Typically the answer to the first question is something like, "Get the visitor to move to the next page in the process." By understanding which of your personas is likely to be engaged in the macro-action, something that would have been clearly established at the persona-definition stage, you will have the answer to question two. The answer to question two provides you the answer to question three—simply consult the motivations and keywords for each of your personas and write marketing language that reflects that information.

Again, as an example, say that Bobby was looking at a particular product on BackcountryStore.com, one that was already being offered at a discount. When we are trying to persuade Bobby to add that item to his shopping cart, based on his persona, the language we are going to use is that describing the quality of the particular product and how the product is preferred by other gear experts. Bobby will have already done his homework and realized that the price is among the best he will get. We know he is a loyal visitor, one likely to come back week after week looking for the best deals. Now all we have to do is make sure that he understands that the product in question is among the best available and Bobby will convert.

Why Is This Relevant?

The author chose to include this discussion on personas and persuasion architecture because it is extremely common for Web site design projects to be run with complete disregard to how the final product will be measured. Web sites are commonly thrown together with a great deal of thought and discussion in the early stages and then most of that work gets thrown out in the eleventh hour when the project is in danger of being delivered late. While this is not always the case, in the author's experience it is more common than not. When everyone is rushing to build out templates, finish marketing copy and optimize images the last thing on anyone's mind is, "How will the effect of all this work be measured?"

Obviously the author sees this as a huge problem, one that needs to be addressed.

The continuous improvement process described in Chapter 2 does not only need to be applied to a finished product undergoing revision. The "design" and "measure" steps are easily applied to any step in the Web design process, regardless of the state of "completeness" of the Web site. Future Now's persuasion architecture blends nicely with the continuous improvement process because it explicitly asks the question, "What should the visitor do next?" This micro-action can be measured in nearly every instance—more often than not you are looking for a simple conversion rate of visitors moving from one page to the next. Bubble this back up to the macro-action and you are looking at a single, measurable step in an action. Continue to bubble this up and you are measuring the effect of a single action on an overall business objective.

Well thought-out design is fundamental to taking advantage of most of the metrics described in this book. If you build without measurement in mind you are likely to back yourself into a corner and have little or no idea how good or bad a job you did with your design. In this regard, the author's recommendation regarding design is as follows:

1. Clearly define the business objectives for your Web site, first and foremost.
2. Make use of personas to provide focus to your designs when important decisions need to be made regarding a page's relevance.
3. Use persuasion architecture to derive the greatest value from your personas and identify the micro-actions that visitors need to accomplish as they effectively accomplish your business objectives.
4. Build measurement in during the design stages, going so far as to establish key performance indicators for each micro- and macro-action.
5. Apply the continuous improvement process whenever possible with all of the above in mind, constantly looking for changes in key personas and how those personas are completing key business objectives.

BIBLIOGRAPHY

Books and Electronic Documents

Berners-Lee, Tim. 2000. Weaving the Web: The Original Design and Ultimate Destiny of the World Wide Web. HarperBusiness, New York, New York.

Creese, Guy and Alex Veytsel. 2002. *Web Analytics: Making Business Sense of Online Behavior.* The Aberdeen Group, Inc., Boston, Massachusetts.

Eisenberg, Bryan. 2003. *What Converts Search Engine Traffic.* Future Now, Inc., New York, New York. (www.cafeshops.com/futurenowinc.8261783)

Eisenberg, Bryan, Jim Novo and John E. Shreeve. 2002. *The Guide to Web Analytics: How to Understand and Use Your Web Trends to Maximize Results.* Future Now, Inc., New York, New York.

Fletcher, Peter, Alex Poon, Ben Pearce and Peter Comber. *Practical Web Traffic Analysis: Standards, Privacy, Techniques, Results.* glasshaus, Birmingham, United Kingdom.

Inan, Hurol. 2002. *Measuring the Success of your Website: A Customer-Centric Approach to Website Management.* Pearson Education Australia, Frenchs Forest, New South Wales, Australia.

Krug, Steve. 2000. Don't Make Me Think: A Common Sense Approach to Web Usability. QUE, Indianapolis, Indiana.

Manning, Harley with Bruce D. Temkin and Nicole Belanger. 2003. *The Power of Design Personas.* Forrester Research, Inc. Cambridge, Massachusets.

Neilsen, Jakob. 2000. *Web Usability: The Practice of Simplicity.* New Riders Publishing, Indianapolis, Indiana.

Neilsen, Jakob. 1994. *Usability Engineering.* Morgan Kauffman, San Francisco, California.

Silverstein, Michael, Harold Sirkin and Peter Stanger. 2003. *Retailing Online: Coming of Age.* Electronic document published and distributed by The Boston Consulting Group (www.bcg.com).

Sterne, Jim. 2002. *Web Metrics: Proven Methods for Measuring Web Site Success.* John Wiley & Sons, Inc. New York, New York.

Sterne, Jim. 2003. *Advanced Email Marketing: Using Email to Achieve Sales and Marketing Goals.* Lyris Technologies, Inc. Berkeley, California.

Sterne, Jim and Matt Cutler. 2000. *E-Metrics: Business Metrics for the New Economy.* Electronic document published and distributed by NetGenesis (www.netgen.com).

Web Sites Referenced

Because of the ever-changing nature of the Internet the author has opted to only provide base URLs for information cited in *Web Analytics Demystified* and would encourage the reader to search the Web site for specific information cited.

Web Site	URL	Referenced In
Aberdeen	www.aberdeen.com	Chapter 1
Gartner Group	www.gartnergroup.com	Chapter 1
PC Webopedia	www.pcwebopedia.com	Chapter 1
HitBox Web Doctor	www.hitboxcentral.com	Chapter 2
Amazon	www.amazon.com	Chapter 2
Wal-mart	www.wal-mart.com	Chapter 2
Microsoft Network	www.msn.com	Chapter 2
Yahoo!	www.yahoo.com	Chapter 2
ESPN	www.espn.com	Chapter 2
Keynote Systems	www.keynote.com	Chapter 2
NetMechanic	www.netmechanic.com	Chapter 2
OpinionLab	www.opinionlab.com	Chapter 2
WebTrends/NetIQ	www.webtrends.com	Chapter 2
WebSideStory	www.websidestory.com	Chapter 2
Wusage	www.wusage.com	Chapter 2
Andromedia (Macromedia)	www.macromedia.com	Chapter 3
NetGenesis/SPSS	www.spss.com	Chapter 3
Accrue (Datanautics)	www.datanautics.com	Chapter 3
IBM Surfaid	www.ibm.com	Chapter 3
Revenue Sciences	www.revenuesciences.com	Chapter 3
Apache	www.apache.org	Chapter 3
Microsoft	www.microsoft.com	Chapter 3
World Wide Web Consortium (W3C)	www.w3c.org	Chapter 3
Coremetrics	www.coremetrics.com	Chapter 3
Omniture	www.omniture.com	Chapter 3
Statmarket	www.statmarket.com	Chapter 3
NetIQ	www.netiq.com	Chapter 4
Best Buy	www.bestbuy.com	Chapter 5
Apple Computers	www.apple.com	Chapter 5
Akamai	www.akamai.com	Chapter 11
Nielsen/NetRatings	www.neilsen-netratings.com	Chapter 11
World Wide Web Consortium (W3C) Library	www.w3.org	Chapter 12
SearchEngineWatch	searchenginewatch.com	Chapter 12
CyberAtlas	cyberatlas.internet.com	Chapter 12
Overture	www.overture.com	Chapter 12
SEO Consultants	www.seoconsultants.com	Chapter 12
ClickZ	www.clickz.com	Chapter 14
Jim Novo	www.jimnovo.com	Chapter 14
CheetahMail	www.cheetahmail.com	Chapter 16
Digital Impact	www.digitalimpact.com	Chapter 16
BeFree	www.befree.com	Chapter 16
ForeSee Results	www.foreseeresults.com	Chapter 16
BizRate	www.bizrate.com	Chapter 16

SalesForce	www.salesforce.com	Chapter 16
Speedera	www.speedera.com	Chapter 16
Hyperion	www.hyperion.com	Chapter 16

Please note that these URLs are only current and active as of the time of this book's publication and may have changed. Please consult the author's Web site, www.webanalyticsdemystified.com for an up-to-date list.

List of Tables and Figures

INDEX